The AMERICAN CIVIL WAR: An ENGLISH VIEW

The Writings of
Field Marshal Viscount Wolseley

*Edited and Introduced
by James A. Rawley*

STACKPOLE
BOOKS

Published by
STACKPOLE BOOKS
5067 Ritter Road
Mechanicsburg, PA 17055
www.stackpolebooks.com

Printed in the United States of America

10 9 8 7 6 5 4 3 2 1

FIRST EDITION

Library of Congress Cataloging-in-Publication Data

Wolseley, Garnet Wolseley, Viscount, 1833–1913
    The American Civil War : an English view / Field Marshal Viscount Garnet Joseph Wolseley.
      p. cm.
    Originally published: Charlottesville, VA : University Press of Virginia, 1964
    Includes bibliographical references and index.
    ISBN 0-8117-0093-3
    1. United States—History—Civil War, 1861–1865—Campaigns. 2. United States—History—Civil War, 1861–1865—Foreign public opinion, British. 3. Public opinion—Great Britain—History—19th century. 4. Confederate States of America—Social conditions. 5. Confederate States of America—Politics and government. 6. Wolseley, Garnet Wolseley, Viscount, 1833–1913—Journeys—United States. I. Title.

E470 .W85 2002
973.7'3—dc21

                                       2001055044

FOR ANN

CONTENTS

Preface to Reprinting   vii

Introduction   ix

A Month's Visit to the Confederate Headquarters   1

General Lee   49

An English View of the Civil War   71

    Part I   73

    Part II   103

    Part III   123

    Part IV   147

    Part V   167

    Part VI   187

    Part VII   205

Index   225

PREFACE

REPRINTING of this book, first published in 1964, testifies to the durability of interest in the views of an English officer who stole from Canada into the Confederacy in 1862 to meet Gen. R. E. Lee and view the Confederate military scene.

An Irishman, Lt. Col. Garnet Joseph Wolseley, the future Field-Marshal Viscount, was renowned for his speedy success in military actions. He brought a sharp eye and experience in India and China to his visit.

While visiting his sister in County Cork in 1861, Wolseley received a telegram ordering him to proceed to Canada as Assistant Quarter-Master General. Writing on board the *Melbourne* in the English Channel, he confided to his friend, Maj. Robert Biddulph, as he apprehended a major war between England and the Union over the latter's seizure of Confederate passengers from a neutral English mail packet.

My own private opinion is that we are now on the verge of the greatest war which has taken place in our days. . . . I cannot say that I have any very sanguine hopes as regards the issue of this winter's campaign, for if the Yankees are worth their salt, they will at once make peace with the south and pour 100,000 men into Canada where they can easily compensate themselves for their losses of the Confederate states, and England will be perfectly unable to prevent it. . . . Do not be in the least surprised if you hear of us all being made prisoners of war before the end of February. Everywhere you go in England now the feeling is the same for war.

A month later Wolseley wrote Biddulph, "Things have changed much since I last wrote you, breathing of war's alarms, peace is now the order of the day."[1]

With the possibility of war between England and the Union quieted, Wolseley continued to study military operations in the divided states. Unlike some European professionals, he believed the fighting between armies composed of civilian volunteers was worth examining and could perhaps provide lessons worth adopting.

[1] Robert Biddulph, ed., "Canada and the American Civil War: More Wolseley letters." *Journal of the Society for Army Historical Research*, 19 (1940): 112–17.

Information coming to Canada from the distant, unfamiliar battle-fields was inadequate for his purposes, so he and a friend decided to visit the United States: one to go to the Confederacy, and the other to the Union. A flip of a coin gave Wolseley his choice. Already holding Gen. R. E. Lee in high regard, Wolseley chose the Confederacy. His outlook on the war's outcome was distinctive. He favored a Southern victory, weakening the immense republic, but not bringing into existence "a government which would be more powerful that it's in our own interests to have established."[2]

Wolseley obtained a two-month leave of absence and letters of introduction from Confederates in Canada to important Southerners. He planned to pass through New York and Baltimore before being smuggled across the Potomac and continuing on to Richmond.

The battle of Antietam had just occurred, and Lee, repulsed from Maryland, lay near Winchester in the Valley of Virginia. Throughout his journey south Wolseley had found friendly souls. He was touched by a note to Lee from the Confederate Secretary of War, reading, "I have not asked Colonel Wolseley to take the usual oath that he would disclose nothing of what he sees to our enemies, because I know I can rely upon the honor of an English officer."[3]

He described the subsequent interview in "A Month's Visit to the Confederate Headquarters," reprinted in this volume. Nearly a quarter of a century later, he published his celebrated sketch of General Lee; and then, invited by the *North American Review*, he wrote a seven-part critique of the four-volume *Battles and Leaders of the Civil War*, written by participants in the great conflict. All of these are included in this work. Together his writings form a unique view, inspiring the interest of many students of the American Civil War.

---

[2] Joseph H. Lehman, *All Sir Garnet. A Life of Field-Marshal Lord Wolseley.* (London: Jonathon Cape, 1964), 117–18.
[3] Ibid., 121–22.

INTRODUCTION

THIS book is a compilation of writings on the American Civil War by a distinguished British soldier. Never previously brought together in book form, they present a nearly complete military history of the American conflict, a review enlivened by the author's firsthand impressions and enriched by his broad knowledge of war in many lands. Viscount Garnet Joseph Wolseley's writings are scarcely known today outside a circle of specialists. In his own time they exerted substantial influence by provoking controversy on the American side of the Atlantic and stirring up a notable British interest in the war.

"A classic of Confederate literature," Douglas Freeman described Viscount Wolseley's sketch of Robert E. Lee. Inspired by a visit with the Confederate leader and by the profoundest admiration ("I have only known two heroes in my life, and Gen. R. E. Lee is one of them"), Wolseley's cameo portrait of "the ideal patriot" has been often quoted.

The delineation of Lee, however, was but one of Wolseley's writings on the American Civil War. At the time of the "Trent" crisis in late 1861 Wolseley, then a lieutenant colonel in the British army, was ordered to Canada to prepare for a possible war between the United States and the United Kingdom. War was averted, and in the fall of 1862 Wolseley stole into the Confederacy, where he inspected the city of Richmond and its battle-scarred environs and visited Generals Lee and Jackson. Later he wrote a thrilling narrative of his exploit, vivid in portraiture, tense with drama, and dyed in the gray of Confederate sympathy.

A generation after these events Wolseley, who had been created viscount for his extraordinary military services and assigned as adjutant general of the British army, was invited by the editor of the *North American Review* to write a series of articles on the newly published *Battles and Leaders of the Civil War,* collected from the *Century.* Wolseley made his work more than an extended essay on that rich repository of warriors' reminiscences; it was virtually a fresh military history of the war. He brought to his task great authority. He had had far-ranging military experience in India, the Crimea, China, Africa, and North America; he had made a close study of the art of war; and he possessed both a keen interest in the Civil War and direct knowledge of it. By 1889 his Confederate bias had mellowed into an appreciation of what was at stake on both sides, and he apportioned praise and blame on military and civilian leaders with a deliberate hand. His candid judgments provoked controversy. General William T. Sherman replied spiritedly to the laudation of Lee; Jefferson Davis published a somewhat churlish self-defense; and Union General James Fry returned a salvo in behalf of the government's direction of the war. Two pen portraits of Generals Nathan B. Forrest and William T. Sherman, published in a British military magazine in 1891–92, completed his contribution to the literature of the American war.

Wolseley's writings on the great contest—his lively contemporary piece, his later evocation of Lee, and his penetrating analysis of the use of arms by American men—are a record of a distinguished military mind. A lesser Wellington, Wolseley beheld his name become a household word in Great Britain. In 1895 he was appointed commander in chief of the British army, and he proceeded to lay "the foundations upon which were built up, both the expeditionary force which saved France in 1914, and the great national army which brought victory to the Allies in 1918."[1]

A brief story of this British soldier's life is essential to an understanding of his literary products. Garnet Wolseley's family—a junior branch of an old Staffordshire house—had secured land in county Carlow, Ireland, under William III. His father sold out as a major and married late in his life Frances Smith, the daughter of a "typical spendthrift Irish landlord." Wolseley was born in a red brick country mansion near Dublin on June 4, 1833; his father died when the boy was seven and left his widow seven children to rear on a modest income.

In these unpromising circumstances family pride was "a spur to the boundless ambition that filled my brain in youth," he recalled. "I was reared in the belief that my family was one of the very few

[1] Douglas F. Freeman, *The South to Posterity* (New York, 1939), p. 157; *Dictionary of National Biography, 1912–1921* (London, 1927), p. 591.

that could trace its direct descent in the male line from ancestors who had lived before 'the Conquest' on lands still held by us, their descendants."[2] His mother, an Irish Protestant, filled her son with her intense if simple religiosity that stayed with him throughout life. His father's military career made it seem natural to turn to army life, a calling to which he took not only an abiding faith in God's providence but a keen ambition, an eager temperament, and a high courage as well.

After studying in a day school and learning draftsmanship and surveying in a Dublin office, Wolseley, not yet nineteen, became an ensign in a battalion sent out for service in the second Burmese War. He quickly won distinction by leading an assault on robber-chief Meeah-Toon's strongly fortified position from which Burmese rebels were capturing British supplies. Severely wounded in the left thigh, the young officer sent his men on to take the stockade; he was mentioned in dispatches, promoted to lieutenant, and awarded the Burma War Medal. Soon he was serving in the Crimea, where he met the later to be famous Charles "Chinese" Gordon—with Lee the other of the two heroes he knew—and where he learned trench warfare. Here he again gained recognition by leading an attack and was again wounded, losing the sight of an eye. Young Wolseley was promoted without purchase to a captaincy in 1855 and recommended for a brevet majority, which he was prevented from receiving until he had completed the required six years of service. He served in India during the Mutiny, was mentioned five times in dispatches, and was promoted to brevet lieutenant colonel just before his twenty-seventh birthday. An exploit on the line of march from Cawnpore to Lucknow earned him a reputation for dash and courage. Wolseley was ordered to see what he could do about attacking a building which had once been a mess house for British forces but was now strongly fortified and held by the enemy. Though given the impression that he probably could not take the garrison and would have to return to report its defenses, he and his men did carry it on the first onslaught. Then,

---

[2] For a brief account of Wolseley's life I have drawn from Frederick Maurice and George Arthur, *The Life of Lord Wolseley* (London, 1924); the sketch in the *DNB;* and his autobiography, *The Story of a Soldier's Life* (2 vols.; New York, 1904). The quotation is from *The Story,* I, 1. Joseph Lehmann, *All Sir Garnet, A Life of Field-Marshal Lord Wolseley, 1833–1913* (London, 1964) appeared after this book had gone to press.

without instructions and at great risk, he proceeded to capture a second fortified area—the "Pearl Palace." He learned that his superior, Sir Colin Campbell, was furious with him for pushing beyond his orders, but the next day Sir Colin shook his fist at him, then smiled and said he was recommending him for promotion.

In 1860, the year of Lincoln's election and of South Carolina's secession, Wolseley took part in the China War and participated in the capture of the Summer Palace at Peking. This experience provided the material for his first book, written while on leave, *Narrative of the War with China in 1860.*

At the close of the China campaign the Irish youth had laid the basis for a distinguished military career. Within less than nine years he had served in four campaigns, had been wounded as many times, and had been mentioned in dispatches nine times. He had shown qualities of dashing resourcefulness and coolheadedness and had risen to the rank of lieutenant colonel by merit alone in an army where birth and purchase counted much. He was marked as a man to watch. His service had made a deep stamp upon the student and thinker, impressing upon him the serious deficiencies in the organization and training of the British army. Afterward he always held as articles of faith the necessity of preparation and organization in peacetime, of reserve training, of overcoming the debilitating purchase system, and of inducing officers to study their profession. Nearly all of the next half-century of his notable life was devoted to putting this faith into practice.

Home on leave he wrote his book on the China war, painted and sketched, and hunted in the Irish countryside where he was staying with a married sister. One winter day early in December 1861 he received an official telegram ordering him to embark at Liverpool for service in Canada as assistant quartermaster general. His orders were an incident of the military preparations for a possible war with the United States, a consequence of the rash seizure by Union Captain Charles Wilkes of two Confederate diplomats, Mason and Slidell, from a royal mail steamer, the "Trent." Statesmanship triumphed over the sense of public outrage within a few weeks, but Wolseley stayed on in Canada for a decade. He and his brother officers were engrossed by the "mighty struggle" raging to the south of them. "It is not easy to describe the breathless interest and excitement with which from month to month, almost from day to day, we English soldiers read and studied every report that could be obtained of the war as it proceeded."³ But because "we could obtain no trustworthy information regarding the Southern plans, or operations, or mode of fighting," he conceived the idea of going to Richmond to learn the facts for himself. Taking two months' leave without disclosing his plans, he passed through New York at the very moment when Lee launched the first Confederate invasion of the North, which was checked at Antietam (September 17, 1862). In company with the London *Times* correspondent, Frank Lawley, he followed an "underground passage" through Maryland and across the Potomac into Virginia.

"A Month's Visit to the Confederate Headquarters," published in *Blackwood's* (January 1863), is first of all an exciting narrative. But more important, it records the fulfillment of his zealous intent "to get to the South and judge for myself as to the condition of its people, the strength of its government, and the organization of its armies." The tour was invaluable for the future historian. It took him through the border states where loyalties were divided, across the Potomac in spite of Union gunboats, and by wagon and rail to the Confederate capital. He felt compassion, more acutely than at any time in his career, for the Confederate wounded; observed the onerous incidence of war on civilians; and thought Richmond singularly beautiful. He inspected the peninsula formed by the York and James rivers where in June McClellan and Lee had engaged in one of the celebrated campaigns of the war, and he noted especially the course of the Chickahominy River and the Federal positions at Harrison's Landing and Drewry's Bluff. Bearing letters of introduction from Secretary of War George W. Randolph, who had received him cordially, he journeyed west to the Shenandoah Valley to meet Lee, now safely back across the Potomac from the Sharpsburg campaign. His impressions of the great commander and his lieutenant, the mighty Stonewall, are of transcendent interest. Wolseley's intimate acquaintance with aspects of the Confederate scene gave him a peculiar vantage in writing of the war; yet it is to be heeded that he did not make a similar visit to interview Union generals and politicians.

Wolseley passed the succeeding years of his Canadian tour in

³ Wolseley, "An English View of the Civil War," *North American Review*, 149 (Dec. 1889), 725.

reading military history, writing a manual of military organization and tactics that sounded the theme of military preparedness and ran through many editions, and commanding the Red River expedition of 1870 to put down the Riel rebellion. In this last enterprise he was confronted with the problem of marching an army through hundreds of miles of Canadian wilderness. He adapted the customs of the Canadian *voyageur* to army methods, and with the aid of *voyageurs* he made the long march, keeping his army well fed and intact, and crushed the rebellion. The incident underscored two salient traits—his adaptability and his capacity to plan.

Further honors followed, and in May 1871 he was brought home to serve as assistant adjutant general in the War Office. In this post he vigorously supported the Cardwell army reforms that the secretary of war was promoting in a bitter struggle against defenders of the purchase of commissions and the long service system. For the next quarter-century Wolseley was the principal leader of the movement in the War Office for fostering efficiency.

Desk duty was interrupted by an assignment to command the expedition in the first Ashanti War (1873–74) in West Africa. By careful planning of a campaign that posed special problems of climate and terrain to Europeans, he scored a quick victory. For his feat he earned promotion to major general, received the thanks of Parliament, and was given a knighthood and a grant of £25,000. Popular acclaim was his. "All Sir Garnet" became a cockney expression for "all correct"; he was the model of the "Modern Major-General" in Gilbert and Sullivan's *The Pirates of Penzance*. Prime Minister Disraeli, who heaped lavish rewards on Wolseley, penned a description of the hero of the hour: "He is a little man, but with a good presence, and a bright blue eye, holds his head well, and has a lithe figure: he is only 40; so has a great career before him."[4]

In 1878 he was promoted to lieutenant general and sent to Cyprus as the first administrator of that Mediterranean island which had been ceded by Turkey to Britain that year. The following year Disraeli proposed to send him to South Africa to pacify Zululand. Queen Victoria objected that Wolseley was too unconciliatory, too ambitious, and too junior in military standing. Disraeli

[4] W. F. Monypenny and G. E. Buckle, *Life of Benjamin Disraeli* (New York, 1920), V, 305.

persisted and was vindicated by the result. He remarked at the end of the year: "Sir Garnet Wolseley has not disappointed me. He is one of those men who not only succeed, but succeed quickly. Nothing can give you an idea of the jealousy, hatred, and all uncharitableness of the Horse Gds. against our only soldier."[5] The year 1882 was notable in Wolseley's life: he attained the post of adjutant general—the key position for military training—and he led the expedition to Egypt that in a small, swift, brilliant campaign suppressed the revolt of Ahmed Arabi and occupied Cairo. Wolseley was advanced to the rank of general, again won the thanks of Parliament, was given a grant of £30,000, and was raised to the peerage as Baron Wolseley of Cairo and Wolseley.

An ensuing action in the Sudan in 1884 showered additional honors on Wolseley. The British imperial interest was menaced by the uprising of a leader called the Mahdi. After the annihilation of the British forces in the Sudan, Wolseley had sent General Charles "Chinese" Gordon to Khartum to arrange evacuation of the Upper Nile. The whole subject was enveloped in controversy. The great British administrator in Egypt, Evelyn Baring (afterward Lord Cromer), advised against the choice of Gordon, whose uncompromising Christianity and attacks on slavery had aroused the hostility of Egyptians. But Wolseley insisted upon Gordon, of whom he later said, "I admired him with a reverence I had never felt for any other man."[6] Gordon delayed evacuation and his retreat was cut off, which forced on the reluctant Gladstone government the necessity of a relief expedition. Wolseley headed the succoring forces and in "the battle of the routes" accepted the risk of an advance up the Nile with its cataracts in preference to a march across an almost waterless desert. He drew on his Red River experience and imported Canadian *voyageurs* and Kroomen from the West Coast of Africa to help his relief force go up the Nile. Two days before the expedition arrived Khartum was stormed, the townspeople slaughtered, and Gordon's head exhibited on a public highway.

Though popular indignation helped bring down the Gladstone ministry, Wolseley, who had early urged relief, was created viscount in 1885, knight of Saint Patrick, and was allowed to resume

[5] *Ibid.*, VI, 473.   [6] *The Story*, II, 90.

his tireless advocacy of army reform. It was soon after this sensational episode that Wolseley was invited by the American publisher to evaluate the *Battles and Leaders* series. The incumbent of a high military post, a world-famous commander (though he had never led large armies), heavy with honors, rich in experience on four continents, ripe in judgment, the holder of a positive military philosophy, a student of the Civil War, he was a discriminating choice.

His later history continues a story of high achievement. While occupying the post of commander in chief in Ireland he wrote *The Decline and Fall of Napoleon* (1895), completed two volumes of the *Life of Marlborough* (1894), and was promoted to field marshal in 1894. This administrative and literary interlude ended with his appointment as commander in chief of the British army in 1895 as successor to the Duke of Cambridge. Enjoying full responsibility but deprived of full authority by a recent act of Parliament, he carried on his fight for the efficient training and preparation of the British military, a need underscored in his last year of office by the lessons of the Boer War. He divested the ministry of control of army patronage and began peacetime spending on supplies and preparations. He retired in 1900, wrote two volumes of an autobiography, and died March 26, 1913—a year and a half before the outbreak of the First World War. By command of King George V every honor was paid to the venerated commander; his body lay in state in the War Office, and after a brief service he was buried in St. Paul's Cathedral.

His career, spanning half a century, personified the British Empire from the pinnacle of its power to the beginning of its eclipse. On his arrival in Calcutta in October 1852 he heard the salute fired on the death of Wellington. On his retirement from active service he saw Britain embroiled in the Boer War, reappraising her vaunted policy of splendid isolation. By the time he reported for duty in North America he was a veteran campaigner in Burma, Turkey, India, and China. He had enjoyed quick advancement because of his combination of dash and sound soldierly qualities; ability, not birth or privilege, won him promotion from ensign to the supreme command. His years in North America gave him knowledge of the New World, revealed his driving curiosity about the Civil War, afforded him time to read military history, started him on his avocation as magazine contributor, and ended full of honor reaped in the Red River campaign. By the time he wrote of Lee and the American Civil War he had acquired administrative experience as high commissioner in Cyprus, had learned something of the complexities of civil-military relationships inside the War Office, and had won spectacular laurels in West Africa and in Egypt.

He never fought a major war or attained the heroic stature of Marlborough or Wellington. At the time of his death a follower murmured, "The tragedy of Wolseley's life was that he never met a worthy foe." Yet his qualities were such as to suggest that had history offered the opportunity, he would have acquitted himself well. The most striking of his qualities were his courage, force (if not brilliance) of intellect, clearness of foresight, ingenious adaptability, and high executive capacity. With these he dealt expeditiously with many difficult imperial problems. He was a bridge between the glamour and romance of the Light Brigade and the blood and iron of von Moltke's modern army. "His real title to fame," a biographer writes, "is that he recreated the British army, which had fallen into inanition and inefficiency after the Napoleonic wars."[7]

Wolseley's literary contribution takes on special interest when one sees it in the context of historical writing on the war. First accounts of the war were contemporary to it—the literature of journalists and soldiers. This was the raw material of history, graphic, sentient, without the benefit of perspective but without the defect of old men's memories. Included in this first outpouring was the work of foreign writers, notably W. H. Russell, correspondent of the London *Times* for the first year of the war, and Lieutenant Colonel Arthur L. Fremantle, the British author of *Three Months in the Southern States,* both of whom treated fragments of the whole fabric. Continental writers soon added two important works. Prussian Captain Justus Scheibert published in 1874 *Der Burgerkrieg in Nord Amerika,* a lively review of military methods and

---

[7] Maurice and Arthur, *Life,* p. 341; *DNB, 1912–1921,* p. 591.

organization, and the Comte de Paris penned from 1874 to 1890 the seven volumes of his pro-Northern *History of the Civil War in America.*

Soon a body of literature dealing with constitutional issues developed, proceeding from Vice President Alexander H. Stephens' *Constitutional View of the Late War between the States* (1867) to Jefferson Davis' arid *The Rise and Fall of the Confederate Government*, published in 1881. These works were partial, justificatory, and scant on military events. The generals themselves made themselves heard early to late, beginning with Jubal A. Early in 1866, going on to Joseph E. Johnston's highly personal *Narrative of Military Operations* (1874), through J. B. Hood's *Advance and Retreat* (1880), and Alfred Roman's *The Military Operations of General Beauregard* (1883). The refighting of the war by the participants themselves found a worthy amphitheater in the *Century* series of the late 1880s.

Apologia, partisan reports, and fractional accounts of the war existed in abundance by 1889. No one of Wolseley's military attainments had undertaken to survey the whole of the American conflict. No British officer who visited the United States during the war became as eminent or influential. Like some of the earlier writers he possessed the advantage of direct knowledge. He had, moreover, been a prospective combatant, and if the "Trent" affair had ushered in an Anglo-Union war, he would have been joined in common cause with the Confederacy. Nevertheless, he was neither rebel nor Yankee, and he saw the war through the eyes of a trained and experienced British army officer with a wide knowledge of military history and a profound concern about the role of the military in the industrial and imperial age in which he lived.

He took a large view. Unlike Russell or Fremantle he surveyed the four years of the war, not a few months, and not just one army. Douglas S. Freeman claimed him as a Confederate historian, but Wolseley may properly be described as a historian of the whole. His point of view, nonetheless, was not national but universal, for what he wanted to determine was the lesson of the American conflict "to the soldiers of all armies." In yet another sense he wrote a tract for Anglo-Saxons, calling on them to comprehend modern war in a threatening world.

The Americans, like the Britons, depended upon sea power and volunteer armies. Wolseley recognized that the British could profitably study the American war, and he used the war's lessons as a means of forwarding his ideas at home. At a time when English officers were dazzled by Prussian success over France in 1870–71 and were studying German methods of warfare, he directed English officers to the study of the American war, helping to make it and its heroes Lee and Jackson a legacy to Britain as well as to the United States. Some of the best writing on military history has come from Britons since the day Wolseley kindled an interest: Colonel G. F. R. Henderson, Sir Frederick Maurice, Liddell Hart, Major General J. F. C. Fuller, W. Birkbeck Wood and Major J. R. Edmonds, Colin R. Ballard, and Winston Churchill.

Not a journalist or a politician, but a soldier who had served in campaigns about the globe, Wolseley, with his native perspicacity, combined the qualities of the fighting man and the staff officer with those of the professional student of war. With instruction and penetration, he brought his long-sustained interest and study to bear on the most massive war of his time.[8]

What then, did Garnet Wolseley, who possessed this rich background, see to be significant in the American Civil War? Living in a century without world war, between Waterloo and Sarajevo, he recognized the American conflict to be the longest since Napoleon. He often drew comparisons between it and the Napoleonic and Franco-Prussian Wars. As early as 1887 he discerned the future power role of the United States and, unlike Alexis de Tocqueville half a century before, forecast a coming struggle of titans, not between the United States and Russia, but between the United States and China. Wolseley's main interests, however, were not in international relations, nor in domestic politics, slavery, or secession, but in matters that we may examine under four rubrics.

The professional soldier was drawn first and foremost to the strategy and tactics employed by the combatants. We have earlier seen with what absorption he followed the armies' movements while he was in Canada and how he risked censure if not capture by stealing behind Southern lines for firsthand knowledge of Confederate warfare. He was fascinated by "the conduct of war—the

[8] Jay Luvaas, *The Military Legacy of the Civil War* (Chicago, 1959), *passim;* Freeman, *op. cit., passim.*

xix

most difficult of all arts."[9] He also saw a didactic value for England in the American war—"Its campaigns are replete with instruction" —and he hoped that "the large numbers of educated volunteer officers whom we now have in England" would study it.

Wolseley's estimations of strategy and tactics stemmed, as he repeatedly declared, from the material presented in the *Century* series. He assayed the often conflicting evidence and formed his judgments without the full benefit of the massive documentation made available by completion of the publication of *The Official Records* in 128 volumes. Those Civil War buffs who today take the highest interest in the Virginia operations may find a kindred spirit in Wolseley. But this soldier from an insular nation thought, as a matter of fact, that the lessons of amphibious warfare were the most important from a European point of view. And this pronouncement he made from a surprising source: not from Grant's operations on the western rivers, not from McClellan's campaign on the York and the James, not even from Farragut's drive up the Mississippi to New Orleans. "No! as always in war, Farragut's success," we are flatly told about this last exploit, "was almost purely the result of the moral effect which his movement produced."[10]

Rather it was in the operations around Charleston harbor where Union forces under Admiral Samuel F. DuPont and General Quincy A. Gillmore sought to wrest the well-fortified harbor from General Pierre G. T. Beauregard that he found his moral. "This cooperating action of the naval and military services, mutually supporting each other, and the fact that neither can be neglected without direct detriment to the other, seem to be among the most important lessons taught in the whole history of the American Civil War. Those lessons are of world-wide interest."[11] We may question the example he cites but subscribe to the general principle, elsewhere well exemplified, of the importance of amphibious warfare.

In his analysis of First Bull Run—"certainly one of the battles of the war which have been most talked about and written about in Europe"—he minimizes the traditional stress on the arrival on the afternoon of the battle of fresh Confederate troops who rushed from railway cars to turn the tide. Taking a larger view he held the

[9] Wolseley, "An English View," *North American Review,* 149 (Sept. 1889), 292.
[10] *Ibid.* (July 1889), p. 32.   [11] *Ibid.* (Nov. 1889), p. 597.

railway served to put the Confederates "on interior lines" with regard to the Federal armies. "The really decisive fact of the campaign was the strategical transfer of Johnston's force from the Shenandoah region, unknown to Patterson."[12] Beyond all this, he lays McDowell's defeat to the blunders made in Washington, a subject we shall save for separate discussion.

So far as western operations were concerned, it was not Grant's success at Forts Henry and Donelson or even his masterly siege of Vicksburg, but the repulse he met at Shiloh in between these victories that occupied his interest. Freeman found Wolseley's narrative "an excellent analysis of Shiloh . . . one of the best even now." Shiloh, a favorite subject of postmortems, the "severest battle fought at the West during the war,"[13] occurred when Grant, oversanguine from victory in Kentucky and Tennessee and thinking he had the Confederates on the defensive, allowed his armies to lie exposed, especially at Shiloh Church. Without entering into the rival claims of Generals Beauregard and J. E. Johnston for originating the scheme, Wolseley pronounced it "in every respect a sound military operation." He censured Grant, who was waiting for expected reinforcement under D. C. Buell before assuming the offensive, and also W. T. Sherman, who made the error of believing the enemy to be restricted to one course of action, viz., defense —both mistakes analogous to those of Wellington and Blucher before Quatre Bras and Ligny. Yet if the Federal commanders were at fault in making this almost fatal assumption which explains the failure to entrench and set up outposts, the Confederates should have attacked a day earlier, before the arrival of Union troops that threw the graycoats back to Corinth on the second day. It was to a failure of staff work that Wolseley ascribed the Confederate delay; they neglected to reduce to writing orders to corps commanders. For lack of this precaution General Leonidas Polk had not understood in conference he was to march at a designated time without waiting for written orders; hence his army was delayed and the attack postponed from Saturday to Sunday. Polk's biographer, J. H. Parks, prefers to fix blame on General William J. Hardee whose corps had to move before Polk's, but he agrees that verbal orders

[12] *Ibid.*, 148 (May 1889), p. 560.
[13] Freeman, *op. cit.*, p. 158; Robert U. Johnson and Clarence C. Buel, eds., *Battles and Leaders of the Civil War* (New York, 1956), I, 479.

had proved inadequate for the general advance. By one day's delay, Wolseley thought, the Confederacy forfeited its advantages—the opportunity to take Pittsburg Landing, to cut off and capture General Lew Wallace's division, and to make difficult if not impossible Buell's advance. The delay proved fatal to the Confederacy's chance to destroy Grant's army. "No wonder that the battle has been looked upon, on both sides, as the turning event of the Western War."[14]

There was another flaw in the execution of the brilliantly conceived Confederate plan, and this was the lack of a supreme command. Albert Sidney Johnston, the Confederate general, became absorbed in particular operations to the neglect of the general movement, leaving staff officers to go their own ways. On Johnston's death his successor Beauregard was in ill health and unable to provide the needed overall direction. "A committee directing a battle is an appalling condition of things to contemplate; but a dispersed committee, not even able to consult together, is a yet more certain cause of failure."[15] From another vantage point of strategy Wolseley believed Shiloh might have been a decisive Confederate victory had a policy of concentration of forces been adopted. The uniting of strength under Beauregard, Earl Van Dorn, and Sterling Price "would have left the whole West in the hands of the Confederacy," at least for a year.[16] As it was, Beauregard retreated from Corinth skillfully, unopposed by the Federals. The appointment of his successor Braxton Bragg and the "ill-advised invasion of Kentucky," Wolseley deemed a misfortune for the Confederacy.

Stonewall Jackson's Valley campaign excited the Briton's highest admiration. Operating while McClellan was readying his assault on Richmond by way of the Peninsula, Jackson sought "to prevent any re-enforcements from being sent to McClellan, and, above all things, to create an alarm at Washington for the safety of that capital." He carried out these missions brilliantly, moving with incredible rapidity and mystifying an enemy who had superior numbers. His surprise attacks on N. P. Banks at Front Royal and Strasbourg "appear to me to be models of their kind, both in con-

[14] Joseph H. Parks, *General Leonidas Polk, C. S. A.* (Baton Rouge, La., 1962), pp. 227–28; Wolseley, "An English View," *North American Review,* 148 (May 1889), 549.
    [15] Wolseley, *ibid.,* p. 555.   [16] *Ibid.,* 149 (Oct. 1889), 451–52.

ception and execution. They should be closely studied by all officers who wish to learn the art and science of war." Jackson's conduct of the battle of Cross Keys "against Fremont, by which he kept him apart from Shields, contriving first to fight Fremont's 10,500 men with 13,000 in a favorable position, and then to crush Shields with 3,000 men, was an operation which stamped him as a military genius of a very high order."[17]

Stonewall's maxims were, to Wolseley's mind, "golden sentences" "which comprise some of the most essential of all the principles of war":

Always mystify, mislead, and surprise the enemy, if possible; and when you strike and overcome him, never let up in the pursuit so long as your men have strength to follow; for an army routed, if hotly pursued, becomes panic-stricken, and can then be destroyed by half their number. The other rule is, never fight against heavy odds, if by any possible manoeuvring you can hurl your own force on only a part, and that the weakest part, of your enemy and crush it. Such tactics will win every time, and a small army may thus destroy a large one in detail, and repeated victory will make it invincible.[18]

Wolseley recurred more than once to these essential principles and contrasted them particularly with the Union conduct of the Peninsula campaign to which Jackson's exploits in the Valley had been ancillary. The Englishman entered dauntlessly into the battle of the generals and historians over one of the most controversial campaigns of the war, that waged on the Peninsula. McClellan's failure rested more on Washington's interference than on the general's ineptitude, he charged. In choosing to proceed against Richmond by the James instead of by direct overland movement south from Washington, McClellan had selected "the shortest and safest, as well as the most decisive, route to Richmond." Wolseley recognized the force of Lincoln's contention that the Federal capital had to be protected against Jackson or other Confederate assailants, but he believed McClellan had made adequate arrangements for its protection. His flaw, then, was a failure to satisfy Lincoln on this point, or in a larger view, "a want of knowledge of the working

---

[17] *Ibid.* (Aug. 1889), pp. 165–66.
[18] *Ibid.* (July 1889), p. 39, quoted from *Battles and Leaders* II, 297.

of popular governments in times of great national danger."[19] The withdrawal of troops by Lincoln and Stanton to keep Washington secure undermined a cardinal tenet of strategy—the concentration of energy. At the same time Wolseley found Lee at fault in letting McClellan escape because his orders were not accurately executed. Freeman cites this judgment with approval in his analysis of the campaign, calling it "a very conservative summary of the case."[20]

In the Fredericksburg campaign, where the Army of the Potomac under Union General Ambrose Burnside was decimated, Wolseley subscribed to the view that "the especial brilliancy of that campaign . . . depended upon the mode in which Lee succeeded in bringing up Jackson exactly at the right moment." More striking, though, is his judgment that Lee committed his greatest mistake of the war in failing to seize the chance to deliver a death-blow to the Northern armies. Wolseley recognized that Lee's position was better adapted to defense than offense and that his losses would probably have been severe, but the battle had been a "brilliant success." "Lee ought to have made it a crushing, if not a final, victory."[21] The critic holds Lee's reasons given in dispatches—that he did not know the extent of Burnside's losses or that Burnside did not intend to renew the attack—to be "most insufficient." These were shortcomings rather than justifications in the Englishman's view.

When we turn to the battle of Gettysburg we see Wolseley siding with Lee against General James Longstreet, not only on the question of grand strategy in waging an offensive on Northern soil, but also on the day-by-day decisions made after Federal and Confederate forces had collided in southern Pennsylvania. He scored Longstreet's fixation on defensive warfare, the arena for which had been Fredericksburg, and sympathized with Lee in the cruel blow administered to him in his relations with the "carping lieutenant" left him as his right arm after Stonewall's death. Longstreet's delays on July 2 and 3 were due to an inability "to subordinate his own views heartily to the views and orders of his great chief. The impartial military critic must admit that at . . . Gettysburg, the Confederacy paid dearly for that defect in his character."

[19] *Ibid.*, pp. 36–37.   [20] Douglas S. Freeman, *R. E. Lee* (New York, 1940), II, 233.
[21] "An English View," *North American Review*, 149 (Sept. 1889), 282, 285.

This harsh, if traditional, estimate of Longstreet contrasts with the more favorable view taken by Glenn Tucker, who argues that Longstreet was less a culprit than a scapegoat. Tucker has shown that Lee never issued a "sunrise attack" order on July 2 and that Longstreet did not delay attack. It was a different matter on July 3, when Longstreet seemed "singularly reluctant." But on the whole Tucker believes the South could never forgive Longstreet for being right.[22]

On two disputed points in General George G. Meade's management of the Union army Wolseley tends to favor Meade. The critic reminds us that Meade had just assumed command of forces whipped at Chancellorsville and now unexpectedly engaged with the victor's army. In this unpremeditated campaign "he seems to have used considerable judgment in the mode in which he brought up his reserves to the right place and at the right time." Following the Confederate failure to take the Union left on the second day, Meade that night held a council of war which decided to stay on the defensive. "This decision cannot be taken as a model for future imitation, though it happened in this instance to be the right course, as it turned out."[23]

Halleck's criticism, shared by many students, of Meade's neglect to pursue the retreating Lee elicits anger from Wolseley. Halleck, the desk general ("Old Brains") and ineffectual commander when in the west, was not the one to cast the first stone against the general who had won the first great victory of the war over Lee. The generals in the field at Gettysburg did not deem pursuit possible. General Meade "appears to have done all that any one but a man of quite transcendent military genius could have done to organize an effective pursuit."[24]

Coming finally to an examination of the last year of the war, Wolseley underscores the difference in the command positions of Grant and Lee. Lincoln's long search for a winning general had culminated March 9, 1864, in the choice of Grant, who then had been given general command of the Union armies. He was then in

[22] *Ibid.*, p. 291; Glenn Tucker, "Longstreet: Culprit or Scapegoat?," *Civil War Times Illustrated*, I (April 1962), 5ff., and *High Tide at Gettysburg* (Indianapolis, 1958), p. 347.
[23] "An English View," *North American Review*, 149 (Oct. 1889), 449.
[24] *Ibid.*, p. 448.

a station to unfold a grand strategy to cover the whole field of war. The Confederacy, on the other hand, did not unify its command under Lee until February 6, 1865, and it acted in the meantime with a sort of headlessness. Lee, then, did not have the authority, military information, or responsibility which he alone in the Southern armies was equipped to deal with; yet his prestige stood so high that Richmond disliked making a decision without consulting him.

The Confederacy's failure to achieve a unified, modern command system, however severe a handicap, did not prevent Lee from outgeneraling Grant from the Wilderness to Cold Harbor. Wolseley praised Lee's exact anticipation of the place which Grant chose to cross the Rapidan and deemed "the most brilliant stroke which Lee had prepared" in the campaign was the position he occupied on the North Anna River, May 24, 1864. Powerless to prevent Grant from crossing the easily fordable river, Lee took optimum advantage of his south-side position by forming his army in an inverted v—apex to the north, his left flank protected by Little River, his right by a swamp. With his communications thus shortened and one flank in a position to reinforce the other, he separated the two wings of Grant's army. But then he fell ill of an intestinal complaint and spared Grant a stunning blow. After two days' fighting the Union general, forced to give up a direct assault on Richmond from the north, slipped away. Lee had won a strategic victory as Grant went on to his colossal mismanagement of the Cold Harbor maneuvers northeast of Richmond.

From the beginning of this series of campaigns up to the confrontation at Cold Harbor, the balance "was heavily in favor of the South."[25] It was at this point, however, that the balance was tipped. Grant's doggedness became plain, and Confederate soldiers, though unwavering in their confidence in "Marse Robert," began to realize that the Union, notwithstanding its cost in men, might win. And while these operations were occurring in Virginia, General Sherman was moving from southeastern Tennessee to push Joseph E. Johnston back from Dalton, Georgia. When he had fallen back almost to Atlanta, Johnston was ordered by President Davis to hand over his command to General Hood. Wolseley plunged

---

[25] *Ibid.* (Nov. 1889), p. 605.

vigorously into what is called the Hood-Davis-Johnston controversy. He supported the Fabian policy and defensive warfare of
Johnston, depreciated Hood's claims for the possible success of
offensive tactics, and scored both Richmond's replacement of Johnston and the lack of a single military head. The result, as the world
knows, was the fall of Atlanta and Sherman's devastating march to
the sea. Yet Wolseley agrees with Sherman's judgment that the
swath cut across Georgia was less significant than the strategic position he attained at Savannah, from where he could march north
through the Carolinas to join forces with Grant. All the while the
Confederacy was losing the advantage that Jackson's earlier campaign in the Shenandoah Valley had given it, for General Philip
Sheridan, after demoralizing the graycoats under Jubal Early, had
devastated an important source of subsistence for Lee's "doomed
army."

In the final operations at Drewry's Bluff, Petersburg, and Richmond, Wolseley found further reason to indict Confederate statesmanship for its failure to name a commander in chief over all its
armies. Had Lee been given this "all-decisive" unity of command,
he and Beauregard might have effectively cooperated in the battle
of Drewry's Bluff, and the outcome might have been different. Enjoying his advantage, Grant moved the armies of Meade and Butler
upon Petersburg, and Lee was immobilized until Sheridan's victory at Five Forks forced his retreat and ultimate surrender at Appomattox.

Wolseley's reflections upon the strategic and tactical noteworthi-
ness of the American Civil War are perhaps his most consequential
contributions. At the same time he, in company with others who
have found inspiration in the history of great wars, discerned valuable lessons in the example of noble lives. To Wolseley the figure
of R. E. Lee transcended all others on the American scene: he
found him the greatest soldier of his age, "the most perfect man I
ever met."[26] During his visit to the Confederacy Wolseley, trav-
eling in discomfort from Richmond to Lee's headquarters near
Winchester, had sought out Lee. His contemporary portrait of the
great commander is remarkable:

[26] "General Lee," *Macmillan's Magazine,* LV (March 1887), 321.

He is a strongly built man, about five feet eleven in height, and apparently not more than fifty years of age. His hair and beard are nearly white; but his dark brown eyes still shine with all the brightness of youth, and beam with a most pleasing expression. Indeed, his whole face is kindly and benevolent in the highest degree. In manner, though sufficiently conversible, he is slightly reserved; but he is a person that, wherever seen, whether in castle or a hovel, alone or in a crowd, must at once attract attention as being a splendid specimen of an English gentleman, with one of the most rarely handsome faces I ever saw.[27]

The young Englishman was awed by Lee's inherent greatness, and forty years later he recollected, "I never felt my own individual insignificance more keenly than I did in his presence."[28]

Wolseley was struck also by the extreme simplicity of Lee's headquarters, so different from the pomp and circumstance surrounding those of European generals. He noted the spontaneous respect paid the general by officers and men and agreed with General Winfield Scott that Lee's accession to the Confederacy was worth 20,000 men.

Wolseley's admiring, yet not unmeasured and withal perceptive, sketch of Lee ("a classic of Confederate literature") swiftly traces Lee's ancestry, boyhood, and youth through his education at West Point and service in the Mexican War "to the most important epoch in his life, when the Southern States left the Union." Wolseley deals understandingly with the crosscurrents which then beset Lee: nationalism and state sovereignty, secession and love of the Union, slavery and emancipation, resignation from the United States Army and the offer of its supreme command. His love of his own state, Virginia, "his unselfish patriotism, caused him to relinquish home, fortune, a certain future, in fact everything for her sake." Without peer in the tableau of Union and Confederate warriors, he had a parallel in Marlborough, "difficult to equal between any other two great men of modern times."[29]

A striking quality of this brief biography, perhaps the most eloquent of Wolseley's writings, is the author's emphasis upon the problems Lee faced in organizing, equipping, and commanding his Southern soldiers. The Virginian, anticipating a long struggle,

---

[27] "A Month's Visit to the Confederate Headquarters," *Blackwood's Edinburgh Magazine*, XCIII (January 1863), 18.
[28] *The Story*, II, 135.   [29] "General Lee," p. 326.

pleaded for enlistments for its duration, deplored soldiers' election of their officers, and withstood the popular outcry for a quick victory while he methodically went forward with the formation of an army. "He knew what he wanted. He knew what any army should be, and how it should be organised, both in a military as well as an administrative sense. In about two months he had created a little army of fifty thousand men, animated by a lofty patriotism and courage that made them unconquerable by any similarly constituted army."[30]

His army equipped itself with abandoned Federal arms and supplies. But throughout the war Lee was handicapped by bad staff organization that frustrated his truly great strategy and unquestionably sound tactics. "Over and over again was the South apparently 'within a stone's throw of independence,' as it has been many times remarked, when, from want of a thoroughly good staff to organise pursuit, the occasion was lost, and the enemy allowed to escape."[31] Lee's disadvantage was, however, offset by the same flaw in the Union army until the war entered its fourth year.

Lee's trials brought into relief certain qualities of his character: his lack of bitterness toward enemy generals, remarkable in civil war; his softness of heart, a fault in a soldier; his subordination to civil government; and the "dignified resignation" with which he bore defeat. The equal of George Washington, he "towered far above all men on either side in that struggle." "I have met many of the great men of my time, but Lee alone impressed me with the feeling that I was in the presence of a man who was cast in a grander mould, and made of different and of finer metal than all other men."[32]

Such praise, stressing Lee's personal qualities, prompted a sharp dissent from General Sherman in the *North American Review*. The American criticized Lee for his decision to resign from the United States Army, for his limited conception of the war (in Virginia and not the continent), and for his failure as an aggressive soldier. Sherman placed Grant, the continental strategist, dogged fighter, and generous conqueror, and Thomas, victor of Nashville, the only battle which "annihilated an army," above Lee.[33]

[30] *Ibid.*, p. 327.   [31] *Ibid.*, p. 328.   [32] *Ibid.*, p. 331.
[33] W. T. Sherman, "Grant, Thomas, Lee," *North American Review*, 144 (May 1887), 437–50.

Like many contemporaries Wolseley did not at first perceive the greatness of the Union president. His upper-class partiality for the Southern cause that flashes through "A Month's Visit to the Confederate Headquarters" betrayed him into branding Lincoln "an insignificant lawyer."[34] Time corrected this misjudgment; nearly a quarter of a century later Lincoln had become "the far-seeing statesman of iron will, of unflinching determination" and, along with Lee, one of "two figures who stand out in that history towering above all others, both cast in hard metal that will be for ever proof against the belittling efforts of all future detractors."[35] Wolseley now counted Lincoln one of America's greatest presidents, shrewd, modest, nobly doing his duty, a rival with Lee as favorite of the gods. The English critic, however, restricted his laudation of Lincoln to the President's civilian achievements, and censured him unsparingly for interfering with the generals in the field. "Entirely ignorant of war," was Wolseley's charge, which is in diametrical contrast with the modern judgment of T. Harry Williams who says Lincoln was "a great natural strategist, a better one than any of his generals."[36] Whatever one may think of this controversy, it seems plain that Wolseley, whose military insight was superior to his political, never fully grasped the brilliance of Lincoln the statesman.

When we turn to Wolseley's treatment of Stonewall Jackson we can see even more clearly that though Lincoln earned Wolseley's respect, he failed to stir the Englishman's imagination as perhaps only a soldier—and a God-fearing soldier—could. The pen portrait is notable:

He has a broad open forehead, from which the hair is well brushed back; a shapely nose, straight, and rather long; thin colourless cheeks, with only a very small allowance of whisker; a cleanly-shaven upper lip and chin; and a pair of fine greyish-blue eyes, rather sunken, with overhanging brows, which intensify the keenness of his gaze, but without imparting any fierceness to it.[37]

Wolseley's analysis of Jackson's Valley campaign has already been presented in detail, and we have seen his praise of the mas-

[34] "A Month's Visit," p. 29.   [35] "General Lee," p. 322.
[36] *Lincoln and His Generals* (New York, 1952), p. vii.
[37] "A Month's Visit," p. 21.

terly strategy and tactics, the loyal dispatch of Lee's wishes, and the resolution to win independence for the South that he brought to the fighting. Stern soldiering and determined patriotism moved Wolseley to admiration, but it was the annexed qualities of a Christian hero that claimed his highest praise. In his autobiography Wolseley recorded his meeting with Jackson and how he asked the general, who had none of the refined physical characteristics of the aristocratic Lee, what he loved best to remember about his visit to England. Jackson "thought for a couple of minutes, and then, turning upon me those remarkable eyes, lit up for the moment with a look of real enthusiasm, he answered, 'The seven lancet windows in York Minster.' "[38]

His esteem for Jackson served to give the Southerner a worthy biographer. After reading an anonymously written book, *The Campaign of Fredericksburg,* Wolseley searched out the author, a British major, G. F. R. Henderson, who had toured Virginia battle-fields in 1883–84. He had Henderson assigned to Sandhurst as instructor in military topography and encouraged him to write *Stonewall Jackson and the American Civil War,* the classic that appeared in 1898. At Henderson's request Wolseley wrote the introduction to the second edition.

Little need be added here to what has been previously told about the prototypes of noble lives Wolseley discovered in the American war. Wolseley found Grant not of the same order of genius as Lee, but towering head and shoulders over all other Federal captains in 1863. He applauded the ability and vision with which he grasped the whole strategy of victory and the pluck and determination with which he later effected the realization of his strategy. The Union owed its life to him.[39] As to McClellan, Wolseley noted that Lee spoke of him with the most respect and regard among Union generals and that he had an inspiriting quality on his men. After the demoralization of Second Manassas McClellan "had the wand of the enchanter" over the "disorganised rabble" of Pope's army; commanding it at Antietam, he saved the city of Washington. Hamstrung in executing his well-conceived Peninsular campaign, he could not give the Union the victory Lincoln and public opinion were demanding. In an essay on "Military

---

[38] *The Story,* II, 140–41.
[39] Wolseley, "An English View," *North American Review,* 149, (Nov. 1889), 600.

Genius," in which he ranked Lee among Caesar, Hannibal, Marlborough, and Napoleon, Wolseley observed that McClellan, never able to estimate accurately his enemy's numbers, lacked "intuitive genius for war."[40]

Jefferson Davis suffered a stinging indictment: "a third-rate man, and a most unfortunate selection for the office of President." Wolseley subscribed to the animadversions made by the Southern fire-eater Robert Barnwell Rhett in *Battles and Leaders* and wryly declared the Northern troops wrong in wanting to "hang Jeff Davis to a sour-apple tree," because he "unwittingly worked for them." Puffed up with a belief in his superior wisdom, rejecting the urging of his military advisers to adopt the policy of concentration, he and his civilian associates lost the war in 1862.[41] Present-day historians, and some of them Southern-born, subscribe to such strictures, but Jefferson Davis himself answered the Englishman's aspersions on his conduct of the Confederacy.

Davis did not, could not, deal with the paramount question of his own fitness for the presidency. Nor did he, in an article called "Lord Wolseley's Mistakes," defend his interference in the plans of his field commanders, his tardy tightening-up of a command system, or the matter of favorites among generals. He sought, instead, to treat specific points made by Wolseley: his refusal of 360,-000 men at the start of the war, expectation that 10,000 Enfield rifles would overawe the United States, neglect to buy the East Indian fleet, failure to keep the ports open, and rejection of all means to place Confederate finances on a sound basis. On all but the last point the palm must be given President Davis, for he adduces good supporting evidence in his own behalf. Modern historians, however, do censure Davis for his financial policies, especially his failure to combat inflation; a division of opinon as to the feasibility of using cotton as a means to finance the war exists among historians. Davis's self-defense, particularistic in character, does not go to the heart of the matter—his wartime leadership.[42]

[40] "A Month's Visit," pp. 18–19; *Fortnightly Review*, XLIV (September 1888), 309.
[41] "An English View," *North American Review*, 148 (May 1889), 539; *The Story*, II, 119.
[42] Jefferson Davis, "Lord Wolseley's Mistakes," *North American Review*, 149 (Oct. 1889), 472–82.

In Nathan Bedford Forrest, Wolseley found one of the few memorable civilians who commanded troops in the Civil War. Forrest was an exception to one of the critic's favorite themes: that the professional soldier was almost invariably superior in war. But Forrest was "nature's soldier." Wolseley regarded the famous raider as a product of the borderland, one who superimposed upon a true military instinct the qualities of "great self-confidence, self-reliance, and reticence . . . of quick resolves and prompt execution, of inexhaustible resource, and of ready and clever expedients." He knew military tactics not through books but "in accordance with common sense and business principles"; his mode of fighting was distinguished by "the invariable hardihood and recklessness with which he dashed upon the enemy." In a sketch that for the most part stressed character rather than military operations, Wolseley did find Forrest's defeat of General Sturgis worthy of the military student's attention; within the space of thirty hours Forrest fought a battle and pursued the enemy for nearly sixty miles, "killing numbers all the way." Perhaps Wolseley saw something of himself in Forrest—a soldier who without military education or governmental favor corroborated Napoleon's dictum: "In war men are nothing; a man is everything."[43]

In an essay written on the occasion of General Sherman's death, Wolseley saw him as the right arm of Grant, just as Stonewall Jackson was the right arm of Lee. Sherman and Jackson "were the two most brilliant and dashing executive leaders in the war." Wolseley lauded Sherman for foreseeing a long war and the need for large forces; a trait that he singled out for remark was Sherman's scrupulous subordination to Grant in their campaigns and his deference to the government at Washington in its decisions about his command assignments. This trait displayed itself most admirably in the Vicksburg campaign where Sherman's strategic views were overruled by Grant; nevertheless, Sherman threw himself heart and soul into the project of taking the river fortress.

Wolseley thought Sherman ought to have struck harder at first in the Atlanta campaign, since it would have been advantageous to

[43] Wolseley, "General Forrest," *United Service Magazine*, CXXVII (April–May 1892), 1–14, 113–24 (available on microfilm, Alderman Library, University of Virginia). Wolseley's essays on Forrest and Sherman are not included in my compilation of his works because they are in some measure repetitious.

fight as close as possible to his base. The critic ascribed Sherman's overcaution to respect for Johnston; once he had confronted Hood, he gained a sense of confidence that gave him an easier victory. Wolseley's judgment of the march to the sea was not unconventional: by this exploit, which was his own idea, Sherman will be best remembered; the campaign had a most important bearing on the destruction of the Confederacy, for it deprived Lee of subsistence and transport animals.

A faithful subordinate, yet one also capable of originality and dash, Sherman was "endowed with that true genius which enables men to win battles." In the unimpassioned judgment of history, Wolseley believed that three names would stand out among those who saved the Union. Apparently ranking them in order of greatness, he named Lincoln, Grant, and Sherman.[44]

The third great lesson the Englishman read in the war was the need of the United States and England to have a "well-organised standing army in the highest state of efficiency, and composed of thoroughly-trained and full-grown men." This is a recurring theme in his pages and a major theme of Wolseley's life as well. He had seen the effects of war coming to a nation unprepared: improvised armies, often composed of mobs or rabble, inadequate supplies, incompetent officers, who had been appointed because of their political influence or elected because of their popularity, leading men who had never known the benefit of reserve training.

At the war's start the United States could call upon only a skeleton military establishment. There were in all only 16,402 officers and men before the Southerners left. Wolseley argued "that had the United States been able, early in 1861, to put into the field, in addition to their volunteers, one Army Corps of regular troops, the war would have ended in a few months."[45] Not all students would agree with this, for military preparedness requires good generalship to take advantage of it, but it is abundantly plain that the United States gained from the Civil War lessons for the future of organization and administration useful for the First World War

[44] Wolseley, "General Sherman," *United Service Magazine,* CXXV (May–July 1891), 97–116, 194–216, 289–309 (available on microfilm, Alderman Library, University of Virginia).
[45] "Introduction" to G. F. R. Henderson, *Stonewall Jackson and the American Civil War* (London, 1906), I, x.

and the continuing crisis of the mid-twentieth century. During the conflict, moreover, the Union did resort for the first time to conscription, did settle for subsequent generations the controversy over the value of West Point training, and did evolve a modern command system.

Finally, Wolseley found instruction in the civil-military relationships that existed on both sides in the war. As he stated in a pithy paragraph:

The . . . lesson is that to hand over to civilians the administration and organisation of the army, whether in peace or war, or to allow them to interfere in the selection of officers for command or promotion, is most injurious to efficiency; while, during war, to allow them, no matter how high their political capacity, to dictate to commanders in the field any line of conduct, after the army has once received its commission, is simply to ensure disaster.[46]

We should not misconstrue his views. What he is saying is not a challenge to the supremacy of the civil branch of government over the military, the principle embedded in the Constitution of the United States. He recognized the subordination of the soldier to the statesman, but he stressed the grave danger of political interference with the field commander. He had no doubt that Lincoln's interference with McClellan in the spring of 1862 probably cost that commander and his country victory over Lee and the Confederacy. At the same time in the Confederate capital, Secretary of War Judah P. Benjamin was committing the same error and causing Stonewall Jackson to offer his resignation.

Wolseley believed that the general pattern of the war vindicated his stand. While Lincoln and Secretary of War Edwin Stanton were meddling with the armies, the Union fortunes languished; when Grant was given a free rein, they prospered. So too in the South during the brief period of Lee's authority. Nor did either general, despite traditional fears of Caesarism, pose any menace to civilian government or national finances. The soldier, trained to be obedient and patriotic, "is less likely than others to run counter to constituted authority."[47] A professional man, administering a difficult art, bearing an immense responsibility, a general must be trusted to make the requisite decisions once assigned to command.

[46] *Ibid.*   [47] *Ibid.,* p. xv.

Two further points loom in Wolseley's analysis of civil-military relationships during the Civil War. The first of these is the error made by politicians North and South in pursuing the policy of local defense which entailed retention of large forces to defend unimportant places. The strategy of concentration, he believed, would have effected Confederate successes in the west—in the trans-Mississippi region, in Kentucky, Tennessee, and at Shiloh. On the Union side we have noted that he thought McClellan would have profited by a concentration of Federal forces.

Wolseley's other observation was concerned with the terrible pressure facing generals because of ignorant public opinion. "The true criminal," "Public Opinion," with the cry "On To Richmond!" brought the rashness of First Bull Run, where a greenhorn army was thrown into battle; it turned McClellan's petty success in West Virginia into a Napoleonic victory, and was responsible for the disaster of Chancellorsville. The danger to military men of "that hoary-headed and cruel old rascal, Public Opinion," was greater in Britain than in the United States, he reflected, where the Constitution provided for "an appeal from him when he is drunk to the time when he is sober." Could a "chastened and wise public opinion" be formed, it "would be an incalculable future benefit to all self-governing nations."[48]

General James B. Fry wrote a salutary corrective to Wolseley's views about civil interference with generals. Fry asserted that the war was not strictly a military matter but a vast sectional struggle reaching beyond mere feats of arms and requiring civil direction. On the McClellan controversy he argued that the young, dilatory general needed prodding; and on the moot question of whether McClellan might have taken Richmond in his Peninsular campaign, he pointed out that the Union general had "the best two-thirds of McDowell's corps, before the enemy drove him back to the James River." Fry also defended Halleck against Wolseley's criticism that he had not carried out a pursuit after Shiloh; Fry observed that Grant was in charge and that Halleck, who had been in St. Louis during the battle, did not arrive in the field until the enemy was safely in Corinth. (We may note here that Halleck's general reputation has been recently rehabilitated by stress on his

[48] "An English View," *North American Review,* 148 (May 1889), 562–63; 149 (Sept. 1889), 292.

work in modernizing and professionalizing a national army.) Fry concluded by affirming his belief that history would sustain the administration against the generals for misfortunes in the field—a prediction that finds much support today.[49]

We may note several shortcomings in Wolseley the military critic. One is his propensity towards hero worship, at its most full-blown in his treatment of Lee. General Sherman's reply was a good antidote, though it perhaps went overfar in deflating the Confederate leader. A second deficiency is in his estimation of the Union army. In the first place, he exaggerated Union numerical superiority in battles, whereas in fact reducing numbers to effectives will often markedly narrow the differences. Second, he betrays a Confederate bias. To cite some of the most unfavorable phrases about the Federals, we read: "a vast mob," "the offscourings of every European nation," and "Mr. Lincoln's mercenaries." On the other hand: "I have seen many armies file past in all the pomp of bright clothing and well-polished accoutrements; but I never saw one composed of finer men, or that looked more like *work*, than that portion of General Lee's army which I was fortunate enough to see inspected."

Lessons in strategy and tactics, examples of noble lives, illustrations of the need for a well-organized standing army, and the dangers of civil interference with the army—such were the four dimensions of the educative value of the American Civil War. It is a soldierly estimate. One may be struck by the absence of strong interest in such vital questions as, Why the Civil War? Who was responsible? Was slavery evil? Was secession right? Wolseley briefly expressed opinions on these topics, but only incidentally. Not the least interesting part of his writings is the opaque plea he made in the winter of 1862–63 for British recognition of the Confederacy. Nevertheless, in his mature judgment he celebrated the outcome, a reunited nation, the future powerful protagonist of Christianity against heathendom, a country already in 1903 "the foremost nation in the world."[50]

[49] James B. Fry, "Lord Wolseley Answered," *North American Review*, 149 (Dec. 1889), 728–40.
[50] *The Story*, II, 144.

A MONTH'S VISIT TO THE
CONFEDERATE HEADQUARTERS

OF WOLSELEY'S WRITINGS ON THE CIVIL WAR, HIS "A MONTH'S *Visit" is the only contemporary piece. It has a freshness and a sense of excitement unique in his work, and is the most pro-Confederate of his literary products. The essay was published in* Blackwood's Edinburgh Magazine *of January 1863.*

The personal reconnaissance recorded here was made in September and October of 1862. The "Trent" crisis that had taken Wolseley to Canada had long since been resolved, and the Civil War had passed through an initial phase which embraced the two battles of Bull Run, McClellan's Peninsular campaign, and Antietam—actually fought while Wolseley was beginning his visit. From an autobiographical point of view, we have here a record of an adventurous man, willing to subject himself to arduous travel at personal hazard in order to satisfy his mind on questions about the Southern people, their government, and their armies. Throughout the summer of 1862 he had been following every move of the two armies on the maps, but had been unable to obtain re-liable information about Confederate plans, operations, or style of fighting. He secured two months' leave and made his way through New York to Baltimore.

Especially interesting are his descriptions of his stealthy entrance into the Confederacy, the civilian scenes on the way to Richmond and in that capital, his interviews with Lee and Jackson, and indications of his strong partiality for the South. On this last subject one may demur at Wolseley's somewhat overdrawn charges of Yankee harshness and des-potism and yet recall that the Union government, confronted by the real or potential disloyalty of thousands of persons, abridged traditional Anglo-Saxon safeguards of civil liberty and resorted to martial law and the suspension of the writ of habeas corpus.

The final pages of this essay, with their thinly masked plea for Eng-lish recognition of the Confederacy, disclose a conservative and aristo-cratic view shared by many Britons of the upper class. It is significant that he wrote for Blackwood's, *a journal noted for its animus toward the Northern cause. At the very time Wolseley was making his visit the British government was deliberating on taking the precise steps he advo-cated—mediation and recognition—steps postponed (and never taken)*

by Northern success at Antietam. Wolseley saw the Confederate strug-
gle as one for country and liberty, and advantageous to England and
Europe in cutting down to size the arrogant American republic. From a
later perspective he would see the advantages to England and the Chris-
tian world of a united, strong American republic.

A MONTH'S VISIT TO THE
CONFEDERATE HEADQUARTERS

KNOWING how little reliance can be placed at any time upon the information published in American newspapers, I was very anxious, if possible, to get to the South and judge for myself as to the condition of its people, the strength of its government, and the organisation of its armies.[1] I had often, during the last year, tried to conjecture what Richmond was like, and felt quite curious to know how the public and private business of the Government was carried on. I confess I entertained a wholesome dread of being taken prisoner by the Yankees in my endeavour to get through their lines, having personally learnt from others who had had the misfortune to come under the displeasure of local military autocrats, how disagreeable they were in the habit of making a prison residence—in many instances, indeed, evincing a barbarity of conduct disgraceful to any nation claiming English descent. But the desire of knowledge, or the promptings of curiosity, as the case may be, determined me upon running all risks, and making my way into the forbidden land of Dixey, despite all the blockading, gunboats, and Federal patrols along the Potomac River. There was, however, one great drawback to my happiness in starting upon this expedition—namely, the necessity which existed for my being back in New York by the 20th of October, and it was already the 11th of September when I left that city. As every one is aware who has travelled in America, letters of introduction are almost indispensable to the comfort of a traveller; certainly so to one whose time being limited makes him necessarily anxious to compress much sight-seeing and amusement into the briefest period possible. Before starting, therefore, I had furnished myself with a number of these "open Sesame" billets, many of which were from persons with whom I was but very slightly acquainted, and in some instances

[1] The text of this article and of the others by Wolseley presented in this book are reproduced here without correction or alteration.

5

addressed to parties but little known to the writers of the epistles in question. This, however, is a matter of little importance in the States. In England, except in particular cases, a very general prejudice against giving letters of this description exists. But brother Jonathan, more pachydermatous and less particular, seems wholly to disregard such little punctilios. And although you may have but just made his acquaintance, if he stops to speak to any gentleman for a few moments when walking with you, he considers it necessary to introduce you to him. In this way it is easy to provide one's self with letters of introduction, the acquaintance of to-day in one town being quite ready and willing to introduce you to the notice of whatever friends he may chance to possess in the next to which you are going—and so on from place to place.

It is scarcely necessary to mention that messengers go backwards and forwards from Richmond to the Northern States almost daily. Now and then some unlucky fellows have been caught, but before their capture they have generally succeeded in destroying the papers and letters of which they were bearers. The frontier to be guarded is so very extensive, that even the vast mob of the half million of men supposed to be in the Federal ranks, if employed only along it, would still be insufficient for the purpose of thoroughly blockading it against the passage of individuals. The inhabitants in and about the neighbourhood of the outposts must be allowed a little liberty of locomotion—their farm duties demand it; and, as a natural consequence when the two contending parties speak the same language, are the same people, and in many districts divided as to their predilections for and against Secession, to prevent the Confederates from receiving information of what goes on at Washington, or effectually to hinder individuals from joining the Southern bands, would be a physical impossibility. The case is different, however, when Englishmen wish to pass over. Our dress, appearance, and, as Americans say, our *patois* English, declare our nationality everywhere in the States. We are all considered as rebel sympathisers; and that we should desire to visit the Southern Republic merely for pleasure and with disinterested views is deemed almost incredible. We must be employed in either smuggling over arms, quinine, tea, or sugar, or engaged in some political conspiracy in aid of "the d——d rebels." Our presence in the border States, when unaccompanied by some Federal official, is consequently viewed with suspicion; particularly if we should leave the large towns and take to roving through the country villages near the actual frontier. Few of *us* will consent, for the mere sake of pleasure, to face the discomfort of travelling about without a change of clothes, a sponge, towel, toothbrush, and other items, which require a small portmanteau for their conveyance; but an American, on the contrary, will travel for weeks with only a few paper collars and a pocket-comb! This dreadful portmanteau of ours, then, is our greatest impediment in getting through the lines. It attracts such attention that, however faithfully an Englishman may copy an American in his black trousers, frock-coat, black satin waistcoat, and unbecoming beard, this fatal encumbrance at once proclaims him to be British, and is also regarded as an offensive claim to exclusiveness, and an affectation of superiority, always hurtful to the feelings of your free-born American. To convey a portmanteau through the debatable ground, so cleared of four-footed animals and carts by the Northern armies, is as great a matter of difficulty as the transport of large stores with a field force is always to a general.

If a man from Maryland or Kentucky wishes to join one of Jackson's regiments, he can always do so easily, as he will find hundreds of men all along the frontier glad to aid him in doing so; but when the same individuals are appealed to by foreigners, they feel naturally disinclined to compromise their personal liberty and private property by aiding people who may be spies endeavouring to entrap them, and of whose real object they must be in any case entirely ignorant. Fortunately, however, the love of gain inherent in human nature, particularly when it is impoverished, here comes to the rescue, and a liberal bribe bridges over most difficulties. These and some other circumstances which I shall mention as I proceed in the narrative of my "underground journey," as getting from the Northern to the Southern lines is called, are serious obstacles in the way of a tour through the Confederate States; but, as I have before stated, the strong desire to obtain some personal acquaintance with the Secession leaders and generals was rather increased than otherwise by the difficulties to be encountered in doing so. To enter into particulars as to the exact route I took, the various houses I stopped at, or the point at which I crossed the Potomac, might compromise others. Suffice it to say, therefore, that I travelled in a two-horse waggon, doing about

7

thirty miles a-day, until I reached the village from which I had arranged that my final start should be made; and where I was informed certain people, with whose names I had been furnished, would arrange all matters for me. The country I passed through was very picturesque, undulating, and well cultivated; but the roads were infamous, winding about from farm to farm, with gates to be opened and shut whenever you passed from one plantation to another. There were not any turnpikes, and no trouble seemed ever to have been expended in even repairing the farm communications that existed. As we approached the Potomac the land became much richer, and tobacco crops more numerous. This season has been a fine one for the "weed," but it was melancholy to see such quantities of it running to seed, and badly cared for, from the scarcity of farm hands, as the plantation slaves are called. Many farmers told me they had not had such a fine crop for years past, but that they must lose a large portion of it from want of hands to cut and spear it. These men were the descendants of those who had joined the Union upon the stipulated faith of their slaves being guaranteed to them, and who would never have joined with any State which would have refused to surrender a fugitive slave. In the face, however, of this treaty, I may call it, the Northern States not only now refuse to give up these runaways, but actually do their utmost to seduce them from their owners. No cavalry patrol ever passes through a village or plantation in that part of the country without carrying away some negro, for whom perhaps a large price had been paid. I am not now going into the vexed question of slavery; no man abhors the institution more than I do; but I love justice, according to the established laws, more dearly than any wild theory regarding abolition: of which all that we know is that, as carried out in our West Indian possessions, it has been a failure in every respect. I need scarcely add that, by all to whom I spoke in those districts, the Northern rule was detested. Every man now feels that the bayonet of the military despot is at his breast, that he is held in subjection against his will by force; and further, as it would seem, that the Lincoln Ministry are desirous of effacing still more completely any superstitious allegiance which he might be expected to owe the Stars and Stripes. The safe retention of personal property is made to depend upon the will and pleasure of some petty provost-marshal of the neighbourhood—a functionary who has also the power of consigning the owners, and perhaps their families, to the miseries of Fort Warren, where even the advice and aid of a lawyer will be denied them. I subsequently passed through districts in Virginia almost reduced by Yankee depredations to their primeval state of waste. But even there I did not hear such expressions of deep hatred, and I may say intense longing for revenge, as in some of the slave-owning counties on the left of the Potomac. These sentiments were only expressed in secret, however. Gentlemen now fear to give their opinion at table, lest the slaves who stand behind them should desert, and play the intelligent contraband's part at the nearest Federal post, and there impeach their master's loyalty.

The white population look cowed.

Tyranny and illegal arrests have stricken them with terror. Many will at first declare that death would be preferable. But though such lofty sentiments are very fitting for young men untrammelled by family ties, and have been often avowed by the bachelors in the border States, when a man has a wife and children, for whom he has no means of providing except by the produce of his farm, more matter-of-fact considerations naturally outweigh the heroic promptings of his nature, and he bridles his tongue in public, though with curses not loud but deep he speaks of his oppressor in private. If in the final settlement of this war the border States are retained in the Union, a very large number of these men will sell off their plantations and move south. The present state of affairs cannot exist much longer. Human beings may and do often submit quietly to coercion for years; but when such coercion descends from great to little matters, from depriving men of a voice in public affairs to all the little minor vexations which narrow-minded, short-sighted despots have resorted to from the era of curfew-bells down to the strictly-maintained passport system of the present day, the iron enters into the soul with such an irritating power that the recklessness of despair will often cause the meekest to turn round and strike his oppressor, even though perfectly aware that the blow must be followed by certain death. Every species of minor annoyance has been resorted to by the Federal authorities, with the avowed determination of coercing men into the Union. Gentlemen cannot now buy boots, clothes, or supplies for their servants in Baltimore or Washington without taking the oath of allegiance; and when driving in their carriages from those cities, every parcel they may have with them is carefully searched. Whilst we were in the former place, no goods could be shipped from thence unless the buyer, seller, and captain of the ship took the oaths of allegiance, and swore that the goods were intended for loyal people. The slaves will not live upon fresh meat —nothing has a greater tendency to drive them to mutiny than cutting off their supplies of salt provisions; and the present Ministry, aware of this fact, hope by so doing to cause all the servants of men favourable to the South to desert, if not to rise against their masters. I know several instances in which violent Secessionists have, to prevent such a catastrophe, sworn the necessary oaths; which, however, from being taken, so to speak, *nolens volens,* they do not consider binding; and those of more rigid principles, who will not thus forswear themselves, suffer heavily in consequence.

The draft had not yet been enforced when we passed through the country, but preparations were being made everywhere for enforcing it. Provost-marshals were drawing up the rolls, and it was curious to hear of the various ailments and long-standing bodily injuries that men were urging as pleas for exemption. In some cases they escaped the enrolment on most frivolous pretences, whilst in others, men with so much stronger claims to exemption had their names inserted upon the drafting lists, that there were fair grounds for believing that the officials employed were not proof against the temptation of a bribe. The draft has since been enforced, and, although it has supplied the Northern ranks with some hundreds of unwilling soldiers, it has also had the effect of swelling the Southern ranks; as all those not having large property at stake whose names were drawn, have fled across the Potomac— men who are naturally disinclined to fight, but who, if forced to do so, are determined at least not to carry a musket against the cause they love.

For the first few nights of our journeyings we stopped at different gentlemen's houses, where we were entertained with patriarchal hospitality. It was interesting in some instances to hear the history of these old homesteads; many of them had been built before the declaration of independence, and more than one was of brick imported from England. All the proprietors boasted of their English descent from good families, and seemed to attach far greater importance to blood and ancient pedigree than even we do. The times have impoverished a vast number of families, so that, although you are still received with as much honest warmth as ever, their ability to entertain you is not the same as it was in former days. Indeed, some of them have been so reduced in circumstances that their children are unprovided with shoes, and the young sons of men, once wealthy, may in many places be seen running about barefooted. The internal appliances of comfort now to be found in the smallest English country houses are unknown amongst them; and in no case did there seem to be any attempt made to substitute modern furniture for the old uncomfortable chairs and sofas of the past generation. The only modern article I saw in any sitting-room in these old country houses was the Yankee rocking-chairs—in which, in every part of the States, the mistress of the house is sure to be seen moving backwards and forwards, with the regularity of a pendulum. There, as in all other places that I visited in the South, hatred of Northern rule seemed to glow far more intensely in the breasts of the ladies than in those of the men. A lady told me that in Norfolk, when passing a Federal officer, every woman gathered up her skirts close to her side, lest they should be contaminated by even grazing a Yankee; and that all females, rich and poor, turned away their heads when a Northern soldier approached. Nothing tends to wound the sensibilities of an American more than such conduct, for the one soft point in his character is a sort of religious veneration for the fair sex, and a desire to be remarked, if not admired, by every one of them, young and old, alike in public and private.

The first night our fortunes led us to an inn, we were shown up to a dingy little sleeping apartment with only one bed in it. To expostulate, however, and assure the host that English gentlemen are always accustomed to the luxury of a bed each, would have been perfectly useless—it being an established custom of the country for two, and sometimes even three, men to sleep together. We consequently accepted what was provided for us without remark, and as soon as the landlord withdrew, we cut the Gordian knot of the difficulty by dividing the bed-clothes, which enabled one to sleep on the floor. But, unfortunately, the blankets were so thickly inhabited by a race of insects which shall be nameless, that I cannot say I "took mine ease in mine inn." My first night's experience of a Southern country hostel, therefore, was far from being agreeable.

On the following morning we started in a two-horsed waggon for the house of a gentleman who we were informed would instruct us as to our best means of getting across the Potomac. But when we arrived at his residence, he came out with terror depicted on his countenance, and, assuring us that he was in hourly expectation of a visit from the Yankees himself, he advised us to turn back, it being perfectly useless, he said, to attempt a crossing in that neighbourhood, where every point was strictly guarded, and patrols always on the alert. This was sufficiently discouraging; but being determined not to be daunted by difficulties, we proceeded to an inn not far off, the landlord of which we knew was to be trusted. By his advice, we did not continue our journey until the next day, when he procured us a conveyance, which took us to a farm-house on the river, the owner of which was to provide us with a boat. But to get the boat proved a more difficult matter than we anticipated; and it was not until after a series of disappointments and fruitless endeavours that we were at length directed to a smuggler on the river, who had a craft of his own, in which he consented to take us over. We remained for a night at his abode, sleeping in a garret destitute of windows, but abounding with rats, which recreated themselves during the silent hours after such a noisy fashion that my friend's rest was sadly disturbed. Being myself accustomed to rough it in every part of the globe, and to sleep amid horrors of every description, I was soon in the arms of the twin brother, and did not awake until the sun, streaming in through the parts where windows ought to have been, warned me that it was time to be up and starting on our cruise.

It proved a most lovely morning, not a ripple on the water, not a cloud upon the bright blue sky, and with only just sufficient wind to stir the leaves gently without affecting the branches of the trees. The creek into which we had hoped to run on the Virginian shore was about a couple of miles higher up than the point from which we started, but, unfortunately, a gunboat lay off the entrance to it, and there were two others at no very great distance. After due deliberation, it was determined that we should make for a spot about five miles higher up, and endeavour to get there by running close along the left bank of the river, so as not to attract attention, and, when clear of all gunboats, to push out into the centre of the stream, and then watch a favourable opportunity for steering into the desired haven. The tide being in our favour, we dropped slowly up on it, until about mid-day, when it turned, and, the wind dying away, we were obliged to make close in for shore, and anchor. My friend and I landed, and spent the day in an old ruined shed surrounded by reeds and rushes. Large steamers and gun-vessels of various sizes kept passing and re-passing all day; but none of them seemed to notice our little craft. On one occasion we saw a boat put off from one of the gunboats and come in our direction; but instead of visiting us, its crew boarded a small cutter which lay becalmed in the centre of the river, and then returned to their own vessel. At sunset a slight breeze arose, before which we glided gently up the river. Directly we passed the mid-stream and approached near the Virginian shore, the owner of the boat became quite nervous, and began lamenting his fate in having to turn smuggler; but the hard times, he said, had left him no alternative, his farm having been destroyed by the Northern troops. He seemed to have a superstitious awe of gunboats, too; and told us he had heard that the officers on board of them possessed telescopes through which they could see distinctly for *miles* at night. Several steamers passed us when we were about two-thirds of the way over, but although the moon every now and then emerged brightly from behind the drifting clouds, we had got under the shade of the land, and managed so that she always shone upon our sails on the side away from the "enemy." We could hear the steamers for about twenty minutes before we caught sight of their light, and during that time the anxious face of the smuggler would have made a glorious study for an artist of the Rembrandt school. The cargo consisted of coffee and sugar, and if safely landed would be in itself a small fortune to the owner of the boat; that he should feel alarmed for its safety, therefore, was not surprising. As we approached the shore, the wind died away, so we were obliged to punt the little craft along: the men thus employed taking off their boots, lest they should make any noise in moving upon the deck. Now and then one of the gunboats, to which I have before alluded as being anchored off the neighbouring creeks, would, by means of a powerfully reflecting lantern, throw a light along the waters in all directions; and though we had fortunately passed beyond the distance to which such light could reach, still our old pilot invariably grew quite restless each time it appeared: and once we all fancied that it was approaching nearer to us. On another occasion we thought we heard the sound of oars, and as there was not a breath of wind to help us along, and punting is a slow process, we felt far from comfortable, though it must be confessed that the amusement afforded us by the smuggler's undisguised and quaintly expressed fears, often served to render us forgetful of our own. Half-past ten found us safe in a little creek almost land-locked, so there was no danger of discovery there; and a run of about a mile and a half up it took us to the point of landing. After a dreary walk of five miles over a forest road, we reached a small village, and, having spent a considerable time in knocking at the door of the house to which we had been directed, we at last succeeded in gaining admittance. The landlord was absent, being in concealment at a farm-house in the neighbourhood; but his niece, a very nice girl, did the honours in his stead. She told us that the Yankees had made a descent upon the village, and carried off several of the inhabitants as prisoners to Washington. The place was suspected of containing smugglers, consequently the Federal troops frequently visited it in search of contraband goods.

The next day, after a long, tiresome drive in a cart without springs, and over the very worst road I ever travelled on, we reached Fredericksburg, crossing the Rappahannock river, upon the right bank of which the town is situated. It has a population of about six thousand inhabitants, and before "the troubles" was a place of rapidly increasing importance, from the establishment of cotton-mills, where a large number of white men and women found employment. The following morning we started, a little after daybreak, in a waggon drawn by two mules, and reached Beaverdam station, on the Virginia Central Railroad, in time for the afternoon train, which took us to Richmond. All the carriages, or *cars*, as they are called in America, were crowded with passengers, of whom a large proportion were the sick and wounded coming from General Lee's army at Winchester. They had been all day on the railroad, and some of the poor fellows seemed quite worn out with fatigue. But there were a few hale men amongst them who were going home for ten days' furlough, and even the most poorly clad of the number looked happy and confident, and all gave me the impression of being earnest men, fully satisfied of the importance of the cause to which they were devoted.

My friend and I stood on what is called the platform of the car, during the journey of two hours and a half, as the regular passenger-cars were full, and those containing the sick and wounded were anything but inviting. Men with legs and arms amputated, and whose pale, haggard faces assumed an expression of anguish at even the slightest jolting of the railway carriages, lay stretched across the seats—some accompanied by civilian friends who had gone from Richmond to the front to fetch them back, and others by wives or sisters, whose careworn features told a tale of sleepless nights passed in painful uncertainty regarding the fate of those they loved. At every station where we stopped, a rush for water was made by crowds of men carrying the canteens and calabashes of those whose disabled condition prevented them from assisting themselves: and it was not surprising that the poor fellows should long for a cool draught, for, in addition to the thirst which they suffered, the filth and stench within those moving hospitals were intolerable. Indeed, the revolting side of war was on that occasion presented under such a repulsive form, that could many of our young soldiers, who now dream of glory and long for active service, have but obtained a view of that ghastly company, I fancy they would pray instead for a continuance of the piping times of peace. For my own part, though well inured to the sight of human suffering, I never remember feeling so moved by it as during that short railway journey.

Upon reaching Richmond we found a dense crowd on the platform and around the terminus—men and women searching for brothers, fathers, husbands, and lovers. A military guard with fixed bayonets was endeavouring to keep order and clear a passage for those on crutches, or limping along with the aid of a stick or the arm of some less severely wounded comrade. We succeeded in getting a carriage for ourselves, and, after a scramble round the baggage-waggon, secured our scanty luggage.

The Spottiswood Hotel is the largest and best in Richmond; to it we accordingly drove; but, after having elbowed our way through a crowd of officers and soldiers standing near the office, we were informed that there was not even one room vacant. The same

15

answer was given us at "The American"; but at the "Exchange" we obtained a little double-bedded apartment up four flights of stairs. The hotels at Richmond just now are as uncomfortable as they well could be. Congress was sitting during our stay there, so the best rooms at most houses were engaged by the members of the legislature, and wounded men occupied almost all the other available bedrooms.

When black tea is selling at sixteen dollars a-pound, and everything else except bread and meat is proportionately expensive, it may be readily imagined that the fare is far from good. Four dollars a-day, however, which is all they charge for board and lodging, is not very exorbitant; and we latterly found out a French restaurant, where we were at least able to get something that we could eat. But no wine or spirits is to be procured at any hotel, the manufacture and sale of all intoxicating liquors having been prohibited by Government.

Few men are fonder of spirits than the Southerners, so this law must affect them sensibly; yet I never spoke to any man in the Confederacy who did not recognise the wisdom of it. Amongst a wild set of fellows collected together in large numbers from every Southern State, if the sale of spirits had been allowed, I feel convinced that it would not only have been impossible to keep order, but that the great things which have been effected by their armies could not have been achieved. From what I saw of the men in the various divisions of their force, I do not believe there are many of them who could not finish a bottle of brandy or whisky at one sitting; and as drink makes them quarrelsome, under its influence rows and blood-shedding would most certainly have ensued. When the army was first enrolled, each man received a daily ration of spirits; but this practice has been long since discontinued, and, strange to say, without causing any discontent amongst the men—a practical refutation of the assertion that a certain amount of stimulants is absolutely necessary for soldiers, and that without it they cannot endure the fatigues of active service. For what army in modern times has made the long marches, day after day, that Jackson's corps of "foot-cavalry," as they are facetiously called, have accomplished? Doubtless there are circumstances when an allowance of grog is very beneficial to health—such as bivouacking in swampy places and during heavy rains; but in ordinary cases, and in fine

16

weather, I am convinced that men will go through as much continuous hard work without any stimulants whatever as with them.

Richmond, which now contains nearly 60,000 inhabitants, stands upon the left bank of the James River, about 120 miles S.S.W. from Washington, and is almost entirely built of brick, with but few stone or wooden houses. Its site was well chosen at the head of the river navigation, as about five miles above the city there is a series of gentle falls, and the river becomes thickly studded with numerous rocks and craggy islands; but the latter being clothed with clustering trees and rich underwood, the whole scene is not only one of varied and singular beauty, but wears such a familiar aspect that it reminded me of many river-scenes at home.

The city is built on a steep bank, rising abruptly in many places, and running parallel with the river-bank, from which it is only from about fifty to a hundred paces distant. The higher ground contains the principal part of the city, while the lower is thickly covered with houses, tobacco-stores, and warehouses of various descriptions. The ground surrounding it is very undulating, and the streets themselves vary almost every quarter of a mile in their height above the river. In the centre of the city, and on its highest point, stands the Capitol. It is a miserable copy of the Maison Carrée at Nismes; built of brick plastered over, and studded with unsightly-looking square windows, the sides being quite destitute of pillars, and those in front bearing no resemblance whatever to the exquisite fluted columns at Nismes. To speak in the mildest terms, the architect has at least proved himself a most unskilful copyist. Standing in the center of the Capitol, and beneath the dome, is a beautifully executed statue of Washington, by Houdon. There is also a bronze equestrian statue of him outside the building, but the base on which it stands is so disproportioned to the size of the man and horse, that, when looking at it, one almost feels nervous lest it should topple over and crush the statues of Jefferson, Mason, and other notabilities which stand around. The grounds about the Capitol, or State-house, are nicely laid out and well kept. The governor's house stands at one end of them, and is a substantial-looking residence, in good repair. Most of the streets are bordered with trees; but the paving, as in many of the large cities in the States, is very bad; and the horrible institution of street railways has penetrated even to Richmond, though there are

17

not so many of them there as there would be in a town of the same size and importance in the North. It is curious to examine the shops in passing. With the exception of book-shops, their shelves are generally more than half empty, and some altogether cleared out. I do not know of any city whose environs are prettier so long as you keep within sight of the James River; and the views from the cemetery above, and from Chapel Point below the town, are really quite lovely. The roads, however, in the neighbourhood, and those running into the country, are sandy and extremely bad. The President's residence, called the "Grey House," in contradistinction, I suppose, to the "White House," is a large, well-built private residence, hired for the purpose, until such time as the Government shall decide upon the future capital of their Republic, wherever that may be. But every one seems agreed with regard to its not being Richmond; and objections to selecting that city are raised by all classes of the people, from every one of the States, and, strange to say, particularly from Virginia. With us, most counties and cities would be ambitious of such an honour, as it would raise the value of property and inevitably give an increased impetus to trade and business. But Virginia objects for several reasons; the chief being, that in whatever State the general seat of Government is located, it will be necessary for that State to give up all jurisdiction in and around the city, as Maryland and Virginia did before with regard to Washington, around which a space of ten miles square was marked out and called the District of Columbia; and within the boundaries of that district the Federal Government ruled exclusively, no particular State having anything whatever to do with the management of the laws within its confines. The necessity for this arises from the fact that the representatives of foreign states who must remain at the general seat of Government, can only hold official intercourse with it; whereas, if any one State had jurisdiction there, they would be constrained to communicate with that State individually upon many minor matters. In fact, a State legislature could at pleasure order any particular ambassador to leave the district; and if State sovereignty is recognised, the general Government could not interfere. The people of Virginia would never consent to relinquish Richmond upon such terms. They are very fond of their State capital, and proud of recalling its many historical associations. But the general objection to selecting it as the

18

future capital of the Confederate States consists in its being considered not nearly central enough, and far too close to Yankeedom for safety. New Orleans and Charleston are open to the same objection, with the addition of being very unhealthy at certain seasons. As, however, it is not deemed necessary that the future seat of Government should be a place of much trade, I think it highly probable that some spot will be selected in the high lands of Georgia, where at present no town exists, but where the climate is most salubrious. Several hotels and other large buildings throughout Virginia, but chiefly in the vicinity of the State House, have been hired and temporarily converted into public offices. The War Office and Treasury are the departments where the greatest amount of business seems to be transacted. General Randolph, the Secretary for War, was most obliging in furnishing us with passes to go wherever we liked, and giving us letters of introduction to the various military authorities. In his room it was surprising to see the numbers of Yankee regimental colours that were heaped in corners and piled up in bundles. Regarding, as we are always taught to do, the standard of our corps with something little short of religious veneration, and being educated to consider its loss as the greatest slur which could be cast upon the honour of those to whose charge it is committed, the absence of all true military spirit, which must have existed in an army who had lost in action the pile of national flags I now saw around me, at first inclined me to feel pity for a people so destitute of proper feeling. But my next impulse was to smile at the utter folly they exhibited in rushing into a great war of conquest, with the avowed object of bringing into subjection those every way superior to themselves, in all qualities essential to good generalship and the formation of a soldierlike character.

Engraving, like most other trades before Secession, was almost entirely neglected in the South, so that at first much difficulty was experienced in providing for the extraordinary issue of notes, which, as in the North, have now completely taken the place of all specie in the South. The Confederate banknotes are worded thus:—"Six months after the ratification of a treaty of peace between the Confederate States and the United States, the Confederate States of America will pay bearer." The first issued were very rudely executed, being but poor lithographs; but those of a later

19

date are better, being from steel plates engraved in England. All these notes possessed an interest for me from the fact of their being signed for the "Register" and "Treasurer" by ladies rendered destitute by the war—their fathers or husbands having been shot, and their property either destroyed or carried off by the Northern troops. They now earn a livelihood by daily signing some hundreds of these Treasury notes.

I need scarcely say that all the menial work in Richmond is performed by negroes, almost all of whom are slaves. The word slave, however, is never used by Southerners in alluding to them; that of *servant* being substituted universally. So that, when a man talks of his servants in the South, he is always understood to mean his slaves. It is for this reason that in the North no white man is ever called a servant; the term *help* being used instead. All the hotels and establishments requiring a large number of hands have slaves hired from masters, who let them out precisely in the same manner that a livery-stable keeper in England lets out his horses. The slaves in large towns are inferior in moral character to those upon plantations; and amongst the former there is always a large admixture of white blood, which is very rare, indeed, amongst farm hands. In many, or I might say in most States, if a woman upon a plantation gives birth to a child of any but ebony hue, it is considered a sort of slur upon the owner of the estate; and she is usually sold to some city master as soon as the fact becomes known, in order, if possible, to hush up the scandal certain to arise in the neighbourhood from the circumstance. I have been informed by many planters that, as a rule, the negresses on estates are a moral class; and as their appearance is repulsive in the extreme, I can well understand there being so few half-caste children in neighbourhoods where the only white men are those of the better classes.

When at Richmond, I visited the scene of several of the battles which took place in its vicinity last June. In some places the numerous graves and pits filled with dead bodies but slightly covered over, testified to the severity of the fighting there. Most of the country fought over was very thickly wooded, so that, without an accurate knowledge of the ground, to direct any operation well would be impossible. No general could see what was going on to his right or left; nor without closing upon his enemy could he form that just estimate of the numbers of those opposed to him, or the position of reserves, &c., which is so essential to success. The *débris* of all things pertaining to an army which lay strewn about on the ground camped on by M'Clellan's troops, was immense. In many places the blackened embers of flour-barrels, clothing-cases, and commissariat stores covered large spaces, showing the haste with which the general retreat was commenced, and the great quantity of stores which it had been found necessary to destroy. In some parts the very trunks of the trees were riddled through: huge pines being cut down by round shot, and great branches torn off by bursting shells.

The Chickahominy River, along the course of which General Lee's operations commenced when he assumed the offensive upon the 26th of last June, is an insignificant sluggish stream, fordable at many points; but, having muddy banks and a soft bottom, no army could pass over it easily without bridging it. The valley through which it flows averages about a mile and a half in width near Gaines's farm, and is rich in meadow land, which after any heavy fall of rain becomes covered with water and impassable for all arms. General M'Clellan had made some corduroy roads across these meadows, and thrown several bridges over the river, when he was attacked by Lee in front and by Jackson in flank. His position, at all times one of hazard, then became untenable; and it was solely owing to the non-execution of General Lee's orders that he escaped utter destruction.

The staff organisation in the Confederate army was not so well established then as it is at present. As will be readily imagined, it is no easy matter to improvise an army and its several departments—making all hang well together at once. Experience as well as judgment is needed for so difficult a task. Every one in the South will tell you that M'Clellan's army was saved, first, by General Lee's orders not being accurately executed, and, secondly, by his gunboats, under the fire of which he halted at Harrison's Landing. Confederate soldiers seem to have some superstitious dread of gunboats, which have been several times the means of saving Northern armies during this war. With soldiers lately raised, such as fill the ranks of both North and South, who possess no traditions of how their regiments in such and such former wars stormed batteries and performed other feats in action, it will always be found that an overweening confidence is placed in artillery fire, and an undue dread felt of its effects. As a rule, none but highly disciplined troops without guns will attack those supported by them; and a very heavy artillery fire brought to bear upon raw soldiers, although from the nature of the ground they may not suffer much from it, will disconcert them terribly. I believe that round shot frightens far more men than it kills. And if this is the case as regards field artillery, how much more so when the missiles are ten-inch shells, such as are thrown by gunboats. The country around Harrison's Landing was so closely wooded that no amount of gunboats in the river could have prevented a disciplined army, flushed with victory, from driving such a mob as that under M'Clellan into the water. The gunboats could only have fired at random into the woods, in many cases doing equal injury to friend and foe. I had subsequently an opportunity of viewing the position from the river, and I was confirmed in this opinion, which I had previously come to from a study of the map.

Before leaving Richmond I spent a day at Drury's Bluff, or Fort Darling, as it is called in the North. My readers may remember that the position there was attacked by the Monitor, Galena, and some other Federal iron clad gunboats, when M'Clellan's army was on the peninsula, and that the second named vessel was disabled and almost destroyed. The works are now beautifully finished. I cannot enter into a description of them, but woe to the vessels which next have the hardihood to attack that position! When the former attack was made only three guns were in the battery, one of which was for nearly two hours unserviceable, from the falling-in of the wooden casemate in which it was placed. But notwithstanding this inferiority in the number of guns to those opposed to them in the iron-clad vessels, the latter were beaten off, as I have before mentioned, and the Galena finally towed down the river in a crippled state.

So much for the often-disputed question of shore batteries *versus* floating ones. Captain Lee, formerly of the United States Navy, commands the troops and position there. He was most obliging in showing us round the works, and pointing out all the new improvements in guns, carriages, and projectiles. He is brother to General R. Lee, commanding the Confederate army, and father of Major-General Fitzlem [Fitzhugh] Lee, commanding a division.

Upon my return to the city from Drury's Bluff, I went on board the Richmond, or Merrimac No. 2, as she is more generally called, and I must say that the efforts made by the Southerners to attain perfection in the arts of shipbuilding, making gunpowder, and other munitions of war, reflect great credit upon the people and authorities. An indolent race, who, before the commencement of hostilities, despised all manual labour, and thought only of amusement and how to spend the money earned for them by their slaves in the pleasantest manner, have now shown that when a necessity for exertion arises, they not only do not shrink from it, but meet it nobly, sparing neither themselves nor their resources. Being destitute of workshops, they have had to create everything, and the makeshifts they have resorted to in many instances are most curious, and display an amount of natural talent which proves that it was not incapacity which kept them from turning their attention to manufactures before. In discussing with Southerners the frequently-mooted subject of recognition by England, they invariably laid great stress upon the advantages which must hereafter accrue to us from having the Southern market thrown open freely to our manufacturers, as they declare that, with the exception of making warlike implements, they never wish to be more than producers of the raw material. I believe myself that they are sincere in saying this; but it would be imprudent to place any reliance upon such assurances. It is certain that after the war is over a large revenue will be required, and indirect taxation must be resorted to for raising it. A high tariff upon all imported goods will quickly give birth to manufactures within the country, which, if not started by Southerners, will soon be established by the Yankees, who are always alive to the advantages to be derived from such a protection. I look upon all promises of free trade as illusory, even though it is said to be the true interest of producing countries to be able to buy manufactured goods in the lowest market. White labour, which is necessary in work where machinery is used, can be profitably employed in the border States and Virginia; and there can be no doubt but that the vast mineral resources, water-power, and coal-beds of the latter State will ere long be developed. Even at this present moment there are several cotton-mills at work, and the iron-works increase daily in size and importance.

Having been furnished by General Randolph, the War Minister, with letters of introduction to General Lee, and the necessary

23

passes, we left Richmond at seven A.M. by the Virginia Central Railroad, and reached Staunton about six o'clock in the evening of the same day. We crossed *en route* the South-west Mountains and the Blue Ridge—the former at a pass through which the Ravanna River forces its way, and then, after running in a southeasterly direction, falls into the James River at Columbia. A canal runs nearly parallel with it within a couple of miles of Charlottesville, on which the produce of the highlands in its neighbourhood is brought down to the James River, and thence to Richmond. Immediately within the pass to which I have alluded lies the town of Charlottesville, distinguished as being the seat of the University of Virginia, which stands outside the town, and close to the railroad. The scenery from thence to the Blue Ridge along the line of railroad is as fine as any I have ever seen. And I fancy there is no spot on this continent where the beauties of a North American forest at the "fall" can be seen to greater advantage than in Albemarle county, Virginia, through the centre of which the railway passes. Valleys within valleys, and chain after chain of mountains, were presented to view as we journeyed along, while the autumn woods, flushed with that hectic brilliance peculiar to the declining year, were hanging out their banners of crimson and gold, and displaying the deep red of the maple, and the vivid scarlet of the shumac and Virginia creeper, contrasted with every imaginable variety of brown, burnt sienna, and yellow,—the whole forming a series of panoramic views, in which the depth and richness of nature's colouring exceeded in warmth and loveliness even the finest of Claude's dreamy conceptions. When I add that the day on which I beheld these fair scenes was one of hushed unbroken stillness, with a radiant atmosphere spreading a golden glow over all things, and a sky of clear unclouded beauty, it may easily be imagined that this bright page of nature is painted on my memory in colours which will not quickly fade away.

On a hill commanding an extensive view of the surrounding country stands Monticello, the residence of the famous Jefferson, one of Virginia's most highly gifted sons, and remarkable even at a time when America could boast of great men and honest statesmen. Up to the year 1861, the history of the United States was only that of the rebellion of our North American colonies. This fact will strike the travelling Englishman before he has been a week in

America; for wherever he wanders, his fellow-passengers in railway carriages or stages will invariably begin talking to him about Smiths, Browns, and Tomkinses in the same strain that we are accustomed to hear allusions made to the Pitts and to Marlborough or Wellington, and localities will be pointed out to him as being the spots where "Jones" was raised, or where "General Thomson" won some glorious battle fighting against the Britishers, &c. The bewildered Englishman, never having heard before of any such men or events, tries to look very wise, and says, "indeed!" but the journey over, he vainly searches through a biographical dictionary for the notabilities of whom he has heard such honourable mention, and no record of the "great battle" is to be found anywhere. Upon looking diligently over some old "annals of the wars," however, he will eventually discover the details of the "glorious victory," in which the numbers engaged on both sides would not have made up a strong company. If this war has no other result, therefore, it will at least afford American historians something to write about, and save them from the puerility of detailing skirmishes in the backwoods or on the highlands of Mexico, as if they were so many battles of Waterloo or Solferino. In ascending the pass by which the railway winds its way over the Blue Ridge, the ascent is in some places so steep that it was only after several ineffectual attempts that the engine at last succeeded in dragging the train up. It stopped two or three times, and twice actually slid backwards for a considerable distance, and was only brought to a standstill at last by having every brake in the train turned on. I don't believe that upon any line of railroad there is a steeper gradient, or one that is in every way more dangerous; the sharpness of the curves exceeded anything I had ever before seen, and the engine at several points seemed to be going at right angles to the hindermost carriages.

Staunton, a town containing about 4,000 inhabitants, is now in a forlorn condition; no business doing there, and many shops closed altogether from the owners having sold off their entire stock, and being unable to lay in fresh supplies. I searched in vain through a number for a teapot or kettle of any description; and I had to go a long journey through the principal streets before I was able to obtain the very commonest description of clasp-knife, for which I paid 2 dollars 50 cents, its real value being, I should say, one shilling. The town lies in a hollow, hemmed in on all sides by hills, and looks sufficiently picturesque when viewed from the high ground; but at present its streets present a melancholy aspect. Being at the end of the railway and the commencement of the turnpike road line of communication with the army, it has necessarily become an entredepôt for stores, waggons, and ambulances, &c. &c. Most of the best houses have been converted into hospitals, from which sick and wounded men seemed to be constantly coming and going, some from the front, others being sent off to the rear by the railway. Throughout the war it has been the practice to send all sick and wounded men who require time to recover to their own friends, where, of course, they receive the kindest treatment; and in this manner the regular hospitals have been greatly relieved, and the service in every way benefited. There is one hotel in the town called the "Virginia House," which, like all those on the army's line of communications, was crowded to excess, every little room being filled with men sleeping on the floor in all directions. The clerk in the office was an Englishman, who, taking pity upon his three compatriots, gave us a room to ourselves with three beds in it, although he was at first very anxious that we should only occupy two of them; one, as he affirmed, being quite large enough for two people, and he wanted to put a stranger into the third. A regular stage, drawn by four horses, runs between Staunton and Winchester. But as there are daily crowds of men going up along the road to join the army, many of whom have what is called "transportation" found them by order of the Quartermaster's Department, and all being very properly allowed a preference over civilians, we were informed that it was hopeless attempting to get seats unless we were content to wait several days for that purpose. As time was a great object to me, and as we were all three most anxious to get to headquarters as soon as possible, this was not to be thought of, so we were determined, if the worst came to the worst, to walk the ninety-two miles, trusting to get our small quantity of baggage taken on in some of the many supply-waggons going daily along the road. We most fortunately met a colonel in the railway to whom one of our party had been previously introduced, who very good-naturedly volunteered to assist us, and through his influence we succeeded in getting an ambulance-cart, one of a large number going up to carry back sick and wounded men. It was four-wheeled, covered over with a tarpaulin-hood, and drawn by two horses, the body of the cart being made to carry two men on stretchers, with room for another man beside the driver. It was mounted on very tolerable springs, but being one of a batch lately made in Richmond after the Yankee pattern, and having been hastily put together by unskilled workmen, its construction was so bad, and the wheels so weak, that I feel convinced the whole affair must have tumbled to pieces in one day's march over the ordinary country roads of Virginia. Very fortunately, however, the road down the Shenandoah valley is macadamised, being, I believe, the only regularly metalled road in the State. There were thirteen ambulance-carts in the train with which we travelled, all under the charge of an officer of the Quartermaster's Department. We had not proceeded more than about six miles when two or three of the carts had to halt at a smith's shop for the purpose of having the wheel-tires cut and reduced in size, the dry weather having so affected the new wood, that the spokes in some of the wheels were rattling loosely about like lucifer-matches in a box. This delayed us some two hours, so that we did not make more than five-and-twenty miles the first day, halting for the night in a field a few miles short of Harrisonburg. The night was cold, with a very heavy dew, but we soon lighted good fires, and, squatting around them, made ourselves tolerably comfortable. The waggon would only admit of two sleeping in it, so one had to lie out with his feet to the fire in correct bivouac fashion. The country we had passed through during the day's march was highly cultivated with maize, wheat, and barley, of which, however, nothing but the stubble then remained in the fields. This valley of the Shenandoah and its tributaries is about the most fertile portion of the State, and by many called the garden of Virginia. The farms are extensive, with larger fields than in most of the other counties I had passed through; and in a number of places well-built walls of loose stone had been substituted for the usual snake and rail fences. Happy men those were whose fathers had thus enclosed their farms, for all the stone walls remained in perfect order, whereas many of the wooden posts and rails had disappeared altogether. Wherever a column had halted for the night, these posts had been used for firing; for, with every desire to protect private property, it is idle to suppose that men will see fine logs, cut regularly so as to burn well, around them, and yet go without a fire—the soldier's only solace and comfort in a bivouac. The country has been so long under cultivation, and land has become in that fertile region of such value, that nowhere is there even a belt of timber left; therefore an army marching along that route must either burn the fence rails, or go without fire. For all such injuries done to their property the farmers are well paid, and in many instances, particularly where men of Union sympathies are concerned, the Government are cheated by having to pay several times over for the same farms. As, since the commencement of hostilities, this valley has been the theatre of operations, it is now almost exhausted of supplies, and it is so difficult to purchase even bread there, that I fear the residents will suffer severely this winter. The next night we bivouacked between Mount Jackson and Woodstock; and on the third night, though we had hoped to have reached Winchester by that time, we had not got farther than Middletown, about thirteen miles from it. It had rained all day, and the prospect of a bivouac was far from agreeable; but having fortunately halted near the village, we shouldered our baggage and marched for the inn there. As usual the place was crowded to excess, men even sleeping in the hall; so we, being tired, wet, and hungry, were consequently prepared to pay any amount that might be asked, provided we could only get a room to ourselves. It was a very dark night, and the street almost ankle-deep with mud, when my two companions, one carrying a candle, sallied forth in search of a lodging for the night, I remaining sentry over our traps the while. They were sent from house to house for some time, no one caring to take in three strangers, but at last a good old woman's heart was touched by our forlorn condition, and she consented to give us shelter. She proved to be most kind and hospitable, giving us a good breakfast the next morning, and seemed quite disinclined to accept any remuneration for the inconvenience we had caused her.

The man who drove our ambulance was a soldier who had been wounded in one of the battles round Richmond, and had been sent home on two months' furlough to recover. He still suffered considerably, and was so weak from fever, superinduced by his wounds, that he could scarcely walk. I asked him why he did not remain longer at home, and he said that his furlough was up, and he would rather die than overstay it. He was married, and the son of a rich farmer, and not only had never done a day's work until he became a soldier, but was of that listless disposition which is so very common amongst the Southerners. He had not sufficient energy even to make himself comfortable at night, or at least as comfortable as circumstances would admit of; but would lie down close to the fire as soon as it was lighted, and fall asleep without his blanket. We frequently urged him to take some care of himself, but without success; and the consequence was, that upon the morning after the heavy night's rain his clothes were drenched through, and his teeth chattering from fever. Careless, listless, and indifferent to his own comforts as this man was, yet, when spoken to about the war, he would change in a moment—he, and every man in the South, were prepared to die, he said, but never to reunite with the d——d Yankees; and, though unfitted by natural disposition as well as by his state of health for the hard life of a soldier, he still seemed determined to go where he thought his duty called him. Every day during our journey to Winchester we passed batches of convalescents marching to join the army, many of whom were totally unfit for any work. This, of course, spoke very highly for the men; but it evinced a great want of judgment on the part of the medical officers, for such men would be an incubus to any army, and, far from adding to its strength, would reduce its power of movement and action immensely. Each day we also passed batches of sick and wounded going to the rear; those totally unable to march being conveyed in ambulances, or the empty waggons returning to Staunton for more supplies. It was an extremely painful sight to see such numbers of weakly men struggling slowly home, many of them without boots or shoes, and all indifferently clad; but posts were established every seventeen miles along the road, containing commissariat supplies, for provisioning them. We also likewise encountered several long trains of guns and ammunition-waggons proceeding to the rear, amongst which were most of the guns taken at Harper's Ferry. It was amusing to see "U.S." marked upon every waggon and upon almost all ambulance-carts which we passed. The North have not only clothed and equipped the millions of men whom they boast of having had at various times enrolled, but they have also similarly supplied the Southern armies. Into whatever camp you go, you are sure to see tents, carts, horses, and guns all marked with the "U.S." Officers have declared to me, that they

have seen whole regiments go into action with smooth-bore muskets and without greatcoats, and known them in the evening to be
well provided with everything—having changed their old muskets
for rifles! The Northern troops have been so liberally supplied
with all, and, indeed, I may say, *more* than a soldier wants in the
field, that they do not value their knapsacks or blankets, and in action invariably throw them away before they "skedaddle"; knowing that if they succeed by their swiftness in living to "fight another
day," their Government will provide them with a new kit, rifle,
and all. About two hundred Northern prisoners passed us during
our journey, and it was curious to observe the difference between
their costume and that of their escort; the prisoners being well-
clothed in the regular blue frock coat and light-blue trousers,
whilst their mounted guard wore every variety of attire—jackets or
coats, it seemed to matter little to them; and, indeed, many rode
along in their shirt-sleeves, as gay and happy as if they were decked
with gold and the richest trappings.

In two or three places the road crosses branches of the Shenandoah river, and the bridges over it having been all destroyed by
Jackson during his remarkable campaign in the valley, and not repaired since, we had to cross by fords, which at that season were
never more than knee-deep. We reached Winchester at ten o'clock
A.M., upon the fourth day after we left Staunton; but only remained there whilst we were getting passes from the provost-marshal, without which we could not have left the town, as there are
guards upon all the roads to prevent any one from passing in or
out without written permission. The convoy then proceeded on
to General Lee's headquarters, which were close to the Martinsburg road, and about six miles from Winchester; and having presented our letters to the Adjutant-General, we were in turn presented to the Commander-in-Chief. He is a strongly built man,
about five feet eleven in height, and apparently not more than fifty
years of age. His hair and beard are nearly white; but his dark
brown eyes still shine with all the brightness of youth, and beam
with a most pleasing expression. Indeed, his whole face is kindly
and benevolent in the highest degree. In manner, though sufficiently conversible, he is slightly reserved; but he is a person that,
wherever seen, whether in a castle or a hovel, alone or in a crowd,
must at once attract attention as being a splendid specimen of an

English gentleman, with one of the most rarely handsome faces I ever saw. He had had a bad fall during the Maryland expedition, from which he was not yet recovered, and which still crippled his right hand considerably. We sat with him for a long time in his tent, conversing upon a variety of topics, the state of public affairs being of course the leading one. He talked most freely about the battle of Antietam, and assured us that at no time during that day's fight had he more than thirty-five thousand men engaged. You have only to be in his society for a very brief period to be convinced that whatever he says may be implicitly relied upon, and that he is quite incapable of departing from the truth under any circumstances. From what I subsequently learned from others, I believe that the Confederates never numbered more than about sixty-five or seventy thousand men in Maryland, and that, owing to the hurried marches Lee and Jackson had made before the battle, nearly one-half of their men were scattered over the country in their rear, unable to get up in time from sore feet occasioned by want of shoes or boots. As is so frequently the case in war, the different events did not occur at the periods calculated on. For instance, Harper's Ferry, the capture of which was one of the chief objects to be gained by crossing the Potomac, held out two days longer than was expected, which prevented Jackson from joining the main army as soon as he should otherwise have done; and when at last he did reach General Lee's column, it was only by a harassing march, which reduced his strength considerably, as the shoeless men could not keep up with the others. It furthermore obliged Lee to fall back from the advanced position he had taken up for the purpose of covering Jackson's operations, and approach nearer the point on the Potomac where he had determined to recross that river in the event of affairs not turning out satisfactorily. But there was also another matter regarding which the Confederate commander was at fault in his calculations. The disorganised mob under General Pope's command, whom he had lately seen flying before his own victorious troops more like scared sheep than soldiers, had rallied under M'Clellan with a rapidity which filled him with amazement, and not only opposed a formidable front, but actually re-assumed the offensive. From the accounts of those who saw Pope's army return to the Potomac after the second battle of Manassas, I do not believe that any one would have thought it possible that such a disorganised rabble could have been placed in line of battle so soon. But M'Clellan seemed to possess the wand of the enchanter on that occasion. It is generally stated that the Confederate authorities calculated upon a rising in Maryland directly their army entered that State. Nevertheless, everybody to whom I spoke on the subject ridiculed the idea of ever having thought that any such rising would take place, until either Baltimore was in their hands, or they had at least established a position in that country, as it was well known that the inhabitants of Washington and Frederick counties were far from being unanimous in their opinions, and that in many districts there the Unionists were considerably in the majority. The city of Washington was saved to the Union by the reappointment of General M'Clellan as Commander-in-Chief of the army. There is no other Federal general who could have fought the battle of Antietam. Hero-worship seems to be inherent in human nature generally, it is true, but for such armies as those in America an idol is indispensable. No man has yet shown himself capable of leading them to victory, so they have agreed to fall down before the image set up by the press—a Napoleon without glory, and a Fabius without success. M'Clellan, a man of retiring disposition and agreeable manners, with a talent for organisation, has succeeded in making himself so beloved by his armies, that no amount of failure or defeat has as yet shaken their confidence in him. After his return from Harrison's Landing he had been placed by the Lincoln clique in "command of the troops around Washington, not otherwise disposed of," which virtually gave him command of only one hundred and eighty men. In other words, he was put on the shelf, the vainglorious Pope being appointed to reign in his stead. But when the news of Lee having crossed the Potomac reached Mr. Lincoln, he and his advisers were, as might be expected, at their wits' end. A mutinous rabble thronged the streets of Alexandria, and strolled at pleasure along the heights opposite Washington. Officers and men cursed the Government which had handed them over to the reckless guidance of such men as Pope and Macdowall [sic]. The soldiers were calling for General M'Clellan to command them; and, incapable as they were of defending their frontier from hostile invasion, they were powerful enough to have crossed into Washington, and, overturning the vile faction which sits there in the name of a government, to have proclaimed M'Clellan dictator. Such a line of conduct was openly talked of, and many of the best informed men now believe that it would have actually been carried into execution, had not Mr. Lincoln called back the favourite to command the Union armies in defence of the empire's capital. The news of his reappointment was received by the army with enthusiasm, and as all the regiments filed through Washington, they insisted upon marching past M'Clellan's house, and cheering vociferously for their new commander as they did so.

Owing to M'Clellan's late disastrous campaign in the peninsula, and the well-known jealousy of Staunton [sic], Seward, and Halleck on account of the army's attachment to him, his recall was deemed an event so improbable that, when it did occur, the Confederate general's plan of campaign was utterly disarranged in consequence. However, when the results of the expedition into Maryland are calmly reviewed, they will be found to have been highly favourable for the Southern cause. Fourteen thousand men made prisoners—over fifty guns and an immense quantity of ammunition and stores captured—together with the fact of having fought with thirty-five thousand men a decidedly drawn battle, without loss in guns or prisoners, against a force of ninety thousand men—are not only circumstances to be remembered with pride, but also fruitful in substantial advantages. Towards the close of that eventful day, many of the Confederate regiments were without a round of ammunition, and held their position solely by the moral weight which the formidable front they showed the enemy gave them. General Longstreet assured me that, towards evening, if he had had even five thousand fresh men, he must have annihilated M'Clellan's army; but his men were exhausted by their long marches for many days previous, and but few of them had any ammunition.

The Federal cavalry had escaped from Harper's Ferry when the infantry there surrendered; and when *en route* to join their main army, they happened by chance to cut in upon General Lee's line of waggons, just at the point where those with the reserve ammunition were. The baggage-guard were all massed in front, so the Federals were thus enabled to carry off or destroy about forty carts. During the night a small reinforcement reached the army, which enabled General Lee to halt all the day following upon the same ground he had held the day before, and offer his opponent battle again—a challenge that M'Clellan did not feel himself sufficiently strong to accept. Such are the general outlines of the Maryland expedition, gathered from the generals and other Confederate officers to whom I have spoken on the subject.

In visiting the headquarters of the Confederate generals, but particularly those of General Lee, any one accustomed to see European armies in the field cannot fail to be struck with the great absence of all the pomp and circumstance of war in and around their encampments. Lee's headquarters consisted of about seven or eight pole tents, pitched with their backs to a stake fence, upon a piece of ground so rocky that it was unpleasant to ride over it—its only recommendation being a little stream of good water which flowed close by the General's tent. In front of the tents were some three or four wheeled waggons, drawn up without any regularity, and a number of horses roamed loose about the field. The servants, who were of course slaves, and the mounted soldiers called "couriers," who always accompany each general of division in the field, were unprovided with tents, and slept in or under the waggons.

Waggons, tents, and some of the horses, were marked U.S., showing that part of that huge debt in the North has gone to furnishing even the Confederate generals with camp equipments. No guard or sentries were to be seen in the vicinity; no crowd of aides-de-camp loitering about making themselves agreeable to visitors, and endeavouring to save their generals from receiving those who have no particular business. A large farm-house stands close by, which, in any other army, would have been the general's residence, *pro tem.*: but as no liberties are allowed to be taken with personal property in Lee's army, he is particular in setting a good example himself. His staff are crowded together two and three in a tent: none are allowed to carry more baggage than a small box each, and his own kit is but very little larger. Every one who approaches him does so with marked respect, although there is none of that bowing and flourishing of forage-caps which occurs in the presence of European generals: and whilst all honour him and place implicit faith in his courage and ability, those with whom he is most intimate feel for him the affection of sons to a father. Old General Scott was correct in saying that when Lee joined the Southern cause, it was worth as much as the accession of 20,000 men to the "rebels."

Since then, every injury that it was possible to inflict, the Northerners have heaped upon him. His house on the Pamunky river was burnt to the ground and the slaves carried away, many of them by force; whilst his residence on the Arlington Heights was not only gutted of its furniture, but even the very relics of George Washington were stolen from it and paraded in triumph in the saloons of New York and Boston. Notwithstanding all these personal losses, however, when speaking of the Yankees, he neither evinced any bitterness of feeling, nor gave utterance to a single violent expression, but alluded to many of his former friends and companions amongst them in the kindest terms. He spoke as a man proud of the victories won by his country, and confident of ultimate success under the blessing of the Almighty, whom he glorified for past successes, and whose aid he invoked for all future operations. He regretted that his limited supply of tents and available accommodation would prevent him from putting us up, but he kindly placed at our disposal horses, or a two-horsed waggon, if we preferred it, to drive about in. Upon leaving him, we drove to Bunker's Hill, six miles nearer Martinsburg, at which place Stonewall Jackson, now of world-wide celebrity, had his headquarters. With him we spent a most pleasant hour, and were agreeably surprised to find him very affable, having been led to expect that he was silent and almost morose. Dressed in his grey uniform, he looks the hero that he is; and his thin compressed lips and calm glance, which meets yours unflinchingly, give evidence of that firmness and decision of character for which he is so famous. He has a broad open forehead, from which the hair is well brushed back; a shapely nose, straight, and rather long; thin colourless cheeks, with only a very small allowance of whisker; a cleanly-shaven upper lip and chin; and a pair of fine greyish-blue eyes, rather sunken, with overhanging brows, which intensify the keenness of his gaze, but without imparting any fierceness to it. Such are the general characteristics of his face; and I have only to add, that a smile seems always lurking about his mouth when he speaks; and that though his voice partakes slightly of that harshness which Europeans unjustly attribute to all Americans, there is much unmistakable cordiality in his manner: and to us he talked most affectionately of England, and of his brief but enjoyable sojourn there. The religious element seems strongly developed in him; and though his conversation is

35

perfectly free from all puritanical cant, it is evident that he is a person who never loses sight of the fact that there is an omnipresent Deity ever presiding over the minutest occurrences of life, as well as over the most important. Altogether, as one of his soldiers said to me in talking of him, "he is a glorious fellow!" and, after I left him, I felt that I had at last solved the mystery of Stonewall Bridge, and discovered why it was that it had accomplished such almost miraculous feats. With such a leader men would go anywhere, and face any amount of difficulties; and for myself, I believe that, inspired by the presence of such a man, I should be perfectly insensible to fatigue, and reckon upon success as a moral certainty. Whilst General Lee is regarded in the light of infallible Jove, a man to be reverenced, Jackson is loved and adored with all that childlike and trustful affection which the ancients are said to have lavished upon the particular deity presiding over their affairs. The feeling of the soldiers for General Lee resembles that which Wellington's troops entertained for him—namely, a fixed and unshakable faith in all he did, and a calm confidence of victory when serving under him. But Jackson, like Napoleon, is idolised with that intense fervour which, consisting of mingled personal attachment and devoted loyalty, causes them to meet death for his sake, and bless him when dying.

Having left Bunker's Hill towards sundown, we returned to Winchester, which we intended to make our headquarters during our stay in the front. It was a dark and rainy evening when we drove up to the inn, where as usual no accommodation was to be had: but a hospitable lady kindly took us in, and entertained us during our stay in that place. The town is very old—that is, of course, in comparison with others in the State—and ordinarily contains about 6000 inhabitants. But whilst we were there, their number far exceeded that, as there were large hospitals filled with wounded men from the Maryland expedition, and a number of soldiers were attached to the military establishments fixed in the place. As to trade there was none, everything almost having been long since bought up from all the shops, and few civilians were to be seen in the streets. The Federals, when bolting from it, had blown up a magazine on the outskirts, which set fire to some houses, and thus destroyed a considerable portion of the town. They had also, during their stay there, pulled to pieces many dwellings from which the proprietors had fled on their approach. Mr. Mason, the deputed representative of the Confederate States in England, possessed a good substantial residence, in what is, I suppose, called the suburbs, and upon it the Northerners poured out the vials of their wrath to such an extent that it is now merely a shell—the floors, windows, and doors having been torn away and destroyed. The streets are paved, and used to be lit with gas. To the northwest of the place is a ridge of hills, upon which the Federals had erected several redoubts, connecting them by a line of trenches. One was a large work intended to mount about ten guns. They had never been finished, either from want of time, or from their uselessness having been discovered, as a line of hills which runs parallel to that upon which they had been laid out commanded them within easy cannon-shot. Indeed, so exposed is the position, that the fact of the works ever having been commenced in such a place, speaks very poorly for the engineering talent of the Northern armies, or at least for that portion of it which had the honour of being commanded by Mr. and Mrs. Banks. For some distance around Winchester, almost every fence has been destroyed, and cavalry might now be used there to advantage. At the commencement of the war, a railroad existed between Winchester and Harper's Ferry, where it joined the Baltimore and Ohio Railway, by means of which the valuable produce of the valley was conveyed to the Northern markets. The army at Winchester was composed of two *corps d'armée* under the command of Generals Jackson and Longstreet, each consisting of four divisions. I was present whilst the latter officer inspected one of his divisions, and was highly pleased with the appearance of the men, and the manner in which they moved. As is usual in impromptu armies, the chief deficiency lies with the officers, who, though possessed of zeal and high courage, seldom know more of their duty than the men under their command. The system of election, which they unfortunately instituted, from the first has worked badly, and I never spoke with an officer on the subject who did not condemn it. It still holds good as regards the first appointment of officers to be second lieutenants, but all the vacancies of superior grade are filled up according to seniority. When such a system has been once established, it is difficult to abolish it suddenly, especially when the army is in the field. It is now a very common thing to see men of large property serving as privates in the ranks, whilst the captains are in social positions their inferiors, being perhaps merely the sons of small farmers in the neighbourhood of their own plantation. Many of these rich landed proprietors have been shoeless for weeks at a time; and a friend of mine who had seen Jackson's corps on the march, informed me that a number of them had been pointed out to him marching contentedly along with some old tattered flannel shirt and a pair of Yankee uniform trousers for their only clothing, whilst their bare feet bled at almost every step they took.

Will any one who understands what it is that makes and unmakes armies, for a moment believe that such men are to beaten by mobs of Irish and German mercenaries, hired at $15 a-month to fight in a cause they know little and care less about? The artillery has been the favourite branch of the service, and consequently is entirely composed of good men. It was much better drilled than the infantry, and indeed, for all practical purposes, its manoeuvres were executed in the most satisfactory manner. Its harness and entire equipment had been taken from the Yankees. The guns used are Parrots, Napoleons, 12-pounders, howitzers, and 3-inch iron rifled guns, all muzzle-loaders, the last being the only gun made in the Confederate States. There are a few batteries of Blakeley's guns made in England, of which the officers entertain a high opinion. But there are only four pieces in each battery, and they have only one line of waggons in the field. The reserve ammunition for each division is under the charge of an ordnance officer, and marches in the rear with the baggage. The infantry accoutrements are the same as those used in the Federal army; indeed I saw very few that had not been taken from the Northerners. Their cartridge-boxes resemble those which our sergeants used to wear, being nearly square, very thin, and only holding forty rounds. The interior arrangement of these boxes is far from convenient; for, having expended the twenty rounds in the upper division of the tin case, which fits closely inside, it has to be withdrawn altogether, and turned with the other side uppermost, to admit of your getting at the twenty rounds in the second compartment. To be obliged to do this in action would be troublesome; for I have tried the experiment, and found, even when at my ease, that it was often difficult to extract the tin case, owing to the leather outside having shrunk from moisture. The belts are all supposed to be black. I have no doubt they were so when taken from their former owners, but blacking is such a scarce commodity in the Confederate States, that it is only at some few hotels even in Richmond you can have your shoes polished in the morning, and then not without paying extra for the luxury. In the division that I saw inspected, there was not a barefooted man on parade, those without shoes having remained in camp. Large supplies of shoes and boots reached Winchester during my stay there, and were immediately distributed amongst the men. Several thousand pairs of long boots, made in England, and of a similar pattern to those served out to our infantry in the Crimea, had been also issued to the army since its return from Maryland. Almost every regiment had a small band of brass instruments. I cannot say much for the music, but it was at least enlivening, and served to mark the time for the men as they marched. Before marching past, no attempt was made to equalise the strength of the companies, which detracted somewhat from the general effect, as a division of eighty men would frequently be followed by one of only half that number. The officers marched in front of their companies, after the French fashion, the covering-sergeant marching upon the pivot flank, and being responsible for distance and direction. Several regiments were to a man clothed in the national uniform of grey cloth, whilst others presented a harlequin appearance, being dressed in every conceivable variety of coat, both as regards colour and cut. Grey wideawake hats, looped up at one side, and having a small black feather, are the most general head-dress; but many wear the Yankee black hat or casquette of cloth. That which is most unmilitary in their general appearance, is the long hair worn alike by officers and men. They not only allow their locks to hang down the backs of their coats, but many pass them behind their ears as women do. Some, doubtless, are ambitious of imitating the cavaliers of Charles I.'s time in dress and appearance, as I noticed many, particularly of the mounted officers, copy their style as portrayed in Vandyke's pictures in every particular, the colour of their clothing alone excepted. As the regiments marched past me, I remarked that, however slovenly the dress of the men of any particular company might be, their rifles were invariably in good serviceable order. They marched, too, with an elastic tread, the pace being somewhat slower than that of our troops, and not only seemed vigorous and healthy, but each man

39

had that unmistakable look of conscious strength and manly self-reliance, which those who are accustomed to review troops like to see.

I have seen many armies file past in all the pomp of bright clothing and well-polished accoutrements; but I never saw one composed of finer men, or that looked more like *work,* than that portion of General Lee's army which I was fortunate enough to see inspected. If I had at any time entertained misgivings as to the ability of the Southerners to defend their country and liberties against Northern invasion, they were at once and for ever dispelled when I examined for myself the material of which the Confederate armies are composed. Any one who goes amongst those men in their bivouacs, and talks to them as I did, will soon learn why it is that their Generals laugh at the idea of Mr. Lincoln's mercenaries subjugating the South. Every man in that service, whether non-commissioned officer or private, will declare to you that it is his fixed determination to fight for his freedom and resist Yankee oppression as long as he has strength to march. A gulf deep and impassable now divides the Southerners from the old Union; and such is the hatred and loathing entertained by them for those who, forgetting the ties of brotherhood which once bound all the States together, have not hesitated to carry fire and sword into the land of their common forefathers, that many have told me, were it possible that the seceding States should ever be conquered, they would emigrate to England to avoid an oppression more tyrannical than that which in times past had driven forth their ancestors from Great Britain. I have heard many men of influence say that they now believe the great rebellion to have been a mistake, and that the acts complained of in the Declaration of Independence (most of which, by the way, were committed subsequent to the first shedding of blood) were trifles when compared with what had been inflicted upon them by the Northerners. It was pretty generally believed last year, that if Mr. Lincoln had picked a quarrel with us, such was the antipathy felt by all Americans for the "Britisher," that the South would have at least aided the North in prosecuting the war. Indeed, a number of American statesmen seemed at one time to think that the best chance open to them of re-establishing the Union was by engaging in such a war. But such a line of policy would now be scorned by the South; and my own impression is, that many generations must pass away ere it would be willing to fight side by side with the men of New England in any cause whatever. The first question always asked me by both men and women was, why England had not recognised their independence. They reminded me of our conduct recently with regard to Italy, and to Greece, Egypt, Belgium, &c., in years past. Had they not done sufficient to prove their determination to be an independent people, and had they not sufficiently shown already their ability to maintain themselves as a separate nation? Would England allow her manufacturing population to starve from want of cotton? Every Yankee with whom they had come in contact during the war had, they said, declared it to be their determination to chastise us as soon as the present difficulties were at an end; and the Government must be aware of this, because every newspaper in the North breathed a similar sentiment. Why was it then that our rulers could be so ill-judging as to allow our American cousins to postpone the attempt until they could turn their whole attention to us; and why not force on the war at once, and in alliance with the Confederates march an army into the state of New York, and teach the bragging people there that the British Lion was a dangerous animal to arouse? In the cause of humanity, would not England interfere to put an end to the fratricidal war which had every prospect of soon degenerating into one of extermination? Had we no feelings of sympathy for the descendants of our banished cavaliers? Was not blood thicker than water? and would we stand by with folded arms whilst the Northern rabble, descended from the offscourings of every European nation, robbed and murdered those of the same race as ourselves? These were the questions propounded by high and low, educated and uneducated. The best informed men always told me that in refusing to recognise Southern independence at first, they considered England had acted justly and as became a great nation; but that her reasons for continuing to do so after M'Clellan's failure before Richmond, was a mystery to them.

Every person who reflects on the matter must be aware that it is the interest of all nations, but especially of England, to have more than one great republic upon the American continent, as the United States were fast becoming such a nuisance in the republic of nations, that if by any accident they should succeed in their war of subjugation, their insolence and arrogance would be more intolerable than ever. "Why then run the risk of incurring such a misfortune?" I confess that I was frequently sorely puzzled by questions such as these. Ladies have asked them with tears in their eyes, and many of the other sex in a tone that showed how irritated they were by our conduct. Our even-handed justice, exemplified in the neutrality we have adopted, and upon which we are rather inclined to pride ourselves, is never believed in. All great nations are known to be selfish; and our policy is generally attributed to base motives, such as dread of the Federals, and a fear that if we acted otherwise, they would carry out their threat of making the recognition of Southern independence by us synchronous with a declaration of war by them. Thucydides affirms that he who declares for no party is not esteemed by any; and our timid policy has most certainly made no friends for us in the Northern States; on the contrary, every succeeding day of its continuance serves still further to estrange the goodwill of a brave people now budding into an independent nationality. A people, too, who pride themselves upon their English origin, and who, from the first moment of their secession, forgetting all former animosities, looked confidently to the land of their forefathers in their hour of need, expecting, if not actual assistance, at least the moral support of recognition. From the position of our defenceless possessions in North America, surely it will be our true policy for the future, to be on the best terms with the Southern Republic. And if this be so, we are neglecting an opportunity more advantageous than we are ever likely to have again, of cementing politically the bonds of national friendship between it and ourselves. Why is it that France has ever been so cordially and highly esteemed in the United States? Is it not because of the assistance she afforded them in establishing their independence, and also from the fact of her being the hereditary enemy of the only power they dreaded, and from which alone they could suffer punishment? If we in our turn had lent the South the moral support of recognition as a separate nation, is there not every reason for supposing that we should be regarded by it with similar feelings?

There is a general impression in the minds of all, at least with whom I conversed, that the English people sympathise with the Southerners, and would gladly help them if they were permitted to do so, but that Lord Palmerston's Government is opposed to Southern independence. The relative position of the opposing armies in Virginia is not likely to undergo any material change for many months to come, owing to the impossibility of moving large armies there during the winter; and before active operations can be resumed, it is known that our present Premier must meet Parliament. A faint hope still exists with many that he will then be forced by the British nation through its representatives to take some decided course regarding their affairs; or else that France, despairing of English cooperation, will not allow herself to be deterred by our Government any longer from recognising the Confederates as a nation, which she is generally believed to have been long anxious to do.

When questioning Southerners of all classes regarding the form of government they intended to establish when peace had been proclaimed, the answer invariably given was, that the constitution, as framed by Washington, Jefferson, and Co., was to be the basis upon which they meant to form theirs, merely adding to it a clause recognising the right of any State to secede whenever its individual interest demanded separation. They argue that, as the interests of all the Confederate States are identical, such an event is never likely to occur; and that even supposing it were to happen from momentary pique, if that State were allowed to secede peaceably, it would soon seek to be readmitted into the Confederacy. Everybody agrees that had South Carolina been permitted to leave the Union quietly when she demanded separation, she would long since have come back, as they say "she could not remain out long by herself, shivering in the cold." The jealousy between States is is very great, and although the conservative element is powerful, universal suffrage is in disrepute, and there is a general craving for strong government; still the love of State rights exceeds all such feelings. *That,* in the opinion of the Southerners, is the touchstone of republicanism in its extended sense, and the suppression of the principle in the North is the reason why all Europe is now authorised in pronouncing the republican form of government to have failed in America. To place any dependence upon a continuance of that identity of interest common to all the seceding States upon which the Southern people lay such stress, is, I believe, an error. For though such unity may exist at present, when all are

43

slave-owners, and all now manufacturing people in the border States, slavery has already met its death-blow, and separation from the North is sure to be followed by the growth of manufactures. My own opinion is, that in the next generation Virginia and the Gulf States will have but little in common; for as soon as it ceases to be a man's interest to own slaves, he quickly discovers how morally wrong slavery is. It is not easy to harmonise the interests of producing and manufacturing communities. Free trade and protection, it would seem, are as antagonistic as liberal institutions and arbitrary government; and it is as difficult to strike a just balance between them as to establish liberty of thought and action under a strong despotism. For these reasons I am led to think that those States in which, from the climate, a development of white labour is impossible, will eventually stand alone; and that in the Southern Confederacy, as well as in what remains in the North of the old United States, division will succeed division according as population increases.

Of the cavalry I saw but little, as General Steuart [sic] had left for his raid into Pennsylvania the day I reached headquarters, and only returned a couple of days before I commenced my homeward journey. I did remark, however, that all the men rode well, in which particular they present a striking contrast to the Northern cavalry, who can scarcely sit their horses, even when trotting. Indeed, I have no doubt but that all who have seen the Northern troopers on duty in Washington, will agree with me in thinking them the greatest scarecrows under the name of cavalry that they ever saw. Apropos of them: a Southern lady told me that on one occasion, when jesting with a Northern officer about the inability of his troopers to contend with the Southern "chivalry," although the latter were not half so numerous, he said, "What can we do? we can never catch them; for whilst we are opening the gates they are all over the fences." Every white man in the South rides from childhood, and consequently is at home in the saddle; whereas to be on horseback is a most disagreeable position for a Yankee, and one in which he rarely trusts himself. In the North thousands keep horses, but only to drive them. "What is the use of having good roads if you don't drive on them," they say. To have a horse that can trot a mile in two minutes forty seconds, is the pride of a New Englander; but a good fencer would be as useless to him as an elephant. The troopers in the Southern cavalry have their own horses: and upon the breaking out of the war they provided themselves with arms as well. Sabres have since been issued to them by Government, and they have mostly armed themselves with carbines or revolvers taken from their discomfited brethren of the North. Their knowledge of drill is limited, and altogether their constitution resembles much that of our irregular Indian cavalry. As they can never be required to act in an open country suitable for masses of horsemen, they are admirably adapted for the service required of them. Cavalry that could not fence well would be utterly useless in Virginia; but in a close country like it, where the quantity of wood always prevents any extensive view, a body of good riders, such as the Southern cavalry, are invaluable to a general, as by their means alone he can learn the movements, and sometimes the whereabouts, of the enemy. The want of such skilful horsemen is sadly felt in the Federal armies, and accounts in a measure for their general ignorance of where the enemy is, and what he is doing. The Federal generals hitherto have been either extremely rash, or extremely cautious and slow. They spurn the advantages attending upon an irregular army; and, unable to attain the efficiency of regulars, they possess the drawbacks of both systems without the advantages of either. The Southern ranks, on the contrary, have attained an efficiency equal to that of the best irregulars; they are therefore enabled to make long and rapid marches, caring little meanwhile for regularity, so long as they can form line upon the decisive points; whilst their puzzled enemy, clogged with all the routine of drill, without officers able to direct it, or soldiers sufficiently instructed to perform it, is trying in vain to discover their whereabouts. It is owing to these circumstances that the Southern cavalry under Steuart has been able to march round and round M'Clellan, seizing and destroying his reserve of stores in the rear whilst he was blindly feeling for them in front. As the real power of an army rests upon its ability in marching well, the Confederates make up for their deficiency in numbers by rapidity of movement.

The much-admired M'Clellan is slowness and caution incarnate; vigour and promptness of action are undreamed of in his philosophy; and from the first he has not only evinced a want of confidence in his troops, but, from a desire of leaving nothing to chance,

45

he has not succeeded in anything. At the opening of his peninsula campaign, when he had more than a hundred thousand men under him, he allowed himself to be so deceived by General Magruder near Yorktown that he actually opened trenches, erected batteries, and placed a number of ten-inch mortars in position to attack a weak unfinished line of open and continuous intrenchments, about five miles in extent, and defended only by 8000 Confederates. How can any soldier call such a man a great general?

In talking of the several Federal generals, the soldiers of the South invariably give the palm to M'Clellan. They consider him inferior to their own leader, and destitute of enterprise, but all declare him to be the only man in the Northern army who is capable of organising it, and allow that for such work his mind is admirably adapted. I have spoken to many persons who knew him intimately, some of them having been class-fellows of his at West Point, and others associated with him in public life for years. All spoke of him with respect. He was a gentleman, they said, and for that reason superior to the host of newspaper editors and swindling lawyers who had been given generals' commissions by Mr. Lincoln. But they were sorely puzzled by his despatches regarding his operations before and immediately subsequent to the battle of Antietam, in all of which facts were perverted, and the number of the enemy exaggerated to a degree that precluded the possibility of acquitting him on the plea of misconception. Indeed, those who had known him well refused to believe the authenticity of these despatches, and declared that they were always cooked up by Mr. Staunton and General Halleck in Washington.

General Banks and Pope are invariably spoken of with rancour and dislike. The former has been accused of the grossest intermeddling with private property. General Pope's orders to his army upon the opening of his disastrous campaign, were of a nature to exasperate all Southerners, and certainly tended to extinguish any smouldering embers of brotherly feeling which might still exist in their breasts. Indeed, I imagine that, had the Confederates taken himself as well as his camp equipage and clothing by the fortune of war, he would have received no very gentle treatment at their hands; nor could the most lenient say that his conduct was such as to merit it.

The debt incurred by the Confederate Government since its establishment, amounts to about $400,000,000, or £80,000,000, little if anything more than a fifth of the sum now owed by the Northerners. To what amount these figures may be increased, if the war should unfortunately last for another twelve months, it is impossible to say. There is no personal sacrifice that the people of the South are not prepared to make rather than again trust their independence, private fortunes, and liberty, to a paper constitution, guaranteed only by the oaths of such men as Sumner and Lincoln, both doubly forsworn. There are no terms upon which they would re-enter the Union, as the present Washington administration has shown them how inefficient an oath is to bind such men to abide by any agreement. All of them upon entering office swore to observe the articles of the constitution, and all have violated them in the most flagrant manner. Personal liberty, freedom of speech, an independent press, and the glorious principle contained in the Habeas Corpus Act, have not only been trampled under foot by these tyrants, but the populace has looked on approvingly. The South will not give in, but its Government is prepared to treat. To have its independence acknowledged, and to allow the border States to express their own wishes freely as to the side they wish to adhere to, is all the South demands. The only manner in which this could be carried out, would be by the withdrawal of both armies from the border States, which would give their people an opportunity of freely expressing the sentiments of the majority. Although the North might be willing at some future period, or even at the present time, to open negotiations, and even to carry out those measures as regards Kentucky and Tennessee, it will never consent to extend the same principle to Maryland; and under these circumstances, the South will not negotiate. I do not think that the Confederate statesmen are in the least anxious for the adherence of Maryland to their Republic. Indeed, as regards Virginia, such is the rivalry between these two States—one being anxious to maintain the trade of Baltimore and make *it* the great exporting city for the South, whilst the other, wishing to obtain the advantages accruing from having such a port within itself, is desirous of making Norfolk the great emporium of trade —that the "Old Dominion," as Virginia is called, would prefer being the frontier province, and have the Potomac for a line of demarcation.

47

GENERAL LEE

THIS SKETCH, PUBLISHED IN MACMILLAN'S MAGAZINE IN MARCH 1887, took as its starting point a biography of Lee written by his "military secretary," General Armistead L. Long.[1] The practice of book reviewing differs in Britain and America: English reviewers, instead of analyzing the contents of the book, often use the work as an occasion for an essay on the general subject. So it is in this case—to our good fortune.

Here we have a charming depiction, especially meritorious, since it is written from first-hand acquaintance, filled with professional lore, and based on mature judgment. It is the piece Freeman called "a classic of Confederate literature"; the author of Wolseley's obituary in the New York Times described it as "one of the standard works on the conflict between the North and South." A peculiar value of this essay is the insight it gives us into how Lee appeared to military men abroad.

Writing for a British audience Wolseley recognized that because the history of the war was yet to be written Long's biography was a valuable contribution to historical literature. He begins by sketching the rival principles involved in the American war (he accepts secession as a sovereign right) and limns the early life of Lee. Maintaining a consistently broad outlook, he compares the American experience with British and European parallels. He deals understandingly with Lee's dilemma: secession or loyalty to the nation. His treatment of the war addresses itself not to campaigns but to staff and organizational problems of a field commander of an improvised army. Beyond this he executes a portrait in depth of the character and physical lineaments of a man, great but not without blemish. Wolseley's Lee is very like Freeman's later evocation.

Wolseley is at his best here, drawing from life and recording the profile of a noble life and a great soldier. His admiration for Lee—"a true hero," "the most perfect man I ever met"—shines through his pages.

Certain errors need correcting, however. Lee's birthday is January 19, not 9; he graduated second in his class, not first; and Lincoln was not elected president in 1860, "in the abolitionist interest," but in opposition to the spread of slavery.

[1] A. L. Long and Marcus J. Wright, Memoirs of Robert E. Lee: His Military and Personal History (London, 1886).

51

GENERAL LEE

THE history of the war between the Northern and Southern States of North America is yet to be written. General Long's work on the great Confederate general is a contribution towards the history of that grand but unsuccessful struggle by the seceding States to shake off all political connection with the Union Government.[1] It will be read with interest as coming from the pen of one who was Lee's military secretary, and its straightforward, soldier-like style will commend it to all readers. It is not my intention to enter upon any narrative of the events which led to that fratricidal war. The unprejudiced outsider will generally admit the sovereign right, both historical and legal, which each State possessed under the constitution, to leave the Union when its people thought fit to do so. At the same time, of Englishmen who believe that "union is strength," and who are themselves determined that no dismemberment of their own empire shall be allowed, few will find fault with the men of the north for their manly determination, come what might, to resist every effort of their brothers in the south to break up the Union. It was but natural that all Americans should be proud of the empire which the military genius of General Washington had created, despite the efforts of England to retain her Colonies.

It is my wish to give a short outline of General Lee's life, and to describe him as I saw him in the autumn of 1862, when at the head of proud and victorious troops he smiled at the notion of defeat by any army that could be sent against him. I desire to make known to the reader not only the renowned soldier, whom I believe to have been the greatest of his age, but to give some insight into the character of one whom I have always considered the most perfect man I ever met. Twenty-one years have passed since the great Secession war ended, but even still, angry remembrances of it prevent

[1] 'Memoirs of Robert E. Lee: his Military and Personal History.' By General A. L. Long and General Marcus J. Wright. London. 1886.

Americans from taking an impartial view of the contest, and of those who were the leaders in it. Outsiders can best weigh and determine the merits of the chief actors on both sides, but if in this attempt to estimate General Lee's character I offend any one by the outspoken expression of my opinions, I hope I may be forgiven. On one side I can see, in the dogged determination of the North persevered in to the end through years of recurring failure, the spirit for which the men of Britain have always been remarkable. It is a virtue to which the United States owed its birth in the last century, and its preservation in 1865. It is the quality to which the Anglo-Saxon race is most indebted for its great position in the world. On the other hand, I can recognise the chivalrous valour of those gallant men whom Lee led to victory: who fought not only for fatherland and in defence of home but for those rights most prized by free men. Washington's stalwart soldiers were styled rebels by our king and his ministers, and in like manner the men who wore the grey uniform of the Southern Confederacy were denounced as rebels from the banks of the Potomac to the head waters of the St. Lawrence. Lee's soldiers, well versed as all Americans are in the history of their forefathers' struggle against King George the Third, and believing firmly in the justice of their cause, saw the same virtue in one rebellion that was to be found in the other. This was a point upon which, during my stay in Virginia in 1862, I found every Southerner laid the greatest stress. It is a feeling that as yet has not been fully acknowledged by writers on the Northern side.

> Rebellion, foul dishonouring word,
> Whose wrongful blight so oft hath stained
>   The holiest cause that tongue or sword
> Of mortal ever lost or gained.
>   How many a spirit born to bless
> Hath sunk beneath thy withering name,
>   Whom but a day's, an hour's success,
> Had wafted to eternal fame.

As a looker-on, I feel that both parties in the war have so much to be proud of, that both can afford to hear what impartial Englishmen or foreigners have to say about it. Inflated and bubble reputations were acquired during its progress, few of which will bear the test of time. The idol momentarily set up, often for political reasons, crumbles in time into the dust from which its limbs were perhaps originally moulded. To me, however, two figures stand out in that history towering above all others, both cast in hard metal that will be for ever proof against the belittling efforts of all future detractors. One, General Lee, the great soldier: the other, Mr. Lincoln, the far-seeing statesman of iron will, of unflinching determination. Each is a good representative of the genius that characterised his country. As I study the history of the Secession war, these seem to me the two men who influenced it most, and who will be recognised as its greatest heroes when future generations of American historians record its stirring events with impartiality.

General Lee came from the class of landed gentry that has furnished England at all times with her most able and distinguished leaders. The first of his family who went to America was Richard Lee, who in 1641 became Colonial Secretary to the Governor of Virginia. The family settled in Westmorland, one of the most lovely counties in that historic state, and members of it from time to time held high positions in the government. Several of the family distinguished themselves during the War of Independence, amongst whom was Henry, the father of General Robert Lee. He raised a mounted corps known as "Lee's Legion," in command of which he obtained the reputation of being an able and gallant soldier. He was nicknamed by his comrades, "Light Horse Harry." He was three times governor of his native state. To him is attributed the authorship of the eulogy on General Washington, in which occurs the so-often-quoted sentence, "First in war, first in peace, and first in the hearts of his countrymen," praise that with equal truth might have been subsequently applied to his own distinguished son.

The subject of this slight sketch, Robert Edward Lee, was born January 9th, 1807, at the family place of Stratford, in the county of Westmorland, state of Virginia. When only a few years old his parents moved to the small town of Alexandria, which is on the right bank of the Potomac river, nearly opposite Washington, but a little below it.

He was but a boy of eleven when his father died, leaving his family in straitened circumstances. Like many other great commanders, he was in consequence brought up in comparative poverty, a condition which has been pronounced by the greatest of them as the best training for soldiers. During his early years he attended a day-school near his home in Alexandria. He was thus able in his leisure hours to help his invalid mother in all her household concerns, and to afford her that watchful care which, owing to her very delicate health, she so much needed. She was a clever, highly-gifted woman, and by her fond care his character was formed and stamped with honest truthfulness. By her he was taught never to forget that he was well-born, and that, as a gentleman, honour must be his guiding star through life. It was from her lips he learnt his Bible, from her teaching he drank in the sincere belief in revealed religion which he never lost. It was she who imbued her great son with an ineradicable belief in the efficacy of prayer, and in the reality of God's interposition in the every-day affairs of the true believer. No son ever returned a mother's love with more heartfelt intensity. She was his idol, and he worshipped her with the deepseated, inborn love which is known only to the son in whom filial affection is strengthened by respect and personal admiration for the woman who bore him. He was her all in all, or, as she described it, he was both son and daughter to her. He watched over her in weary hours of pain, and served her with all that soft tenderness which was such a marked trait in the character of this great, stern leader of men.

He seems to have been throughout his boyhood and early youth perfect in disposition, in bearing, and in conduct—a model of all that was noble, honourable, and manly. Of the early life of very few great men can this be said. Many who have left behind the greatest reputations for usefulness, in whom middle age was a model of virtue and perhaps of noble self-denial, began their career in a whirlwind of wild excess. Often, again, we find that, like Nero, the virtuous youth develops into the middle-aged fiend, who leaves behind him a name to be execrated for all time. It would be difficult to find in history a great man, be he soldier or statesman, with a character so irreproachable throughout his whole life as that which in boyhood, youth, manhood, and to his death, distinguished Robert Lee from all contemporaries.

He entered the military academy of West Point at the age of eighteen, where he worked hard, became adjutant of the cadet corps, and finally graduated at the head of his class. There he mastered the theory of war, and studied the campaigns of the great masters in that most ancient of all sciences. Whatever he did, even as a boy, he did thoroughly with order and method. Even at this early age he was the model Christian gentleman in thought, word, and deed. Careful and exact in the obedience he rendered his superiors, but remarkable for that dignity of deportment which all through his career struck strangers with admiring respect.

He left West Point when twenty-two, having gained its highest honours, and at once obtained a commission in the Engineers. Two years afterwards he married the grand-daughter and heiress of Mrs. Custis, whose second husband had been General Washington, but by whom she left no children. It was a great match for a poor subaltern officer, as his wife was heiress to a very extensive property and to a large number of slaves. She was clever, very well educated, and a general favourite: he was handsome, tall, well made, with a graceful figure, and a good rider: his manners were at once easy and captivating. These young people had long known one another, and each was the other's first love. She brought with her as part of her fortune General Washington's beautiful property of Arlington, situated on the picturesque wooded heights that overhang the Potomac river, opposite the capital to which the great Washington had given his name. In talking to me of the Northern troops, whose conduct in Virginia was then denounced by every local paper, no bitter expression passed his lips, but tears filled his eyes as he referred to the destruction of his place that had been the cherished home of the father of the United States. He could forgive their cutting down his trees, their wanton conversion of his pleasure grounds into a grave-yard; but he could never forget their reckless plunder of all the camp equipment and other relics of General Washington that Arlington House had contained.

Robert Lee first saw active service during the American war with Mexico in 1846, where he was wounded, and evinced a remarkable talent for war that brought himself prominently into notice. He was afterwards engaged in operations against hostile Indians, and obtained the reputation in his army of being an able officer of great promise. General Scott, then the general of greatest repute in the United States, was especially attracted by the zeal and soldierly instinct of the young captain of Engineers, and frequently employed him on distant expeditions that required cool nerve, confidence,

57

and plenty of common sense. It is a curious fact that throughout the Mexican war General Scott in his despatches and reports made frequent mention of three officers—Lee, Beauregard, and McClellan—whose names became household words in America afterwards, during the great Southern struggle for independence. General Scott had the highest opinion of Lee's military genius, and did not hesitate to ascribe much of his success in Mexico as due to Lee's "skill, valour, and undaunted energy." Indeed subsequently, when the day came that these two men should part, each to take a different side in the horrible contest before them, General Scott is said to have urged Mr. Lincoln's Government to secure Lee at any price, alleging he "would be worth fifty thousand men to them." His valuable services were duly recognised at Washington by more than one step of brevet promotion: he obtained the rank of colonel, and was given command of a cavalry regiment shortly afterwards.

I must now pass to the most important epoch of his life, when the Southern States left the Union and set up a government of their own. Mr. Lincoln was in 1860 elected President of the United States in the Abolitionist interest. Both parties were so angry that thoughtful men soon began to see war alone could end this bitter dispute. Shipwreck was before the vessel of state, which General Washington had built and guided with so much care during his long and hard-fought contest. Civil war stared the American citizen in the face, and Lee's heart was well nigh broken at the prospect. Early in 1861 the seven Cotton States passed acts declaring their withdrawal from the Union, and their establishment of an independent republic, under the title of "The Confederate States of America." This declaration of independence was in reality a revolution: war alone could ever again bring all the States together.

Lee viewed this secession with horror. Until the month of April, when Virginia, his own dearly-cherished State, joined the Confederacy, he clung fondly to the hope that the gulf which separated the North from the South might yet be bridged over. He believed the dissolution of the Union to be a dire calamity not only for his own country, but for civilisation and all mankind. "Still," he said, "a Union that can only be maintained by swords and bayonets, and in which strife and civil war are to take the place of brotherly love and kindness, has no charm for me." In common with all

Southerners he firmly believed that each of the old States had a legal and indisputable right by its individual constitution, and by its act of Union, to leave at will the Great Union into which each had separately entered as a Sovereign State. This was with him an article of faith of which he was as sure as of any Divine truths he found in the Bible. This fact must be kept always in mind by those who would rightly understand his character, or the course he pursued in 1861. He loved the Union for which his father and family in the previous century had fought so hard and done so much. But he loved his own State still more. She was the Sovereign to whom in the first place he owed allegiance, and whose orders, as expressed through her legally-constituted government, he was, he felt, bound in law, in honour, and in love to obey without doubt or hesitation. This belief was the mainspring that kept the Southern Confederacy going, as it was also the corner-stone of its constitution.

In April, 1861, at Fort Sumter, Charleston Harbour, the first shot was fired in a war that was only ended in April, 1865, by the surrender of General Lee's army at Appomattox Court House in Virginia. In duration it is the longest war waged since the great Napoleon's power was finally crushed at Waterloo. As the heroic struggle of a small population that was cut off from all outside help against a great, populous and very rich Republic, with every market in the world open to it, and to whom all Europe was a recruiting ground, this Secession war stands out prominently in the history of the world. When the vast numbers of men put into the field by the Northern States, and the scale upon which their operations were carried on, are duly considered, it must be regarded as a war fully equal in magnitude to the successful invasion of France by Germany in 1870. If the mind be allowed to speculate on the course that events will take in centuries to come, as they flow surely on with varying swiftness to the ocean of the unknown future, the influence which the result of this Confederate war is bound to exercise upon man's future history will seem very great. Think of what a power the re-United States will be in another century! Of what it will be in the twenty-first century of the Christian era! If, as many believe, China is destined to absorb all Asia and then to overrun Europe, may it not be in the possible future that Armageddon, the final contest between heathendom and Christianity, may be fought out between China and North America? Had secession been victorious, it is tolerably certain that the United States would have broken up still further, and instead of the present magnificent and English-speaking empire, we should now see in its place a number of small powers with separate interests.

Most certainly it was the existence of slavery in the South that gave rise to the bitter antagonism of feeling which led to secession. But it was not to secure emancipation that the North took up arms, although during the progress of the war Mr. Lincoln proclaimed it, for the purpose of striking his enemy a serious blow. Lee hated slavery, but, as he explained to me, he thought it wicked to give freedom suddenly to some millions of people who were incapable of using it with profit to themselves or the state. He assured me he had long intended to gradually give his slaves their liberty. He believed the institution to be a moral and political evil, and more hurtful to the white than to the black man. He had a strong affection for the negro, but he deprecated any sudden or violent interference on the part of the State between master and slave. Nothing would have induced him to fight for the continuance of slavery: indeed he declared that had he owned every slave in the South, he would willingly give them all up if by so doing he could preserve the Union. He was opposed to secession, and to prevent it he would willingly sacrifice everything except honour and duty, which forbid him to desert his State. When in April, 1861, she formally and by an act of her Legislature left the Union, he resigned his commission in the United States army with the intention of retiring into private life. He endeavoured to choose what was right. Every personal interest bid him throw in his lot with the Union. His property lay so close to Washington that it was certain to be destroyed and swept of every slave, as belonging to a rebel. But the die was cast: he forsook everything for principle and the stern duty it entailed. Then came that final temptation which opened out before him a vista of power and importance greater than that which any man since Washington had held in America. General Long's book proves beyond all further doubt that he was offered the post of commander-in-chief of the Federal army. General Scott, his great friend and leader, whom he loved and respected, then commanding that army, used all his influence to persuade him to throw in his lot with the North, but to no purpose. Nothing would induce him to have any part in the invasion of his own State, much as he abhorred the war into which he felt she was rushing. His love of country, his unselfish patriotism, caused him to relinquish home, fortune, a certain future, in fact everything for her sake.

He was not, however, to remain a spectator of the coming conflict: he was too well known to his countrymen in Virginia as the officer in whom the Federal army had most confidence. The State of Virginia appointed him major-general and commander-in-chief of all her military forces. In open and crowded convention he formally accepted this position, saying, with all that dignity and grace of manner which distinguished him, that he did so "trusting in Almighty God, an approving conscience, and the aid of my fellow-citizens." The scene was most impressive: there were present all the leading men of Virginia, and representatives of all the first families in a State where great store was attached to gentle birth, and where society was very exclusive. General Lee's presence commanded respect, even from strangers, by a calm self-possessed dignity, the like of which I have never seen in other men. Naturally of strong passions, he kept them under perfect control by that iron and determined will, of which his expression and his face gave evidence. As this tall, handsome soldier stood before his countrymen, he was the picture of the ideal patriot, unconscious and self-possessed in his strength: he indulged in no theatrical display of feeling: there was in his face and about him that placid resolve which bespoke great confidence in self, and which in his case—one knows not how—quickly communicated its magnetic influence to others. He was then just fifty-four years old, the age of Marlborough when he destroyed the French army at Blenheim: in many ways and on many points these two great men much resembled each other. Both were of a dignified and commanding exterior: eminently handsome, with a figure tall, graceful, and erect, whilst a muscular, square-built frame bespoke great activity of body. The charm of manner, which I have mentioned as very winning in Lee, was possessed in the highest degree by Marlborough. Both, at the outset of their great career of victory, were regarded as essentially national commanders. Both had married young, and were faithful husbands and devoted fathers. Both had in all their campaigns the same belief in an ever-watchful Providence, in whose help they trusted implicitly, and for whose interposition they prayed at all times. They

61

were gifted with the same military instinct, the same genius for war. The power of fascinating those with whom they were associated, the spell which they cast over their soldiers, who believed almost superstitiously in their certainty of victory, their contempt of danger, their daring courage, constitute a parallel that is difficult to equal between any other two great men of modern times.

From the first Lee anticipated a long and bloody struggle, although from the bombastic oratory of self-elected politicians and patriots the people were led to believe that the whole business would be settled in a few weeks. This folly led to a serious evil, namely, the enlistment of soldiers for only ninety days. Lee, who understood war, pleaded in favour of the engagement being for the term of the war, but he pleaded in vain. To add to his military difficulties, the politician insisted upon the officers being elected by their men. This was a point which, in describing to me the constitution of his army, Lee most deplored. When war bursts upon a country unused to that ordeal, and therefore unskilled in preparing for it, the frothy babbling of politicians too often forces the nation into silly measures to its serious injury during the ensuing operations. That no great military success can be achieved quickly by an improvised army is a lesson that of all others is made most clear by the narrative of this war on both sides. All through its earlier phases, the press, both Northern and Southern, called loudly, and oftentimes angrily, for quick results. It is this impatience of the people, which the press is able to emphasize so strongly, that drives many weak generals into immature action. Lee, as well as others at this time, had to submit to the sneers which foolish men circulated widely in the daily newspapers. It is quite certain that under the existing condition of things no Fabius would be tolerated, and that the far-seeing military policy which triumphed at Torres Vedras would not be submitted to by the English public of to-day. Lee was not, however, a man whom any amount of irresponsible writing could force beyond the pace he knew to be most conducive to ultimate success.

The formation of an army with the means alone at his disposal was a colossal task. Everything had to be created by this extraordinary man. The South was an agricultural, not a manufacturing country, and the resources of foreign lands were denied it by the blockade of its ports maintained by the fleet of the United States.

Lee was a thorough man of business, quick in decision, yet methodical in all he did. He knew what he wanted. He knew what an army should be, and how it should be organised, both in a purely military as well as an administrative sense. In about two months he had created a little army of fifty thousand men, animated by a lofty patriotism and courage that made them unconquerable by any similarly constituted army. In another month, this army at Bull's Run gained a complete victory over the Northern invaders, who were driven back across the Potomac like herds of frightened sheep. As the Federals ran, they threw away their arms, and everything, guns, tents, waggons, &c., was abandoned to the victors. The arms, ammunition, and equipment then taken were real godsends to those engaged in the organisation of the Southern armies. Thenceforward a battle to the Confederates meant a new supply of everything an army required. It may be truthfully said, that practically the Government at Washington had to provide and pay for the arms and equipment of its enemies as well as for all that its own enormous armies required. The day I presented myself in General Lee's camp, as I stood at the door of his tent awaiting admission, I was amused to find it stamped as belonging to a colonel of a New Jersey regiment. I remarked upon this to General Lee, who laughingly said, "Yes, I think you will find that all our tents, guns, and even the men's pouches are similarly marked as having belonged to the United States army." Some time afterwards, when General Pope and his large invading army had been sent back flying across the Maryland frontier, I overheard this conversation between two Confederate soldiers: "Have you heard the news? Lee has resigned!" "Good G——!" was the reply, "What for?" He has resigned because he says he cannot feed and supply his army any longer, now that his commissary, General Pope, has been removed." Mr. Lincoln had just dismissed General Pope, replacing him by General McClellan.

The Confederates did not follow up their victory at Bull's Run. A rapid and daring advance would have given them possession of Washington, their enemy's capital. Political considerations at Richmond were allowed to outweigh the very evident military expediency of reaping a solid advantage from this their first great success. Often afterwards, when this attempt to allay the angry feelings of the North against the Act of Secession had entirely failed, was this action of their political rulers lamented by the Confederate commanders.

In this article to attempt even a sketch of the subsequent military operations is not to be thought of. Both sides fought well, and both have such true reason to be proud of their achievements that they can now afford to hear the professional criticisms of their English friends in the same spirit that we Britishers have learnt to read of the many defeats inflicted upon our arms by General Washington.

What most strikes the regular soldier in these campaigns of General Lee is the inefficient manner in which both he and his opponents were often served by their subordinate commanders, and how badly the staff and outpost work generally was performed on both sides. It is most difficult to move with any effective precision young armies constituted as these were during this war. The direction and movement of large bodies of newly-raised troops, even when victorious, is never easy, is often impossible. Over and over again was the South apparently "within a stone's throw of independence," as it has been many times remarked, when, from want of a thoroughly good staff to organise pursuit, the occasion was lost, and the enemy allowed to escape. Lee's combinations to secure victory were the conceptions of a truly great strategist, and, when they had been effected, his tactics were also almost always everything that could be desired up to the moment of victory, but there his action seemed to stop abruptly. Was ever an army so hopelessly at the mercy of another as that of McClellan when he began his retreat to Harrison's Landing after the seven days' fighting round Richmond? What commander could wish to have his foe in a "tighter place" than Burnside was in after his disastrous attack upon Lee at Fredericksburg? Yet in both instances the Northern commander got safely away, and other similar instances could be mentioned. The critical military student of this war who knows the power which regular troops, well-officered and well-directed by a thoroughly efficient staff, place in the hands of an able general, and who has acquired an intimate and complete knowledge of what these two contending American armies were really like, will, I think, agree that from first to last the co-operation of even one army corps of regular troops would have given complete victory to whichever side it fought on. I felt this when I visited the South, and during the progress of the war I heard the same opinion expressed by many others who had inspected the contending armies. I say this with no wish to detract in any way from the courage or other fighting qualities of the troops engaged. I yield to none in my admiration of their warlike achievements; but I cannot blind myself to the hyperbole of writers who refer to these armies as the finest that have ever existed.

Those who know how difficult it is to supply our own militia and volunteer forces with efficient officers can appreciate what difficulties General Lee had to overcome in the formation of the army he so often led to victory. He had about him able assistants, who, like himself, had received an excellent military education at West Point. To the experienced soldier it is no matter of surprise, but to the general reader it will be of interest to know that, on either side in this war, almost every general whose name will be remembered in the future had been educated at that military school, and had been trained in the old regular army of the United States. In talking to me of all the Federal generals, Lee mentioned McClellan with most respect and regard. He spoke bitterly of none —a remarkable fact, as at that time men on both sides were wont to heap the most violent terms of abuse upon their respective enemies. He thus reproved a clergyman who had spoken in his sermon very bitterly of their enemies:—"I have fought against the people of the North because I believed they were seeking to wrest from the South her dearest rights; but I have never cherished towards them bitter or vindictive feelings, and I have never seen the day when I did not pray for them." I asked him how many men he had at the battle of Antietam, from which he had then recently returned. He said he had never had, during that whole day, more than about thirty thousand men in line, although he had behind him a small army of tired troops and of shoeless stragglers who never came up during the battle. He estimated McClellan's army at about one hundred thousand men. A friend of mine, who at that same time was at the Federal headquarters, there made similar inquiries. General McClellan's reply corroborated the correctness of Lee's estimate of the Federal numbers at Antietam, but he said he thought the Confederate army was a little stronger than that under his command. I mention this because both those generals were most truthful men, and whatever they stated can be implicitly relied on. I also refer to it because the usual proportion throughout the war between the contending sides in each action ranged from about twice to three times more Federals than there were Confederates engaged. With reference to the relative numbers employed on both sides, the following amusing story was told to me at the time. A deputation from some of the New England States had attended at the White House, and laid their business before the President. As they were leaving Mr. Lincoln's room one of the delegates turned round and said: "Mr. President, I should very much like to know what you reckon to be the number of rebels in arms against us." Mr. Lincoln, without a moment's hesitation, replied: "Sir, I have the best possible reason for knowing the number to be one million of men, for whenever one of our generals engages a rebel army he reports that he has encountered a force twice his strength: now I know we have half a million of soldiers in the field, so I am bound to believe the rebels have twice that number."

As a student of war I would fain linger over the interesting lessons to be learnt from Lee's campaigns: of the same race as both belligerents, I could with the utmost pleasure dwell upon the many brilliant feats of arms on both sides; but I cannot do so here.

The end came at last, when the well-supplied North, rich enough to pay recruits, no matter where they came from, a bounty of over five hundred dollars a head, triumphed over an exhausted South, hemmed in on all sides, and even cut off from all communication with the outside world. The desperate, though drawn battle of Gettysburg was the death-knell of Southern independence; and General Sherman's splendid but almost unopposed march to the sea showed the world that all further resistance on the part of the Confederate States could only be a profitless waste of blood. In the thirty-five days of fighting near Richmond which ended the war of 1865, General Grant's army numbered one hundred and ninety thousand, that of Lee only fifty-one thousand men. Every man lost by the former was easily replaced, but an exhausted South could find no more soldiers. "The right of self-government," which Washington won, and for which Lee fought, was no longer to be a watchword to stir men's blood in the United States. The South was humbled and beaten by its own flesh and blood in the North, and it is difficult to know which to admire most, the good sense with which the result was accepted in the so-called Confederate States, or the wise magnanimity displayed by the victors. The wounds are now healed on both sides: Northerners and Southerners are now once more a united people, with a future before them to which no other nation can aspire. If the English-speaking people of the earth cannot all acknowledge the same Sovereign, they can, and I am sure they will, at least combine to work in the interests of truth and of peace, for the good of mankind. The wise men on both sides of the Atlantic will take care to chase away all passing clouds that may at any time throw even a shadow of dispute or discord between the two great families into which our race is divided.

Like all men, Lee had his faults: like all the greatest of generals, he sometimes made mistakes. His nature shrank with such horror from the dread of wounding the feelings of others, that upon occasions he left men in positions of responsibility to which their abilities were not equal. This softness of heart, amiable as that quality may be, amounts to a crime in the man intrusted with the direction of public affairs at critical moments. Lee's devotion to duty and great respect for obedience seem at times to have made him too subservient to those charged with the civil government of his country. He carried out too literally the orders of those whom the Confederate Constitution made his superiors, although he must have known them to be entirely ignorant of the science of war. He appears to have forgotten that he was the great Revolutionary Chief engaged in a great Revolutionary war: that he was no mere leader in a political struggle of parties carried on within the lines of an old, well-established form of government. It was very clear to many at the time, as it will be commonly acknowledged now, that the South could only hope to win under the rule of a Military Dictator. If General Washington had had a Mr. Davis over him, could he have accomplished what he did? It will, I am sure, be news to many that General Lee was given the command over all the Confederate armies a month or two only before the final collapse; and that the military policy of the South was all throughout the war dictated by Mr. Davis as president of the Confederate States! Lee had no power to reward soldiers or to promote officers. It was Mr. Davis who selected the men to command divisions and armies. Is it to be supposed that Cromwell, King William the Third, Washington, or Napoleon could have succeeded in the revolutions with which their names are identified, had they submitted to the will and authority of a politician as Lee did to Mr. Davis?

Lee was opposed to the final defence of Richmond that was urged upon him for political, not military reasons. It was a great strategic error. General Grant's large army of men was easily fed, and its daily losses easily recruited from a near base; whereas if it had been drawn far into the interior after the little army with which Lee endeavoured to protect Richmond, its fighting strength would have been largely reduced by the detachments required to guard a long line of communications through a hostile country. It is profitless, however, to speculate upon what might have been, and the military student must take these campaigns as they were carried out. No fair estimate of Lee as a general can be made by a simple comparison of what he achieved with that which Napoleon, Wellington, or Von Moltke accomplished, unless due allowance is made for the difference in the nature of the American armies, and of the armies commanded and encountered by those great leaders. They were at the head of perfectly organised, thoroughly trained and well disciplined troops; whilst Lee's soldiers, though gallant and daring to a fault, lacked the military cohesion and efficiency, the trained company leaders, and the educated staff which are only to be found in a regular army of long standing. A trial heat between two jockeys mounted on untrained horses may be interesting, but no one would ever quote the performance as an instance of great racing speed.

Who shall ever fathom the depth of Lee's anguish when the bitter end came, and when, beaten down by sheer force of numbers, and by absolutely nothing else, he found himself obliged to surrender! The handful of starving men remaining with him laid down their arms, and the proud Confederacy ceased to be. Surely the crushing, maddening anguish of awful sorrow is only known to the leader who has so failed to accomplish some lofty, some noble aim for which he has long striven with might and main, with heart and soul—in the interests of king or of country. A smiling face, a cheerful manner, may conceal the sore place from the eyes, possibly even from the knowledge of his friends; but there is no healing for such a wound, which eats into the very heart of him who has once received it.

General Lee survived the destruction of the Confederacy for five years, when, at the age of sixty-three, and surrounded by his family, life ebbed slowly from him. Where else in history is a great man to be found whose whole life was one such blameless record of duty nobly done? It was consistent in all its parts, complete in all its relations. The most perfect gentleman of a State long celebrated for its chivalry, he was just, gentle, and generous, and child-like in the simplicity of his character. Never elated with success, he bore reverse, and at last, complete overthrow, with dignified resignation. Throughout this long and cruel struggle his was all the responsibility, but not the power that should have accompanied it.

The fierce light which beats upon the throne is as that of a rushlight in comparison with the electric glare which our newspapers now focus upon the public man in Lee's position. His character has been subjected to that ordeal, and who can point to any spot upon it? His clear, sound judgment, personal courage, untiring activity, genius for war, and absolute devotion to his State mark him out as a public man, as a patriot to be for ever remembered by all Americans. His amiability of disposition, deep sympathy with those in pain or sorrow, his love for children, nice sense of personal honour and genial courtesy endeared him to all his friends. I shall never forget his sweet winning smile, nor his clear, honest eyes that seemed to look into your heart whilst they searched your brain. I have met many of the great men of my time, but Lee alone impressed me with the feeling that I was in the presence of a man who was cast in a grander mould, and made of different and of finer metal than all other men. He is stamped upon my memory as a being apart and superior to all others in every way: a man with whom none I ever knew, and very few of whom I have read, are worthy to be classed. I have met but two men who realize my ideas of what a true hero should be: my friend Charles Gordon was one, General Lee was the other.

The following lines seem written for him:

> Who is the honest man?
> He who doth still and strongly good pursue,
> To God, his country and himself most true;
> Who when he comes to deal
> With sick folk, women, those whom passions sway,
> Allows for this, and keeps his constant way

69

When all the angry feelings roused by Secession are buried with those which existed when the Declaration of Independence was written, when Americans can review the history of their last great rebellion with calm impartiality, I believe all will admit that General Lee towered far above all men on either side in that struggle: I believe he will be regarded not only as the most prominent figure of the Confederacy, but as the great American of the nineteenth century, whose statue is well worthy to stand on an equal pedestal with that of Washington, and whose memory is equally worthy to be enshrined in the hearts of all his countrymen.

AN ENGLISH VIEW OF THE CIVIL WAR

PART I

THE PUBLICATION UNDER REVIEW HERE GERMINATED IN THE mind of Clarence C. Buel, assistant editor of the Century, in 1883. The magazine had just printed two successful articles with rival points of view on John Brown's raid. Acting on a suggestion from Buel, the Century undertook to assemble and publish a series of articles by Union and Confederate leaders on the principal battles.

Many former commanders were eager to tell their stories. Writers bowed to the editorial decree that sectional politics be left out, and they leveled their charges against members of their own side. Starting in November 1884 and appearing monthly, the articles boosted circulation and ignited controversies such as the hot disputation between Confederate Generals Joseph E. Johnston and P. G. T. Beauregard over First Bull Run. The editors published the three years' series with many additions as the four-volume Battles and Leaders of the Civil War in 1887. The work (verified in detail with the War Department, which was then compiling the Official Records) became a standard reference on the military history of the war. Nothing like it exists for other American wars, and it is probably unique in the chronicling of warfare.

Partisanship had not been eliminated by checking for accuracy, and it was fitting that an outsider, a foreign critic and expert, be invited to review it by a third party—the North American Review. In seven essays Wolseley subjected the work (also called The Century War Book) to a close analysis that became in Freeman's phrase "a critique of many aspects, civil and military, of the War between the States."

PART I

Wolseley's first paper treats four main subjects. One is his estimate of President Jefferson Davis, whom he found "a third-rate man," a judgment that seems excessively harsh to the modern historian. Here also he analyzed the early months of the war in the west, both the trans-Mississippi operations and those extending from the Ohio River to Shiloh. His study of the battle of Shiloh is especially noteworthy. He then turned to the east to appraise First Bull Run and finally to comment on the rise of General McClellan. The critic always has an eye on

73

*the future usefulness of Civil War lessons to Great Britain, and
throughout these pages is an obvious concern for strategy and a with-
ering indictment of the force public opinion exerted on field operations.*

AN ENGLISH VIEW
OF THE CIVIL WAR

I

THE *Century* Company has, in my judgment, done a great service to the soldiers of all armies by the publication of these records of the great War[1] in the United States. The first volume of the re-publication has just reached me, and I propose in the following pages to restrict my comments to that part of the history embraced within the seven hundred-odd pages it contains.

The story of the War, as told by the several actors in it, has not, in this volume, reached the date at which I personally paid a visit to one of the contending armies. I can only, therefore, comment on the evidence supplied to us, as a deeply interested student of the mighty struggle. The characteristic features of this part of the history are very unlike those of the later campaigns. The attention of soldiers in Europe has been so much directed to the long series of campaigns that were fought over the ground between Washington and Richmond, that we are prone to regard them as representing the character of the War throughout. The elaborately-prepared defensive positions of the later campaigns, and the sharp counter-strokes with which Lee, using Stonewall Jackson as his right arm, met the continued and systematic process of attrition applied by the Northern generals, have hardly their counterpart in this earlier period of the War. Nor do those far-reaching raids of mounted men on either side, which afterwards gave such a distinctive character to the War, appear to have yet made themselves felt.

The stately figure of Robert Lee, as yet, remains in the background. It is, however, excessively interesting to get clearer views than we have hitherto had of the circumstances under which Grant, Sherman, Sheridan, Jackson, and others first made their

[1] "Battles and Leaders of the Civil War" (The *Century* War Book).

appearance in this great struggle. The story of the first battle of Bull Run, and of Shiloh, are each told here with much circumstantial detail that supplies most valuable corrections to what we knew of them before. The stories of the capture of Fort Henry and of Fort Donelson have a very different aspect, now that we are able to judge of them from both sides and from many points of view. To English soldiers, all the minor circumstances of the gathering of the Northern and Southern forces have a special interest, as they enable us to realize in a new way the analagous incidents which must have attended the beginning of the war between King and Parliament in Charles I.'s time. The uncertainty as to which side men would take, the acts of vigorous, personal individuality, like those of Captain Lyon in Missouri, were common to both epochs. The trains with recruits for both sides, passing one another almost amicably on the same American railroad, with other kindred incidents, are all just of such a kind as must have happened in England, when men rallied to the standards of Rupert and of Cromwell. In the later instance, however, they were strangely affected in their form by all the elaborations of modern civilization and by the vastness of the theatre of war,—an area in which our whole island would be lost.

It is with the deepest regret that I feel obliged, at this early part of my review of the War, to call in question the fitness of Mr. Jefferson Davis for the high position he occupied. A man weighed down with years, with misfortunes, and, above all, with sad memories of a lost cause, and, I presume, the conviction that he was a failure, appeals to our pity rather than invites our censure. Like all the great actors on both sides, he was, I am sure, influenced in the course he took by the highest motives. He sincerely believed in the justice of the cause he espoused, and he brought to the service of his country an honesty of purpose, a fervid patriotism, an ability of no mean order, a zeal, and a persistent determination which all will admit he possessed. But that he was a third-rate man, and a most unfortunate selection for the office of President, I cannot conceal from myself. The great misfortunes of public servants who have utterly failed in the one great public venture of their lives must not be allowed to silence the voice of censure, much less of criticism. In dealing with private individuals we can afford to indulge our amiable feelings for misfortune. What we owe to historical truth and to the teaching of future generations forbids us, however, to deal similarly with men who have filled high positions. I note it here as a curious and, in my opinion, a regrettable fact, that in this, the first volume of "Battles and Leaders of the Civil War," there is no picture of the President of the Confederate States, although there are likenesses of many much less important men on both sides in this great struggle. The tremendous indictment against his capacity, which is drawn by Mr. R. Barnwell Rhett, so strongly supports my views regarding him that I regret very much that no answer to it has been printed side by side with it, in accordance with the impartial method of "The *Century* War Series." What reasonable answer could be made to it? If the Northern troops had then really known how he unwittingly worked for them, would they have wished to "hang Jeff. Davis to a sour-apple tree"?

It may be said that it was impossible for any one to foresee the dimensions to which the struggle would grow. But surely it is a statesman's business at least partially to gauge the strength of the forces with which he has to deal. The *soi-disant* statesman who began his high duties with the avowed expectation that 10,000 Enfield rifles would be sufficient to overawe the United States; who then refused the services of 366,000 men, the flower of the South, and accepted only a fraction of them, because he had not arms for more; the man who neglected to buy the East Indian fleet, which happy chance and the zeal of subordinates threw in his way; the ruler who could not see that the one vital necessity for the South was, at all sacrifice and at all hazard, to keep the ports open; who rejected all means proposed by others for placing the finances of the Confederacy on a sound basis,—that man, as I think, did more than any other individual on either side to save the Union. I have not attempted to make the charge against him as complete and crushing as it could easily be made by those who trusted him with almost unlimited powers in their behalf. Enough has been said to illustrate what, I think, is, on this point, the commonly accepted verdict of history.

It is the old, old story over again, of civil rulers who blunder, and, failing to foresee events, sacrifice everything to a momentary popularity, in order to divert popular wrath from themselves to the unfortunate soldiers who have been their victims. An illustration of my meaning is to be found in the pathetic story told in this volume of the gallant and high-minded Albert Sidney Johnston. Like Robert Lee, he hated the War, and had also refused the highest military position in the United States Army, at the call of what he considered to be his duty to his State. Those who played the part of statesmen on the Southern side had left Johnston without resources. Despite all his efforts, and despite his zeal and great military ability, he was overwhelmed by the popular fury at a failure for which others had prepared the way, and where the action of his Government had rendered success well-nigh impossible. To do Mr. Davis justice, he no doubt, in this instance, did his best to support by words the soldier whom he had failed to support by deeds.

To pass to other matters: I am struck, throughout the whole story of the minor operations of this period, by the illustrations they afford of the regularity with which the old rules and principles of war assert their supremacy. The battle of Wilson's Creek, on August 10, 1861, and that of Pea Ridge, on March 7, 1862, are curiously alike in their military lessons. In both, the attempt was made to carry out distinctly separated movements by isolated parts of an attacking force, in order to strike upon the flanks or rear of a concentrated defensive force. Both attempts failed, as might have been predicted beforehand. No doubt Sigel's movement round the rear of Price at Wilson's Creek was a more hazardous, as well as a bolder, attempt than that of Price and McCulloch at Pea Ridge, so far as their separation on the field of battle was concerned. But McCulloch, at Pea Ridge, was completely disconnected from the attack made upon the Federal right by Price. The consequences in each battle followed in the same way. McCulloch, at Pea Ridge, and Sigel, at Wilson's Creek, each for the moment gained advantage from a surprised enemy; but when time had been given for the surprised to recover, there was in neither instance a supporting force sufficiently near at hand to meet the supports brought up by the enemy. The advantage gained at first was soon lost, and then the isolated force was crushed. The result was, in each instance, that the depending army was thus soon able to devote its whole strength to meet the remainder of the attack, and to crush that in its turn also. It is worthy of note that, in the general position taken up for the attack, Price had passed completely to the rear of the Federal position. It is clear that he sacrificed as much as he gained by so doing. The Federals were as directly on his line of communications as he on theirs.

I am much struck, in this intricate series of minor actions, by the terrible difficulty under which generals act who are in command of troops that cannot be employed solely to win victory, and to bring about peace by securing it. I refer to the necessity which the leaders on both sides had to yield to, of retaining often large forces for the defence of points of political, but of small military, importance, if of any at all. McCulloch, tied to the defence of the trans-Mississippi region, and especially to that of Arkansas, on the Indian territory, could not, perhaps would not, join with Price in any large military movement. Here, as always, the orders from the Civil Government at Richmond hampered the military movement of the Confederate leaders; otherwise it is clear that a far more effective mode of meeting the Federal advance could have been devised than that of passing round to their rear. The Federal forces, based on St. Louis, had advanced by way of Rolla, Lebanon, and Dug Spring to the Pea Ridge. (See map on page 263.) Van Dorn had his headquarters at Pocahontas. Price had fallen back before the Federal Army as it advanced. McCulloch was, at first, at Maysville. It is not very clear from any of the narratives how much force Van Dorn, who was in command of the whole, had gathered at Pocahontas; but, as he had been contemplating a movement on St. Louis, he must, at least, have collected a considerable quantity of stores at Pocahontas. It would seem that McCulloch might have been at once transferred to the eastern side of the White River, allowing Price to continue his retreat towards the same point. General Curtis, when he reached Pea Ridge with the Federal force, entered a most difficult country; and had Price gradually given him the slip, with a view to a junction with the other Confederate forces, it is clear that an advance northward, directly upon Rolla or Springfield, based on Pocahontas, would have obliged Curtis to abandon his invasion of Arkansas, and would have enabled Van Dorn to fight at far greater advantage than he actually did. The Federal line, even from Rolla to Sugar Creek, was two hundred and ten miles in length, and from St. Louis it was three hundred and twenty miles. It would have been exposed throughout that entire distance to such a stroke from Pocahontas.

I do not, however, say this as a criticism on the generals on either side. No one who has himself realized the practical difficulties of command in the field is much tempted to any slap-dash criticism of those who are engaged in high command. The lesson which is most impressed upon me by a study of these campaigns is the danger there always is of popular irritability and ignorant impatience preventing a general from doing the very thing which would, if time were allowed, surely gain the ends which the people desire. If England were invaded, or threatened with invasion, the general in supreme command would be exposed to the same difficulty. People in Manchester would be uneasy because the Lancashire Volunteer Corps were drawn away from the defence of their own locality, for the purpose of crushing the enemy in the field elsewhere, by the united action of all our available military forces. It is for this reason that I hope the *Century's* admirable narrative of the Confederate War may be read attentively by the large numbers of educated volunteer officers whom we now have in England. Its campaigns are replete with instruction for all our auxiliary forces, as well as for our army.

In 1866, during the western campaign in Germany, very similar events repeated themselves. There, Vogel von Falkenstein, with a numerically very inferior force of Prussians, triumphed over the army opposed to him—an army made up of Hanoverians, Wurtembergers, Bavarians, and troops of various other minor states—because the officers commanding each contingent were hampered by their respective civil governments with orders which had their origin in a desire to keep each its own troops for the defence of its own particular state. Hence the absence of all unity of action, and the impossibility of concentration upon the decisive points. On the other hand, the Prussians triumphed because they were everywhere directed upon the decisive points against enemies whose several interests kept them from working heartily together. I dwell upon this because I have heard English politicians say that, in the event of danger here, we should have great difficulties with localities, which would cry out against having their volunteer corps removed for the defence of distant, though possibly most vital, points.

This great principle of strategy rules everywhere; and although I have every wish to do justice to the ability of General Albert Sidney Johnston, it is impossible to accept the reasons which his son advances for his having allowed General Curtis to attack Fort

Donelson without moving to resist him, when he was, himself, within supporting distance at Nashville. The statement that he was bound to remain at Nashville, because it was the objective point of the Federal campaign, is answered by the facts. He was immediately obliged to abandon Nashville and to fall back on Corinth, as soon as Donelson fell. As long as the point of Federal attack was uncertain, it would seem to have been quite permissible for him to divide his forces between Donelson and Nashville, each of which was of great importance. What appears to me certain is that the course which was pursued by the Confederate commanders, prior to the first Bull Run, would here have been the right one. Whilst Buell's advance on Nashville was delayed, and Grant's attack on Donelson was declared, it would have been well to demonstrate in advance of Nashville, so as to convey the impression of intended aggression from that point, just as in the early summer of 1861 General Joseph E. Johnston did against Patterson, before he moved to support Beauregard, then in position on Bull Run.

If a similar course had been followed in Kentucky and Tennessee in February, 1862, and a rapid movement made with all the troops which General Albert S. Johnston could have then collected to attack Grant before Fort Donelson, it is difficult to believe, considering what actually did happen there, that the Federal forces could have escaped decisive defeat. It is evident that the personal presence of General A. S. Johnston himself was badly needed at Fort Donelson, and the moral effect of his arrival there with fresh troops would have been enormous. Such a success would have greatly assisted Van Dorn's campaign, and if that campaign had been conducted in the way suggested, on the line from Pocahontas towards Rolla, the forces under Johnston and Van Dorn would have occupied a central position between Buell and Curtis, and might have struck with great advantage at either. That such a co-operation between Van Dorn and A. S. Johnston was not rendered impossible by any material obstacles, or by distance, is clear from the fact that, previous to Shiloh, Beauregard was looking for support from Van Dorn (page 574) on February 21, three days before Van Dorn started for the Pea Ridge campaign, and whilst Van Dorn was still at Pocahontas.

I shall not enter into the disputed claims of General Beauregard and of General A. S. Johnston to have conceived the scheme of the Shiloh campaign. Whoever conceived it, the advance to attack Grant where he stood in position was in every respect a sound military operation.

It is curious to see how differently men regard operations in which they have been personally engaged and those in which they have had no special or direct interest. General Grant's own account of Shiloh leaves one the impression that he is conscious that his proceedings there were not militarily defensible. I hardly know of two commanders to whose sound military judgment I would more unhesitatingly commit the following proposition than Generals Grant and Sherman, supposing it were possible to do so, and that it could be put to them regarding an action in which they had not been personally concerned. I cannot do better than state the proposition in the terms, and in what seems to me the unanswerable criticism, of General Buell, given on page 487.

An army comprising seventy regiments of infantry, twenty batteries of artillery, and a sufficiency of cavalry, lay for two weeks and more in isolated camps, with a river in its rear, and a hostile army, claimed to be superior in numbers, twenty miles distant in its front, while the commander made his headquarters and passed his nights nine miles away on the opposite side of the river. It had no line or order of battle, no defensive works of any sort, no outposts, properly speaking, to give warning, or check the advance of an enemy and no recognized head during the absence of the regular commander. On a Saturday the hostile force arrived and formed in order of battle, without detection or hindrance, within a mile and a half of the unguarded army, advanced upon it the next morning, penetrated its disconnected lines, assaulted its camps in front and flank, drove its disjointed members successively from position to position, capturing some and routing others, in spite of much heroic resistance, and steadily drew near the landing and depot of its supplies in the pocket between the river and an impassable creek.

Had not the commander of that assailed army positively invited defeat? Is there a syllable in that summary of the facts which does not accurately represent the incidents of the first day's fight at Shiloh?

It is hoped that no one will imagine for a moment that I wish to throw a stone at General Grant. We are all of us liable to human error. The greatest generals have made great, perhaps some of the greatest, mistakes ever made in war. The matter is looked at solely as a question of military study, and, looking so, it would not appear that General Buell's criticism, in the chapter called "Shiloh Reviewed," admits of any good answer. No satisfactory answer is, in my opinion, supplied to it by General Grant's statements on the battle of Shiloh. As a matter of fact, it would seem that Grant and Sherman before Shiloh, like Wellington and Blucher before Quatre Bras and Lignay, were contemplating an offensive, not a defensive, campaign. By coupling together these names as I have done, I shall perhaps best show that I am not speaking with any disparagement of Grant or of Sherman.

In both instances alike, the error of taking for granted that an active and able enemy is restricted to one course of action, was severely punished. In both cases alike, it very narrowly missed being fatally punished. In no other way, with, perhaps, the reservation that Grant had not at that time acquired the experience he afterwards gained, can I explain the facts. Grant was avowedly waiting for the arrival of Buell's force to begin an offensive campaign with a united army. By means of his gunboats he had complete command of the passage of the Tennessee. Supposing that it was advisable to make the concentration in the neighborhood of Pittsburg Landing, clearly the right course would have been to cover that concentration by the river, and, therefore, to have retained the bulk of his forces concentrated on the east bank, awaiting Buell's arrival. If it were necessary, as perhaps it was, to secure Pittsburg Landing itself, as a means of debouching on the opposite bank, there could have been no objection, and probably would have been advantage, in having a small, strongly-intrenched position near that point, in the nature of a bridgehead, with its flanks thoroughly swept by the fire of the gunboats. Clearly, if, as General Grant says, the troops required discipline and drill more than work at intrenchments, it would have been easier and safer to impart both to them on the east bank of the river, away from the enemy, than on the west bank within his easy reach.

The accidents and mistakes which occurred in regard to the march of General Wallace's division were only such as continually occur when a change in the position of troops, that has not been previously arranged for and worked out beforehand, is suddenly ordered in any sudden exigency. As an admirable illustration of the kind of method that makes all the difference between success and failure in war, the student should carefully compare the arrangements made for the march of General Lew Wallace's division with the—on the surface—apparently very similar steps taken by Napoleon before Austerlitz, for the due arrival of Davoust's corps. Napoleon deliberately kept that corps away from Austerlitz till the actual day of battle, in a way that might, to a careless student, seem similar to that which left General Lew Wallace within a march of the field of Shiloh. The difference lay in this: Napoleon had been for weeks watching closely the movements of the Allies, and had been endeavoring to tempt them to attack him, by not allowing the forces that he knew he could count on for the field of battle to be apparently within reach. Every detail for Davoust's march had been carefully thought out and prepared beforehand. He was destined to arrive on a part of the field where it was important to encourage the enemy to attack, where the enemy's advance must necessarily be slow, and where it was advisable to allow him to secure some temporary advantage. All this had been previously designed.

On the other hand, for days before Shiloh nothing was known of the movements of Johnston and Beauregard. No attack from them was either expected or prepared for. The direction of Lew Wallace's march depended on his correctly interpreting a single loosely-worded order. The very position of his three brigades seems to have been imperfectly known at Grant's headquarters, for the order of march was certainly not made in accordance with their actual position. Time and distance are elements of vital importance in all these matters. Altogether, the more one studies this first day's battle on the Federal side, the more clear it seems that the opportunity presented to the enemy for attack was as favorable as it well could have been. It is hardly necessary to insist upon the point so well made by General Buell in the passage I have quoted, that the risk was enormously enhanced by the fact that this detached and isolated army, unprepared as it was to resist attack, was liable to be driven "into the pocket between the river," which it had so rashly crossed, and an "impassable creek." When the opportunity is presented to a commander for an attack upon any fraction of a hostile army then in the act of concentrating against him, there are two conditions for which he prays. One is that there shall be time and opportunity for defeating the fraction in question before it can be supported. The other is that the position of the fraction shall be such that, when once defeated, it shall be so utterly broken up and demolished that it can render no assistance to the new supporting force which may possibly arrive.

Both these conditions were presented to Generals Beauregard and Johnston when they designed the march to attack Grant at Shiloh. Seeing the enormous change in the whole situation which would have been wrought if the first day's action had been final and conclusive, it is of great interest to consider, from the Confederate side, what the circumstances were which deprived them of the success which seemed so nearly within their grasp.

It seems tolerably clear that, had everything been done as rapidly as it might have been, the Confederates could and would have made their attack on Saturday, April 5, instead of on Sunday, April 6, 1862. If the attack had been thus made twenty-four hours earlier than it was, I think nothing could have saved Grant's army from complete destruction. Buell had pressed his march, despite the fact that Grant had not proposed to send boats to Savannah "till Monday or Tuesday, or some time early in the week," and had always written in the sense of his words on that very Saturday in Nelson's camp: "There will be no fighting at Pittsburg Landing; we will have to go to Corinth, where the rebels are fortified. If they come to attack us, we can whip them, as I have more than twice as many troops as I had at Fort Donelson." Considering the state of the rivers and bridges, as described by Buell, it seems impossible that any portion of his force should have arrived earlier than it did. Nothing would have tended to change the conditions of Lew Wallace's march, and, therefore, as far as one can judge, in all probability Saturday would have placed the Confederates in a position even more favorable than they actually were in by Sunday evening; more favorable because on Saturday their final movement would not have been checked by the arrival of Nelson's division.

In all probability, therefore, even on Saturday evening a final attack would have resulted in the capture of Pittsburg Landing itself, and of the powerful force of reserve artillery concentrated there. In any case, that would have happened on Sunday morning, and, as an incident of the fighting on that day, Lew Wallace, committed, as he would have been, to a position on the Confederate side of Snake Creek, would have been cut off from the only bridge by which he could have returned. Attacked, as he certainly would have been, by overwhelming forces in front, flank, and rear, he must have lost his whole division in a few hours. The Confederates, fully aware of the proximate advance of Buell, would, in that case, have had the greater part of Sunday in which to prepare for him. If Buell had attempted, under these circumstances, to attack, he would have done so under the greatest disadvantages. The whole artillery and all the stores of Grant's army would have been available for employment against him. He must have necessarily landed division by division, because apparently there was not river transport available for more than one division at a time. No doubt the gunboats would have afforded him powerful assistance, but even with their aid the enterprise would have been one which few prudent commanders would have risked. In all probability, he would have been obliged to gather his forces on the further side of the Tennessee, whilst the Confederates, supplied with all the arms and stores of which they stood so sorely in need, would have been joined by thousands of recruits whom they would then have been able effectively to arm and equip. No wonder that the battle has been looked upon, on both sides, as the turning event of the Western War.

What, then, was the cause of the Confederate delay, which proved so fatal to them? It has been remarked by able officers on the Confederate side that, while nothing could have been more admirable than the conception of the attack on Shiloh, nothing could have been more miserable in all details than the execution. That, I take it, was the inevitable result of the condition of the army at the time. Military training and organization would be useless and, certainly, very expensively purchased qualities, if it were possible that an army of recruits, gathered together in the way the army at Corinth was, should be able to execute a well-prepared plan with all the celerity and certainty which attend the movements of veteran armies. The difficulties which the want of experience, the want of drill, the want of discipline, and the want of a highly-trained staff entailed on both armies, are insisted on at every stage by those who took part in the operations. It is, however, in the movements of attack conducted through an intricate country, almost without roads and very imperfectly mapped or known, that these defects of an army tell most severely. An army in a defensive position, requiring relatively little movement, does not feel them nearly so severely. It was in his thorough appreciation of these facts that, later on in the war, General Robert Lee showed his masterly power of adapting means to ends. He always used Jackson's seasoned soldiers for those wide-reaching strokes by means of which he sought to compensate for the inferiority of his less handy troops. The newly-raised battalions, whom he could not trust to manœuvre, but who shot fairly enough, he placed in position where their want of military efficiency was not particularly felt, whilst their strength was evident.

Nevertheless, it is very interesting to note the incidents which, in the mere delivery of orders and in the mode in which they were interpreted, tended to cause delay. The "Notes of a Confederate Staff Officer at Shiloh" (pages 594–603) are in this respect most valuable. General Jordan observes, in a note to page 595: "As I framed this order, I had before me Napoleon's order for the battle of Waterloo, and, in attention to ante-battle details, took those of such soldiers as Napoleon and Soult for models." Now, it is worth noting that, during the Waterloo campaign, Soult on one or two occasions failed Napoleon as a chief of the staff, not in the drawing-up of orders, but in getting them actually delivered and acted on. The whole movement of Napoleon's army on the 15th was seriously hampered because Vandamme's corps did not move in time, owing to his not having received his orders. In the movement on Shiloh, the army was delayed, and the attack was postponed from Saturday to Sunday, largely because General Polk's corps did not march at the appointed time, he thinking it his duty to await written orders. It had, as we learn, been expressly arranged at a meeting between General Beauregard and the three corps commanders that they should march at twelve, noon, on April 3, without waiting for the written orders containing the detail of their respective routes. General Beauregard himself had, when in bed, worked out these routes during the night of April 2–3 "on the backs of telegrams and envelopes." As it was likely to take some time to reduce these plans and orders to shape, it had been arranged, as already stated, that the corps, to avoid delay, should at once advance over

87

that part of the route which was well known and had been explained previously to their commanders by General Beauregard. It was promised that complete instructions in writing should be sent them on the march.

But it is clear that, while General Beauregard and his staff believed that all the corps generals had understood that they were to move off without waiting for further orders, General Polk, whose corps was leading, had not understood this. According to General Jordan's own account (page 595), the written circular order to the corps commanders directed "that each should hold his corps under arms by 6 A.M. on the 3d of April *ready to march,* with one hundred rounds of ammunition," etc. Now, in a conference of several people it is extremely difficult to be sure that anything which has not been reduced to writing has been understood separately by each of them. Men are very apt to think that everybody else understands what they themselves understand. It seems to me, therefore, that as a lesson of staff-work to be deduced from this experience, which is by no means exceptional, the right course in similar cases would be this: A written memorandum, which could have been drawn out in two minutes, should have been noted by each corps commander to this effect:

Camp———, 3d April, 1862.

It is to be understood that the troops will move off at 12 to-day, under the orders of their corps commanders, without waiting for further instructions from headquarters. Full instructions as to the direction and mode of attack will be sent in due course to each corps commander en route.

This is not suggested as a censure on the actual course pursued by the staff on this occasion. It is only by the reiterated experiences of this kind which war supplies that we learn to avoid the possibilities of future error. Nevertheless, this case and that of Soult at Waterloo, which General Jordan has taken as a model, are illustrations for all soldiers of the number of points which ought to engage the attention of a chief of the staff independent of the mere correct drawing-up of orders. War is big with instances of the importance of the links which connect the actual schemes of operations with their practical execution by means of the feet and legs of men. All our accumulated experience of this kind points to the great importance—I may say the necessity—of the presence, at the right hand of the actual commander, of a chief of the staff, who should be the general who is next to him in genius and ability in the army. The most important function of this chief of the staff is to see that the strategic and tactical plans of the commander are practically worked out and properly executed. It is all very well to design a brilliant stroke, such as that on Shiloh; but if the men do not actually march at the appointed hour, if a corps like Polk's "somehow blocks the line of march," if, for some reason or other, a corps like Bragg's is moved "with inexplicable tardiness," the best-laid schemes "gang oft agley," as Burns has it.

It is impossible, without a more intimate knowledge of all the circumstances, and of the actual condition of the ground at the time, than those who were not there now possess, not to accept as actual fact the statement of General Beauregard that any movement of the three corps toward the field in three separate columns was "an absolute impossibility." (Page 581, note.) I cannot see that Colonel Johnston has in any way upset this statement by the man who, certainly, from all his circumstances, had the best means of knowing the character of the ground. No one would doubt that, had it been possible, it would have been better and more rapid to move by three roads. As the Confederate force scarcely exceeded 40,000 men of all arms, the term "three corps" tends to give rather an exaggerated impression of the crowding that must have taken place on the two bad roads they actually followed.

It is difficult to judge with certainty, and with absolute fairness to all concerned, the conduct of a very complex action of the kind which followed. Nevertheless, I cannot, for instance, agree with General Beauregard that the whole sequence of events shows that, when once in presence of the position, it would have been better for Johnston not to attack. A retreat under such circumstances would have been most demoralizing. All, or almost all, the reasons which General Beauregard advanced at the time for not carrying out the enterprise proved, in fact, to be mistaken. The enemy were *not* "intrenched up to the eyes," as he believed they would be, or intrenched at all. The enemy had *not* been roused by the clumsy recognizance in force made by part of Bragg's corps. To all intents and purposes, the enemy were completely surprised. Nothing shows it more clearly than the contrast between Grant's words

89

at Nelson's camp at Savannah, the previous evening, which I have already quoted, saying that no attack would be made by the enemy, and the letter he wrote to General Buell during the attack (see page 492), in which he states that "the rebel forces," actually numbering 40,000, "are estimated at over 100,000 men."

All that occurred bespoke it the surprise it actually was. The postponement of the attack from Saturday to Sunday clearly deprived the assailants of their best hope of gaining a crushing victory. Seeing, however, how successful the Confederates were on that day, it seems to me that they stood to win more by the attack than by a retreat, which would have brought down on them the united forces of Grant and Buell, untouched and in full power. As General Buell fairly urges, the Confederates, considering the extent to which they had been able to re-arm and re-equip themselves, were actually stronger at the end than they were at the beginning of the first day, whilst the Federals had been materially weakened. Moreover, despite all that General Beauregard has urged, as to the impossibility of carrying, before nightfall, the last foot-hold of the Federal Army at Pittsburg Landing with the forces then actually up, it was, as far as I can judge, a case where the attacking general himself ought to have pushed to the front, gathering all the forces he could from every quarter, for a final attack. It was then a question of "neck or nothing" with him to push home his victory. Arrangements could have been made afterwards for the disposal of the ample supplies of food and ammunition captured in the Federal camps. It seems that all the evidence on both sides, as to the situation of things along the river bank, tends to confirm the evidence supplied on this point by Colonel Lockett, who was present on the spot. "In our front only one single point was showing fight, a hill crowned with artillery"; Bragg with his forces on the spot was confident of victory, when he was stopped by a messenger from Beauregard saying: "The General directs that the pursuit be stopped; the victory is sufficiently complete; it is needless to expose our men to the fire of the gunboats."

That seems to me to indicate exactly the condition of General Beauregard's mind. The shells of the gunboats were, according to all testimony, telling upon the far-distant rear of the Confederate forces. They were producing, however, no effect whatever on the front, and did not in the slightest degree interfere with the carrying-out of the final assault. But that was a condition of things in which, from this position at Shiloh, General Beauregard could do nothing. He was very much debilitated by bad health; he had not wished that the attack should be made that day at all; he was occupied with the by no means important fighting which was still taking place on the Federal right; he saw the streams of disordered men who always hang about the rear of newly-raised armies, composed as both those were which contended at Shiloh. He saw the effects of the shells on these stragglers. He does not seem to have realized the importance of pushing the attack home, or the ease with which it could have been made. He failed to see that it was then a question of "now or never." It is clear that not 5,000 men, and those all more or less seriously shaken, were available to avert the final collapse of the Federal Army, had the Confederates pushed their victory home. Moments were all precious; they were lost, never to be regained. It is impossible not to sympathize with the exclamation attributed to General Bragg: "My God! Was a victory ever sufficiently complete?" "My God! My God! Is it too late!"—*i.e.*, to carry out the attack because of the inopportune order to retreat.

General Beauregard's position during the earlier phases of the battle seems to have been more in accordance with the duties of a general in supreme command than were those rapid movements throughout the day, from point to point, of General Johnston. General Beauregard not unfairly observes, upon Johnston's frequent changes of position, that owing to them he was not able to govern the course of battle at all. As he puts it at page 588:

At no time does it appear from the reports of subordinates in any other part of the field that, either personally or by his staff, General Johnston gave any orders or concerned himself with the general movements of our forces. In fact, engrossed, as he soon became, with the operations of two or three brigades on the extreme right, it would have been out of his power to direct our general operations, especially as he set no machinery in motion with which to gather information of what was being done elsewhere or generally by the Confederate Army, in order to enable him to handle it intelligently from his position on the field.

It must be remembered that Johnston was the general in command until mortally wounded a little after 2 P.M. Beauregard,

91

though probably better placed for directing the general operations up to that time, seems to have deprived himself of such staff as was left him, and not to have possessed sufficient authority, or sufficient means, to carry out the duties of command which Johnston had so largely vacated. Both Johnston and most of the headquarters staff seem to have been carried away by that longing, which all real soldiers experience, to be engaged in the close fighting line. It is a fatal mistake for a commander to give way to any such feeling, and a good deal of the incoherence in the execution of that day's well-conceived project—an incoherence which has been commented upon by almost all those who were present—seems to have been due to this. Indeed, there was so little unity of intention and direction throughout the day's operations that the absence of any one controlling spirit was apparent everywhere. Staff officers seem to have been going about issuing orders according to their own lights, without the smallest means of ascertaining what General Johnston's wishes actually were, without any clear knowledge of where he was, or even if he were alive,—and, as a matter of fact, he was not alive during part of the time I refer to. It was probably, on the whole, the less of two evils that orders should have been given even in this way than that troops should have remained out of action for lack of orders; but the chaos that must have necessarily ensued from all this is obvious. A committee directing a battle is an appalling condition of things to contemplate; but a dispersed committee, not even able to consult together, is a yet more certain cause of failure.

It would, therefore, be very unfair, in my judgment, to make General Beauregard, even after Johnston's death, responsible for the want of direction which is conspicuous in a good deal of this day's fighting. At the same time, it must be admitted that, when the Federals had been driven back, and the stress of battle had manifestly passed on towards the bank of the river, the time had come for the general in chief command to go forward. Had he done so, it does not seem that the battle would have ceased when it did. Had he then appeared upon the scene, the evidence goes to show that the reserve Federal artillery must then have been captured, and that, although the battle had been begun by the Confederates twenty-four hours later than it ought to have been, Buell would have arrived too late to save Grant's army from destruction. As has so often happened in war, the fight on either side was, it seems, considerably affected by the state of health of the two commanders. Had Beauregard been in his usual health, he would probably have ridden to the front between four and five o'clock in the afternoon. Had it not been for the severe fall, from the effects of which Grant was then suffering, probably there would not have been that absence of direction on the Federal side of which Buell speaks.

The numerous graphic sketches which are given of the "Hornet's Nest" are very interesting. The peculiar strength of the position seems to have depended on the fact that the assailants had to move out of cover across a rather narrow belt of open ground, against troops well posted under cover on the further side, the open space being also swept by flanking batteries. There is in the Niederwald, on the site of the battle of Woerth, a very similar clear break in the wood. The fire-arms of 1870 were, I suppose, a good deal more punishing than those of 1862. But this space was not flanked by any batteries; yet the whole German infantry of the XIth Corps were checked at this point, and unable to pass because of the conditions I have described. The analogy suggests some curious reflections as to the nature of ground that is most difficult for attacking troops to surmount.

As a student of war, I have endeavored to express, with impartial freedom, but, I hope, without offence to any one, these comments which the circumstances of this very interesting battle of Shiloh have suggested to me. Being in Canada at the time, I followed very closely all the newspaper accounts of it; but its details have never been made so clear as by the accounts from many different quarters with which the *Century* Company have now supplied us. It would be impossible so to reconcile these different accounts as to satisfy all who took part in the action that justice had been done to the views which they advocate upon the responsibility of individual generals for failure and success. I think, however, that soldiers who desire to learn experience from these events will succeed in doing so much better by a perusal of the accounts given by the actors in this great drama, than from any ordinary pleasantly-sounded narrative. After all, it is as individual men, as actual soldiers, that we take our share of duty and responsibility, and the experiences of what other men have actually gone through are

93

interesting, just because they represent the very partial view of a great action which we are, any of us, able to gain. We are able to see better how the swirl and whir of the battle surged round different parts of the field, by having laid before us the statements of what each actor saw and did in the performance of his own part.

I do not propose to touch, in any detail, the part that was played in these campaigns by the naval service on either side; but, for several reasons, very much interest attaches itself to the general scope and method of the combined land and water movements of this War. In the first place, owing to the many wars we have to carry on in wild and distant countries, the bearing of river transport upon military operations is a matter of great importance to our army. The subject is, therefore, especially interesting to us. Then, again, these full accounts of the methods pursued in these great river campaigns are of great value to English soldiers and sailors. Owing to our insular position, all operations of war, outside Great Britain, must necessarily begin with combined naval and military expeditions. It is, indeed,—according to Mr. Kinglake's happy phrase,—on our "amphibious strength" that we depend. The magnificent sea-like rivers of the United States, and the essential dependence of the whole scheme of offence and defence, throughout this war in the West, on the retention or conquest of the course of the Tennessee, the Ohio, the Missouri, the Cumberland, and the Mississippi, make the whole character of the theatre of war and its method of special interest to us. The originality and force with which all the resources and ingenuity of a great industrial and commercial people were thrown into the struggle, give to these combined naval and military movements a modern form, unique of its kind.

Each campaign is full of useful suggestions for us, upon the employment of similar means, should we, as seems more than likely, be forced to throw our whole strength into some—not in point of time—distant struggle for Imperial existence. There was, throughout all the phases of the detailed arrangements for this war, a similar originality in the adaptation of means to ends; as, for instance, in the Confederates' use of the bales of wet hemp during the siege of Lexington. I have preferred to deal first at large with these campaigns in the West, because the whole series hangs closely together, while the campaigns in Western Virginia and of the first Bull Run stand out like isolated combats, as far as this part of the history is concerned, and are much more closely connected with the history of the succeeding years. Indeed, as every one who writes of these campaigns in the West remarks, by the time that Donelson, Henry, Pea Ridge, Memphis, and Shiloh had been lost, the Confederate cause in the West was doomed. Vicksburg was more important as the final death-blow to that cause than as determining to which side victory should incline. The struggle for the great rivers was, during the earlier part of the War, almost as vital to the successful establishment of a Southern Confederacy as the defence of Richmond. When this period ended, the whole interest of the War shifted eastward and was concentrated on the line between Richmond and Washington.

Though, therefore, in point of date, the campaigns in Western Virginia and the battle of Bull Run preceded most of the events in Missouri and Tennessee, those campaigns are really the introduction to the history of the later period of the War. I may add that, except for the personal connection of General Beauregard with both Shiloh and Bull Run, and for the effect which was undoubtedly produced throughout the West by the Confederate success at Bull Run, the two series of events might almost as well have taken place on different continents, as far as any immediate influence which they exercised upon each other was concerned. The battle of Bull Run—certainly one of the battles of the war which have been most talked about and written about in Europe—would appear, from these accounts of it, to have gathered round itself, hitherto, a large margin of fiction and misconception.

As far as General Beauregard himself is concerned, there is a quaint historical parallelism between the battle of Shiloh and that of Bull Run. In neither was he the actual commander in point of seniority. In both, the actual commander seems to have left to him a certain authority on the battle-field, the nature of which has become the subject of subsequent fierce controversy. In the case of both battles, he succeeded in persuading the commander of forces engaged in a neighboring district to form a junction of both armies in his own district, with a view to crush one part of the enemy's forces, before that part which was in the neighboring district could be brought to its support. In both battles, the commander who so joined him was a General Johnston, though, so far as I am aware, there was not any family connection between General J. E. Johnston, who commanded at Bull Run, and Albert Sidney Johnston, who commanded at Shiloh; nor, to judge by the two likenesses on pages 228 and 542, was there the smallest personal resemblance between the two men. In both instances, the ground over which the battles were fought was much better known to General Beauregard than to either General Johnston. In both battles,—though here we enter upon more disputed ground,—the evidence seems clear that the general arrangements of the campaign had been thought out some time beforehand by General Beauregard, and that the other commander, on his arrival, almost inevitably accepted Beauregard's proposals. In both cases, the scheme of battle was so affected by unforeseen circumstances that at one, Shiloh, Beauregard himself, at the last moment, recommended the abandonment of the attack he had so ably planned, and at the other, Bull Run, where the enemy's forward movement left him no choice in that matter, his designed attack was converted into an almost purely defensive battle, carried out by a part only of the forces at his disposal. In both battles, taking account only of the first day's action at Shiloh, incidents occurred toward the end of the day which shook men's confidence in the man who had had the most share in the general planning of the campaign. In both battles, with whatever difference of cause and circumstance, those incidents were connected with a supposed too early stopping of the battle, and failure to drive the enemy to complete and final destruction. In both battles, General Beauregard attributed this early stopping of the action to the fatigue and exhaustion of his men, and to his want of food and ammunition for them. In both campaigns, he complained bitterly that he had not been supported properly by the civil authorities at Richmond. These analogies afford some food for reflection, and I leave readers to draw from them their own conclusions, which will probably differ not a little. The corrections which are supplied to the popularly-received account of Bull Run all seem to tend in the direction of substituting a picture of battle truly representative of what war really is for the kind of imaginative ideal of a battle which people at a distance love to create for themselves. General Beauregard says (page 216):

It was a point made at the time, at the North, that, just as the Confederate troops were about to break and flee, the Federal troops anticipated them by doing so, being struck into this precipitation by the arrival on their flank of the Shenandoah forces marching from railroad trains halted en route with that aim—errors that have been repeated by a number of writers, and by an ambitious, but superficial, French author.

I am sorry to say that the error has been freely repeated by English as well as by French authors, and has even crept into some of our best-known text-books. The matter is of some importance, because it gives a false conception of the possible use of railways in war. It looks very pretty to draw a line of railway running at right angles to an enemy's line of advances, and to represent troops getting out of the trains and coming straight away from them to strike the exposed flank of the enemy. In the case of a pure infantry force, this might be possible, if it had been thought out beforehand. Very rarely indeed would it be possible for cavalry, and still more rarely for artillery. Moreover, where a mixed body of troops were coming by railway to an assigned railway junction, which, like Manassas, possessed some sidings and platforms provided for their disembarkation, it would very rarely be possible to disarrange the sequence of trains so as to disembark the infantry at some other point more important tactically, without disturbing the movement of the whole force, and probably causing much delay in the arrival of the troops upon the battle-field. Now, General Johnston, who actually directed upon the field at Bull Run the troops of Elzey and Early, which troops, in fact, turned the Federal right flank, tells us expressly (page 249) that Elzey, who arrived first with three infantry battalions, came from "Manassas Junction." Early, who came next, arrived with "Stuart's cavalry and Beckham's battery." The cavalry and artillery had evidently come up from Manassas, joining Early en route. It is clear that, essentially, this railway movement was purely one of general reenforcement. Manassas Junction lay far away to the right rear of that part of the Confederate line where the battle was actually fought. The overlapping of the Federal right was accomplished by movements made under General Johnston's own orders, advantage being taken of the concealment afforded by the woods near Chinn's house on the Federal right. Of the movements of General Smith, who at first com-

97

manded Elzey's brigade, Johnston says: "He was instructed through a staff officer, sent forward to meet him, to form on the left of our line, his left thrown forward, and to attack the enemy in flank. At his request I joined him, directed his course, and gave him these instructions."

Moreover, the extreme troops on the Confederate left flank, and those which carried out the ultimate turning movement, were, so far as the infantry was concerned, not those which had arrived by railway at all, but Early's brigade, which had been in reserve behind Longstreet and Jones near Blackburn's and McLean's Ford, being, in fact, a part of Beauregard's own army. Thus it is as clear as possible that the important service which the Manassas Railway did for the Confederates was in putting them, strategically, in a military sense, as Beauregard says, "on interior lines" with regard to the two Federal armies of McDowell and Patterson. The really decisive fact of the campaign was the strategical transfer of Johnston's force from the Shenandoah region, unknown to Patterson. The turning of the Federal right was a tactical incident, due in part to the troops which were put at the disposal of the Confederate commander by that strategical transfer of force. In all essentials, the cause of the Confederate success was a movement like that which preceded the defeat of Hasdrubal by the Romans, or like that which preceded the battle of Blenheim. Almost all great military successes have these simple actions as their basis. Only, as has been said, it is that which is simple which in war is so very difficult.

Here, as in almost every other instance, the defeat of McDowell seems to have been due to the blunders of the authorities at Washington, acting under the influence of popular opinion. McDowell had fully foreseen the danger with which he was threatened. This is shown conclusively by his making it one of the conditions of his movement that General J. E. Johnston's force should be kept engaged by Major-General Patterson. Nothing can be clearer than this fact—that the Bull Run disaster, which so appalled public opinion in the North, was deliberately prepared for itself by that very public opinion taking upon itself to enforce its demands upon the generals in the field through the medium of its recognized exponents. General James Fry puts this well in separate paragraphs which are worth collating: "General Scott, who controlled both

McDowell and Patterson, assured McDowell that Johnston should not join Beauregard without having Patterson on his heels." (Page 181.) "Northern enthusiasm was unbounded. On to Richmond was the war-cry. Public sentiment was irresistible, and, in response to it, the army advanced." (Page 176.)

Yet, again, after showing how completely Johnston gave Patterson the slip, he says, "It rested, however, with higher authority than Patterson to establish between his army and McDowell's the relations the occasion called for" (note, page 183); and then he goes on to show how the public fear in the Capital of attack by the Shenandoah Valley obliged the Washington authorities to insist on Scott's not only keeping Patterson in the Shenandoah Valley, but actually reenforcing him at the moment when every man was required to reenforce McDowell. Furthermore, if Patterson was to keep Johnston from reenforcing McDowell, it could only be done by steady and persistent fighting. But he had been warned against fighting, lest the Capital should be exposed by want of "caution." *Hence,* as General Fry truly says, "as soon as McDowell advanced, Patterson was upon an exterior line and in a false military position."

To sum up, then, the indictment against the true criminal. Let us clearly understand that the prisoner at the bar is "Public Opinion." This is the case against him. He understood nothing whatever of military principles or the conditions of the movements of armies; yet he took into his ignorant hands the entire conduct of this part of the war. Without even realizing the connection between the several things which he required as a sacrifice to his imagined omniscience, he kept Patterson and all his forces in the Shenandoah Valley for fear lest Johnston should move on the Capital. Then, having deprived McDowell of all possible supports and crowded his camps with picnicking parties, "under no military restraint, that passed to and fro among the troops as they pleased," reducing indefinitely the fighting power of his army, the prisoner at the bar sent forward the unfortunate general and army to meet their fate from the two armies whose union he (the prisoner) had facilitated. Whom shall we hang? This thing, or the fine soldier whose portrait is given on page 170? Unfortunately, the number of convictions against the prisoner, and the freedom with which he secures the power to repeat his crimes, are so notorious that there is little use in convicting him. In 1861 he cries out madly, "To Richmond!" In 1870 his mad cry is, "To Berlin!" If only some one would make out a true record of all the crimes with which he has been justly charged, seeing that there is and can be no defence for him, one might hope that perhaps on some future occasion, some one or two of the host that go to swell his power, to tickle his vanity, and to lead his followers to destruction, might pause and consider. Even one or two strong men facing the stampede of an ignorant crowd that knows not where it is going, have often a wonderful power in breaking its force and in turning it aside from ruin. Therefore, it is worth while to seize such occasions as one may, to hold up to this creature, to this self-styled god, a mirror in which it may see its own likeness, and seeing it, and appalled by the image, may cower before perpetrating fresh crime. I doubt very much if the criminal is as powerful or as ignorant in the United States as he is among us. I believe, with Sir Henry Maine, that the creators of your Constitution showed their wisdom mainly in shackling his impatient hands; in at least providing for an appeal from him when he is drunk to the time when he is sober.

I can here only touch upon the first phase of the next fit of madness which, in 1861, seized him in the United States. I have always had a great respect for General McClellan. But to those who, having first caused the destruction of McDowell's army, carried out the next stage of the programme usual in such cases, namely, the discovery that McDowell was responsible for all they had done, and decided to replace him by a "Young Napoleon," the graphic details of the campaigns in Western Virginia, under McClellan's leadership, must be painful reading. If General Cox had tried to complete this part of my indictment against the reckless interference of Public Opinion in the conduct of military affairs, he could hardly have worded it more incisively than he has done, in what he himself describes as the "unvarnished tale" of the attack on Rich Mountain, and in his description of the mode in which it led to its one important consequence—the promotion of McClellan to the command of the Potomac Army. It would not be unfair to sum it up thus: McClellan arranged to detach a small turning force under Rosecrans to attack a flank of Rich Mountain. The success of such a movement ordinarily depends on the vigor with which other forces combine in the attack, and on the support afforded to the small turning force, which is otherwise dangerously risked. McClellan had undertaken to attack vigorously as soon as Rosecrans was heard to be in action. "The noise of the engagement had been heard in McClellan's camp, and he formed his troops to attack, but the long continuance of the cannonade, and some sign of exultation in Pegrans's camp, seem to have made him think that Rosecrans had been repulsed." Therefore, McClellan did nothing whatever; meantime Rosecrans, who had planned his own movement, and had volunteered for it, had, by extraordinary good fortune and good management, succeeded in carrying the whole position entirely with his own force. Thereupon the defence of the remainder of the Mountain collapsed. "On McClellan's part," beyond a rather timidly-conducted pursuit, "nothing further was attempted." McClellan, however, published a dispatch in which he congratulated his troops on having "annihilated two armies, commanded by educated and experienced soldiers, intrenched in mountain fortresses fortified at their leisure." "The country was," we are told, "eager for good news, and took it as literally true." Whereupon McClellan was photographed in the Napoleonic attitude, and duly promoted to the command of the Potomac Army, to be dealt with afterwards according to the time-honored fashion of that hoary-headed and cruel old rascal, Public Opinion, towards his broken idols.

101

AN ENGLISH VIEW OF THE CIVIL WAR
PART II

In dealing with the second volume of *Battles and Leaders* *Wolseley devotes his attention to two principal topics: amphibious war and George B. McClellan. His reference to the historian Alexander W. Kinglake, author of the eight-volume,* The Invasion of the Crimea, *serves to remind us that the critic was drawing on his own deep reading of military history as well as his own participation in war. The indispensableness of cooperation between army and navy, a truth not really grasped by the Americans until Pearl Harbor, is one lesson he draws from these writings.*

His other principal topic is a defense of General McClellan as strategist and organizer of victory. Wolseley admired McClellan for his able and rapid shaping of raw levies into the Army of the Potomac after First Bull Run, for recognizing the magnitude of the task of subduing the South, for his careful planning of the Peninsular campaign, and for his capacity to inspire confidence in his officers and men. At the same time he notes two shortcomings in McClellan's makeup: his failure to understand how popular government works in time of peril and his vanity.

Wolseley continues his strictures on public opinion, fixing fault on Lincoln and Stanton, his secretary of war, for failing to give McClellan the reinforcements he called for in waging his river-route assault on Richmond. The judgment of the English expert is meaningful, since one of the great controversies of historical interpretation has raged about McClellan. Wolseley's criticism of the appointment of Pope appears perhaps colored by his partiality for McClellan and dislike of Stanton. The satirical tone here is not often found in his writing about individuals.

AN ENGLISH VIEW
OF THE CIVIL WAR

II

THE second volume of the "Battles and Leaders" is, in my judgment, even more interesting than the first volume. It introduces
us to the period when General McClellan transformed the armed
masses which had fought at the first battle of Bull Run, together
with the vast numbers of recruits who subsequently joined them,
into the Army of the Potomac. It takes us through the Peninsular
Campaign and dwells upon the deeply-interesting questions involved in its conduct, as well as in its conception as illustrated by
later events. It tells us of those two brilliant champions of a lost
cause whose leadership is full of military suggestion and military
lessons. No matter how doubtful at every point and for all time
may have been the legality or advisability of the War, that two
such men had fought on any one side would, of itself, throw a
halo round the cause they fought for. Their character can never
fail to excite general admiration. Even those who were most bitterly opposed to Stonewall Jackson and to Robert Lee, even those
who believed them to be utterly wrong in their conception of national duty, will readily admit their excellence as soldiers, their
sincerity as patriots.

There is so much to be said on the campaigns in the Shenandoah Valley, on the seven days' fighting near Richmond, on the
campaign against Pope, and on Lee's invasion of Maryland, that I
must pass over somewhat lightly the most important operations of
Admiral Farragut, which led to the capture of New Orleans.
Nevertheless, for us of the old country these "amphibious" operations, as Mr. Kinglake would call them, have a quite peculiar importance. The cooperation of the United States navy with their
army, in producing a decisive effect upon the whole character of

107

the military operations, is akin to what happens with us in nearly every war in which we engage. A German, a French, or a Russian general may frequently, perhaps usually, carry on a campaign without considering what assistance he may expect to derive from the cooperation of his own navy, or what impediments he may expect to encounter from the operations of the naval forces of his enemy. An English general has almost always to make his calculations strictly in accordance with what the navy can do for him. The operations by which the Federal navy, in conjunction with the army, split the Confederacy in two and severed the East from the West, must always, therefore, have for him a profound interest and importance. The great strategical results obtained by this concentration of military and naval power, which were as remarkable as the circumstances under which the successes were gained, deserve our closest study.

I shall not attempt to discuss from a naval point of view the much-debated question whether Admiral Porter's mortar-schooners were or were not largely instrumental in determining the success of Farragut's passage between Fort Jackson and Fort St. Philip. The point is, however, one in which the effect on the forts is as much involved as the action of the navy. I may, therefore, venture the opinion, based on the evidence of the Confederate side, that the bombardment, considering the enormous number of large shells actually exploded within Fort Jackson, had comparatively little effect in preventing that fort from contributing its share toward the result of the operation. Captain Robertson's evidence (p. 100, Vol. II) is distinct that at the time of Admiral Farragut's passage, in the water-battery at least, "every gun in the battery was loaded and pointed toward the river, and the men were kept at their posts"; and again: "No guns were silenced in either Fort Jackson or the water-battery at any time during this engagement. Not a man was driven from his post at the guns in the water-battery, much less from the battery itself."

It is, *mutatis mutandis*, almost the same story that General Sheridan tells of the effect of the Prussian artillery at Gravelotte. There the Prussian officers believed they had absolutely silenced the French artillery and crushed out the resistance of the French infantry. From his experience during the Civil War, General Sheridan told them that when they made their attack they would find out their mistake. One of the most bloody repulses sustained by the Germans throughout the war soon afterwards verified the correctness of his inference.

Had it been necessary to silence by mortar fire the guns of Fort Jackson and the water-battery before the ships ran the gauntlet between Fort Jackson and Fort St. Philip, Farragut would never have achieved his splendid success. No! as always in war, Farragut's success was almost purely the result of the moral effect which his movement produced, and of defects other than material in the force opposed to him. It is clear that there was a complete want of unity of command over the combined naval and military defences for the protection of New Orleans. No doubt the Southern fleet was not properly ready for action, and for this unreadiness it would seem that Captain Mitchell, who commanded it, was not responsible. I do not think, however, it is possible to read the correspondence which passed between Captain Mitchell and General Duncan without feeling that Captain Mitchell was one of those men, common enough in every service, who cannot bring themselves to imagine that any one outside their own particular calling is other than a stupid fool. Such men usually conceive it to be their first duty to ignore, as an impertinent interference, any suggestion which comes from outside their own charmed circle. It is clear that the officers in the forts were in a position to observe the movements and to forecast the intentions of the Federals, and that the officers in the ships were not. As it turned out, the "Louisiana" proved absolutely useless to the defence. General Duncan saw through the intentions of Admiral Farragut, but his correct anticipation that the attempt would be made the night it was actually made was an absurd landsman's guess about matters he was not calculated to express any useful opinion upon. His views were, therefore, contemptuously ignored.

Had Captain Mitchell been a man large-minded enough to rise above paltry professional prejudices, he would not have continued to expend all his energies on preparing the "Louisiana" for a service she was never called upon to perform. But he would, on the other hand, have kept "the river well lit up with fire-rafts," as he was again and again urged to do. The temper shown in this proceeding is one so dangerous that, whenever it appears, it deserves to be castigated by those who review the facts afterwards, whether

109

the lash falls on naval or military shoulders. The same temper, it would seem, crops out in Commodore Mitchell's present defence. "Naval officers," he says, "ought surely to be considered better judges of how the forces and appliances at their command should be managed than army officers." Certainly no one will dispute that statement, but both naval and army officers must be judged by a reasonable examination of the results of their action and of the alternatives open to them. On the question whether certain naval officers properly cooperated with and paid proper attention to the representations of the soldiers, a Naval Court of Inquiry is not likely to be the most impartial of tribunals. It would have been interesting if, in appealing to the final judgment of history, Commodore Mitchell had not relied merely upon a naval verdict, which, as he admits, was given without any reception of the evidence on the other side. It would have been well for him to explain why no fire-ships were sent down the river; why the forts were left to fight in the dark during the actual night of attack. Granting that he is correct in urging that by the evening of the 24th April he would have had his ships ready, it would be interesting to know what service he considered he was rendering the Confederacy by preparations which, it was pointed out to him, could not be completed in time for the attack that others believed would be made on the night it actually occurred. To weigh fairly the evidence and to estimate justly the soundness or unsoundness of the reasons and motives which determined Commodore Mitchell's action at the time, it is not necessary to be either a soldier or a sailor. When that officer alleged that he did not take steps to meet the attack on the night between April 23 and 24, because the "Louisiana" would be ready for service by the evening of the 24th, any man of ordinary common-sense will understand that he disbelieved the evidence supplied to him. The evidence went to show that the attack would be made twenty-four hours before the evening of the 24th. Yet surely those reasons for expecting the attack to be made when it did actually come off were absolutely sound.

Such, I think, will be the verdict of independent naval officers, who examine the facts without prejudice. I would sooner have exposed such a line of conduct on the part of a soldier, because my views upon it would then have been more manifestly impartial. But I feel it is important, in the interest of all naval and military states, that these miserable little professional prejudices should be exposed wherever and whenever they occur, for the encouragement of the large-minded men of both services. To do so frankly at all times will, I think, check one of the most fatal tendencies by which the success of any joint naval and military operations may be imperilled, as, in my opinion, the interests of the Confederacy were seriously injured in this instance. To me it seems clear that Admiral Farragut's splendid achievement was made possible, first, by the inadequate previous preparation of the naval part of the New Orleans defences; secondly, by the want of harmonious working between the Confederate naval and military forces; and, lastly, by his own clear appreciation of the moral effect he would produce by forcing his way past the defences of Fort Jackson and Fort St. Philip and by his appearance before New Orleans. For, after all, the forts were never captured by actual attack. They fell because the Confederate soldiers in Fort Jackson mutinied against the continuance of the defence when New Orleans had been captured. It is a curious fact to note that, at that very time, New Orleans—which, however, could not itself be defended—was surrendering avowedly because those forts had fallen! This brilliant result is a striking instance of the due appreciation by a commander of the effect which daring achievements exert on men's minds, although, as in this case, those daring acts do not actually, directly, or materially make certain the end or the surrender they may have secured. In other words, Admiral Farragut's attack was based on a knowledge of the superior importance in war of moral over material force. One can hardly offer a higher compliment to any naval or military commander.

I pass now to the appointment of General McClellan to the command of the Army of the Potomac, and his subsequent accession, for a time at least, to the general command of the armies of the United States. I entertain the strongest possible belief, which has been confirmed by all the evidence supplied by the *Century* papers, that for the failure of the Peninsular Campaign the Administration at Washington was far more to blame than General McClellan. It is, therefore, only fair that I should turn first to the defence of the Administration which has been attempted by Lieutenant-Colonel R. B. Irwin (p. 435, Vol. II), and examine it in the light of the evidence supplied elsewhere.

General McClellan was appointed on July 25, 1861, to the command of the army in the department of the Potomac, and on November 1 following "to command the whole army" of the United States. He had to create out of purely raw materials an army of which the part he proposed to employ in the Peninsula alone was 156,000 strong. The more one studies the nature of this force as it manœuvred and fought in the Peninsula, and as, despite all its subsequent disasters, it substantially remained throughout the War, the more marvellous does the ability, as well as the rapidity, with which General McClellan organized it appear to soldiers who understand the magnitude and difficulty of the task he undertook. Throughout his whole army, with few exceptions, this appears to have been the view taken by all, from the most senior general to the youngest recruit. But outside the army this was different, although in newspaper articles he was commonly referred to, with more effusion than sense, as the young American Napoleon. They did not hesitate to puff this untried leader as they would have advertised the talents of some rising dentist. As time wore on without bringing any decisive action, there arose throughout the mass of the people an impatience at the delay of preparation, which became daily more apparent. That most cruel tyrant, the "public," had no means of realizing the difficulties to be overcome. It did not understand what organization meant, but it shared with all peoples the very common article of faith that you have only to gather together hundreds of thousands of men, and to arm them, in order to form an army.

As the months of 1862 went by, the universal feeling was one of impatience and restlessness at what was deemed the waste of time and the useless delay which were taking place. Under that impression, and under the force which this so formed Public Opinion was exerting, the Administration at Washington found itself compelled to act. That is evident enough from the most interesting and striking letters which Colonel Irwin quotes as written by Mr. Lincoln to McClellan. It is clear in all of them that the President felt he was being driven by a power superior to his own, and by one to which McClellan, like himself, must yield. "Once more let us tell you," he writes, "it is indispensable to *you* that you strike a blow! I am powerless to help this." The Administration was merely giving expression to the decrees of an entirely ignorant public opinion. If all those who wield the pen would only kindly wait until commanders have quite accomplished the mission entrusted to them before they decide that soldiers, "with their guns and drums and fuss and fury," are to pass away and leave the glory to others, it might matter little to the state. But when in the middle of a war they take it upon themselves to drive or to force those whom they influence to decide what the naval or military commander should do, the result will certainly be, as it was in this instance, to protract, perhaps for years, the duration of the war which they, in their self-conceit, imagined they could settle off-hand at once.

If these *Century* articles could be as widely read among us as they have been in America, we might possibly be saved in the future from disasters such as were entailed on us in the Crimea by very similar action. In particular, I should like those articles by Mr. Warren Lee Goss, the "Recollections of a Private," duly studied. For, after all, questions of strategy, of tactics, and of the importance of organization of all kinds turn upon the effect which is ultimately produced on the spirit and well-being and fighting efficiency of the private soldier. Whilst the organs of public opinion and their humble servant, the public Administration, were grumbling at the slow movements which only carried General McClellan's army forward fifty-two miles in sixteen days (Colonel Irwin, p. 437), Private Lee Goss and his companions were learning "in time that marching on paper and the actual march made two very different impressions," and though they could "easily understand and excuse our fireside heroes, who fought their own or our battles at home over comfortable breakfast-tables, without impediments of any kind to circumscribe their fancied operations," they found out also that it is "much easier to manœuvre and fight large armies around the corner grocery than to fight, march, and manœuvre in wind and rain, in the face of a brave and vigilant enemy."

There are, however, matters beyond the immediate view of the private which must be considered. From the moment when, thanks to those mistakes of Mr. Jefferson Davis of which I spoke in the last article, the Federal navy had asserted its absolute supremacy at sea, it is clear that the shortest and safest, as well as the most decisive, route to Richmond was by a movement based on the

113

James River. To carry this out arrangements for the adequate protection of Washington were essential. But whilst McClellan with the main army marched upon Richmond, it was necessary to protect the force allotted for the defence of Washington from a counter-stroke by Lee or by his lieutenant, Stonewall Jackson. To effect this it was desirable to keep it close to Washington, and thus as far away from Richmond as was possible with due regard to the safety of the former city. In order that the army on the James River, intended for offensive operations, should be made as strong as possible, the force detailed for the protection of Washington should have been as small as was consistent with the accomplishment of its object, and should have had a strictly defensive role allotted to it. This concentration of energy on a single aim at a time is such a commonplace of ordinary business life that it is passing strange why it should be so difficult to persuade men who have not had the experience of war that in all military operations it is the one thing most needful. Military history, had it been known to Mr. Lincoln and his ministers, would have taught them that, under the then existing circumstances, the Confederate army could not venture far away from Richmond. That threatened capital was not only the seat of the Confederate government, but it was also the base from which the Confederate armies between Richmond and Washington drew their supplies. Whenever attacked, those armies must have returned to defend it.

I think General McClellan ought not to have left Washington without convincing himself that Mr. Lincoln and the Secretary of War were satisfied with the arrangements he had made for the defence of the capital. That those arrangements were in themselves adequate is beyond doubt. In omitting to come to this understanding with the President, he evinced, it would seem, a want of knowledge of the working of popular governments in times of great national danger. He thus exposed himself to, or, at least, he gave an excuse for, the very thing which happened—that which ruined his chances in the campaign; namely, the withdrawal from his command of at least 63,000 men. Nor was this mere withdrawal of McDowell's corps, of Blenker's division, and of the 10,000 men of General Wool's command, the only disastrous consequence which was entailed on McClellan by the exaggerated fears of the Government at Washington. Secretary Stanton appears to have been encouraged by this first interference with McClellan's plans to take upon himself the general direction of the whole campaign. It was he who thrust forward the force under McDowell, and so entailed upon McClellan the necessity of placing himself in that false position astride of the Chickahominy which led to all the misfortunes of this campaign. It is scarcely possible to imagine any military arrangements more futile than those which were devised by this civilian Minister of War, Mr. Stanton. His scattering of the Federal forces throughout the Shenandoah Valley gave Jackson the opportunity for carrying out his brilliant campaign in that region. The necessity of maintaining connection with the armies which were to come to his support from the North obliged McClellan so to divide his force that, had General J. E. Johnston's orders been properly carried out, the Federal army ought to have had its left wing annihilated at the battle of Seven Pines, as it actually had its right wing crushed at Gaines's Mill.

As already stated, I think General McClellan should have satisfied Mr. Lincoln as to the steps he had taken for the defence of Washington, because that was a subject on which the President had fairly every right to be satisfied; but I cannot admit that this omission on the General's part was any adequate excuse for the complete upsetting of his whole plan of campaign. Mr. Lincoln, though doubtless one of the greatest men who have ruled the United States, was entirely ignorant of war. Able and wise as he was in all matters of civil government, he failed here most disastrously. By the course he pursued he wrecked an ably-devised plan for the advance upon Richmond of all the available Federal forces by one single line, whilst the troops intended for the defence of Washington were kept as passive as possible. Instead of that plan, a divided command was inaugurated and a disjointed series of movements were ordered, which ended in the transfer of the initiative to Lee. The change ordered by Mr. Lincoln in McClellan's plans gave the Confederates an opportunity for throwing their united forces, at pleasure, upon any part of the scattered Federal army. I cannot admit, as Colonel Irwin appears to expect we should all at once do, that McClellan was wrong in refusing to explain publicly to the Cabinet the details of his proposed scheme. At that time it was notorious that what was said to the Cabinet in Washington leaked out at once into the streets, and was thence conveyed promptly to the Confederate authorities. I know, from what I learned at Richmond in the autumn of 1862, how well Lee was kept informed of everything done or intended by the Northern army.

Let us hear Stonewall Jackson on this subject, and compare his methods and principles of action in each particular with those that were pressed on McClellan by the Washington Administration, or, rather, by their master, public opinion. We have to thank General Imboden for those golden sentences of Jackson's which comprise some of the most essential of all the principles of war:

Always mystify, mislead, and surprise the enemy, if possible: and when you strike and overcome him, never let up in the pursuit so long as your men have strength to follow; for an army routed, if hotly pursued, becomes panic-stricken, and can then be destroyed by half their number. The other rule is, never fight against heavy odds, if by any possible manœuvring you can hurl your own force on only a part, and that the weakest part, of your enemy and crush it. Such tactics will win every time, and a small army may thus destroy a large one in detail, and repeated victory will make it invincible.

Compare those principles, and the mode in which Jackson carried them out, with the ideas current at Washington, and you will see that they are direct inversions. The orders which emanated from there may be described thus:

Go straight at the enemy at the very point where he expects you, and where he has long been expecting to receive you. Let everyone know what you are going to do, so that we may announce it in the public press, and chuckle and crow over your coming victory. Scatter your forces in as many directions as possible, so that the enemy may always be able to bring superior forces against you. Arrange your force so that it is rigidly tied to one particular point, and that the enemy cannot doubt where you will be. Go ahead without preparation, forethought, or care; only let us hear that you are moving, so that the newspapers may brag.

These—I declare I have nothing exaggerated and naught set down in malice—these are the principles and practice which Colonel Irwin has undertaken the task of defending. It is a difficult one. I frankly admit that, when dealing with this fatuous folly, General McClellan did not behave with the meekness of an amiable schoolboy under discipline. I think he was unjust to Mr. Stanton in supposing that he (Mr. Stanton) had any personal hostility to him. Mr. Stanton really believed that the orders he gave were transparently sound and wise, and that any one who differed from him must be wrong. I do not know, however, that, placed in General McClellan's position, most generals could possibly have realized this. In order to understand Mr. Stanton it is necessary to read General Pope's account of his interview with that gentleman, given on page 449. One of my friends assures me that in reading it he literally "laughed till he cried," and never fully understood what the expression meant before doing so. I can quite understand it. Laughter is said to be due to our being impelled by two contradictory feelings at the same time. That certainly is the condition under which one reads those pages. There is scarcely any folly possible in relation to the command of an army which Mr. Stanton does not propose with the gravest face to General McDowell. At the same time, the man is evidently sincere, and convinced that, being a clever politician and holding the position of War Minister, every principle of war—*as he understood war*—which he enunciated must be right, and therefore ought to be obeyed without question. It is difficult to pronounce whether the image that rises before us is that of the ignorant stage charlatan who, because his legs are decked with military boots, thinks himself every inch a soldier, or that of a grave Minister who is charged with the solemn responsibility of a great Nation's destiny and with the lives and fortunes of thousands of his fellow-citizens. Let me put a few of the points together.

If there be one thing more important than another in the command of any army, but more especially of one recently gathered together in a hurry from civil life, it is that officers and men should have confidence in their leader. It is essential that they should know and understand him, and, from their previous experience, should feel sure he is going to lead them to victory. "Therefore," says Mr. Stanton, "I cannot be wrong in withdrawing General Pope from the Army of the Mississippi, where he is known and liked and has been doing very well, to take command of the army of Virginia, where no one knows much more than his

117

name, his previous military operations not having been on a scale to command universal attention."

Promotion of a junior over the heads of men very senior to him in the service is often very wise and necessary; but unless it is done for reasons which are known and appreciated by the army as a whole, such as tend to inspire the army with confidence, it is pretty sure to lead to serious friction. "Therefore," says Mr. Stanton, "let us proceed as follows: There are those three corps, which have been chiefly formed under McClellan and are extremely proud of themselves as forming part of the old Army of the Potomac. They have already begun to acquire a certain spirit of their own; disasters have overtaken them for the moment (in consequence, as they believed, of their having been withdrawn from McClellan and foolishly scattered). Let us, therefore, select an officer from a far-off region, belonging to a force of which the Army of the Potomac has a certain amount of soldierly jealousy. The deeds of that distant hero will certainly not be appreciated at their full value by the followers of McClellan. But never mind; let us put this unknown leader over the heads of the three men now holding high command in that army, each well known to his own corps, and each senior to the man we select to command them." With disadvantages of such a nature against him, it may still be necessary sometimes to put an able junior over his seniors, in order that he should undertake some special task, provided he clearly sees his way to accomplish it, and feels confidence in himself. "Therefore," said Mr. Stanton, "let us select General Pope to undertake a task which he himself regards as a 'forlorn hope.' Despite his imploring remonstrances that he may be sent back to his old army, we will order him to 'submit cheerfully,' which will, of course, inspire him with all the confidence he needs." Surely, surely, so far at least every man who manages a large business concern will follow me in seeing that all these propositions denote an insanity that would be ludicrous, if it were not, in such a matter, so terribly criminal.

Upon General Pope, not a strong commander, was now forced the monstrous scheme of moving forward his already hopelessly-scattered army to "demonstrate" within striking distance of Richmond just at the time when McClellan, deprived of that very force, was about to be reduced to inaction by the battle of Gaines's

Mill and the retreat to the James River at this junction. General Pope showed his appreciation of the position by urging the appointment of some one general to command the two armies, who could then combine their action for a common purpose. It was a necessity entailed by the attempts to operate at once with both armies, instead of keeping one of them on the defensive and weakened so as to make the other very strong for rapid, offensive operations along the most telling line for an advance. It is obvious that the retreat of McClellan to the James River did make General Pope's position, to the north of Richmond, exceptionally dangerous. It placed the Confederate army absolutely between the two Federal armies, and greatly increased the distance between them. It is not, however, I think, the fact, as General Pope assumes, that the Confederates were "ready to exchange Richmond for Washington." For Jackson's movement to oppose Pope was not made till Lee was convinced that McClellan's army was not in a condition to carry out any further offensive movement. The wide turning movement of Jackson on Manassas Junction, and the movement northwards of Longstreet's corps, did not take place till McClellan had begun to evacuate the Peninsula.

Whatever mistakes General Pope may have made, it is clear that the disasters of this campaign were due to the order from Washington which required him to maintain an advanced position on the Rappahannock, and which gave him reason to suppose that his communications with Manassas would be guarded by troops independent of his own army, but which were nowhere within reach when they were wanted. For that failure General Halleck was no doubt directly responsible; but the great mistake lay in that action of the Administration, which can hardly be better described than in Mr. Lincoln's words applied later in the War: they "swopped horses whilst they were crossing the stream." They allowed McClellan to go off with his army to the Peninsula whilst he was at least nominally in command of the armies of the United States, and as soon as he was fully committed to the enterprise, they so completely upset all his arrangements as to bring about the condition of things which made it necessary to have with the Government in Washington a "General-in-Chief" of all the National forces. General Halleck was selected for the post—a most unhappy, most unfortunate selection.

I do not much appreciate any part of General Halleck's conduct in the War, either when he was in the West or after he arrived at Washington. He appears to have chiefly distinguished himself in the West by snubbing the two ablest soldiers he had under him, Generals Grant and Sherman. He appears to have chiefly distinguished himself at Washington by first snubbing General McClellan, then by placing Pope in a hopeless position, then, immediately after, by giving a positive assurance that Pope was in no danger, to be followed quickly by a complete loss of heart when that General's army came hurrying back in confusion to the Potomac. Then we find him, when panic-stricken for the safety of Washington, throw all responsibility on McClellan, the man he had previously snubbed. As soon as McClellan's presence had restored confidence and *morale* to Pope's demoralized army, he does his best to prevent McClellan from striking effective blows against the very much weaker and, for the time, necessarily dispersed army of General Lee, and we see him, ignorantly and stupidly, incidentally throwing away the forces which were compelled to surrender at Harper's Ferry. It is not, therefore, from any special sympathy with General Halleck that I am induced to think he was, from the first, placed in a false position. He had to take up and accept for better or worse the fatuous plan devised by Secretary Stanton, against which both McClellan and Pope had equally protested. He had to face immediate emergencies before he could possibly have made himself really acquainted with all the circumstances of the new field of war into which he had been suddenly pitchforked.

Hence my own conviction that for this, as for most of the other misfortunes experienced by the Federal troops, the verdict of history will ultimately hold responsible the Administration at Washington rather than the generals who commanded in the field. And yet it is both striking and interesting to see how much the personal character of Lincoln himself rose superior to his surroundings. His very modesty unfortunately left him, as regards all military operations, too much in the hands of his Secretary for War. But compare Mr. Stanton, with "large eye-glasses," "dishevelled appearance," "presence not imposing," "abrupt manner," "speech short and rather dictatorial," employed in dictating orders which were rank nonsense, with the quiet, modest manner, the simple, natural dignity, the genial humor, the shrewd common-sense, which appear in every story told of President Lincoln. One sees clearly enough that, though General McClellan was probably wrong as to the cause which he assigned for Mr. Stanton's opposition to him, he was right enough in attributing his difficulties to the Secretary for War, and not to the President. Mr. Lincoln was, from a military point of view, clearly mistaken in believing that *the* one way to get at Richmond was by making straight there from Washington. It is impossible, however, if one puts one's self at all in his place, not to see how nobly he faced the difficulties of his position, and how anxiously he endeavored to do his duty to his country.

AN ENGLISH VIEW OF THE CIVIL WAR
PART III

IN HIS THIRD PART WOLSELEY TRAVERSES THE SAME EASTERN campaigns as in the second article—but from a Southern viewpoint. Two heroes stand out: Jackson the tactical genius and Lee the unexcelled master of Confederate strategy. We have an expert assessment of Jackson's principal military monument, the Shenandoah Valley campaign, with an eye to how it illustrated Jackson's military principles; a dissection of the Peninsular campaign, with stress on the error of separating the Union armies; and a further evaluation of McClellan and his vain attempt on Richmond, his dismissal, and his restoration to command in time to frustrate Lee's first invasion of the north.

McClellan is censured for placing his army astride the Chickahominy River and for his tendency to exaggerate his enemy's strength, exemplified both on the Peninsula and at Antietam. The last named battle is interpreted simply as a Confederate victory on the field; the modern historian, of course, would claim for Antietam much influence in Britain's debate over mediation and in the issuing of the Emancipation Proclamation.

125

AN ENGLISH VIEW
OF THE CIVIL WAR

III

IN MY last article the conduct of the War was chiefly examined from the Northern side. Turning now to the South, the contrast in its management by the Confederate leaders during this part of the War is very conspicuous. Already the general scheme of the War had practically passed under General Robert Lee's direction, though in the earlier period he acted only as adviser to the President, whilst Johnston commanded the army between Richmond and Washington in the Peninsula. There are some who think that war is a game of pure chance, in which great leaders form their plans on some unintelligible inspiration which guides them as to the right course to be pursued, that they draw nothing from the experience of earlier wars, and that none can tell why one man succeeds and another fails. Let those who think thus call to mind the words I have quoted from Stonewall Jackson, drawn absolutely and merely from his knowledge of war, as learned from the great leaders of former days. Then let them observe how, in practice, both Lee on the larger and Jackson on the minor scale applied them, and to how great an extent the triumphs of their armies were due to the skilful application of those principles. Moreover, since, as Burns tells us, the best-laid schemes "o' mice and men gang aft agley," let them note how, when the men failed, the principles asserted their importance.

In the first place, consider the respective forces in the Shenandoah Valley and neighboring departments. Jackson had an available force at first, in the beginning of March, 1862, of about 5,000 men, strengthened at the beginning of May by Ewell's division, which raised his army to perhaps 14,000 men. According to the careful estimate of the editors (note page 285), there were opposed

127

to him in the Valley 44,840 men. In addition, there were in the neighboring departments, available for the march on Richmond, a number of troops that brought up their forces to 80,000 men. As a great strategic question, the object desired by the employment of Jackson's little army in the Shenandoah Valley was to keep occupied and retain there as large a number of the Federal forces as possible, so that the main Confederate army engaged in the decisive issue against McClellan should have every possible chance. In fact, it was Jackson's rôle to prevent any reenforcements from being sent to McClellan, and, above all things, to create an alarm at Washington for the safety of that capital.

In his first action at Kernstown, when he was acting purely on the defensive, Jackson's object was simply to "mystify" the enemy as to his actual numbers. This he accomplished, time after time, by the choice of strong positions, where, without committing himself to a decisive action, he was still able to deal with considerable portions of the enemy's forces. In these operations, therefore, he qualified his general principle, "to remain quiescent in presence of superior force," by giving battle whenever attacked by fractions of the Union forces. He succeeded in his larger purpose, for the alarm he created at Washington was sufficient to stop any further troops being withdrawn from the Valley, and Banks's corps, then on its march to the Potomac, was stopped and turned back towards Winchester. This action at Kernstown took place on March 23, 1862, and it was on his arrival at Fort Monroe, on April 2, that General McClellan received a telegram withdrawing 10,000 men from his command. It is, therefore, reasonable to conclude that this weakening of the Army of the Potomac was consequent upon Jackson's demonstration towards Winchester with a tiny army, whose vigor caused its strength to be, as usual, so greatly exaggerated. Thus he had already begun "mystifying and misleading" his enemy.

It is, however, his next moves which afford the most brilliant illustrations of his military principles. His sudden disappearance and supposed flight from Port Republic, allowing despair to settle on the minds of all of his friends in the Valley, had the result he intended; that is, their genuine beliefs and anxieties at once reached the enemy. This led to a hasty pursuit, which enabled him to use the very trains he had collected for a supposed start for Richmond, to take him back in time to crush the foremost pursuers at the village of McDowell. So completely, despite the disparity of numbers between 14,000 and 44,800 men, had he shown how "a small army may destroy a large one in detail" that, as General Schenck, who commanded against him, tells us, "the only question was, how best to extricate ourselves from this disadvantageous position in the presence of a force of the enemy largely superior in numbers."

Then came another mysterious disappearance. Again with superior numbers he struck Fort Royal, surprised it, scattered the force opposed to him, and then "never let up in the pursuit" as long as his men had strength to follow. He then passed round the rear of Banks's intrenchments at Strasbourg and struck him in flank as he retreated, capturing 3,000 men and enormous quantities of stores, and creating the wildest alarm at Washington, which incalculably multiplied the effect of his action. McDowell, then on the march to join McClellan, was ordered back, and told to detach 20,000 men to the Shenandoah Valley. It was impossible for Jackson to maintain himself long in the field with such greatly superior forces opposed to him. These brilliant successes, however, appear to me models of their kind, both in conception and in execution. They should be closely studied by all officers who wish to learn the art and science of war. His action at Cross Keys against Frémont, by which he kept him apart from Shields, contriving first to fight Frémont's 10,500 men with 13,000 in a favorable position, and then to crush Shields with 3,000 men, was an operation which stamped him as a military genius of a very high order. It must be remarked that McClellan was not taken in by these operations. He saw through them, and understood their object: not so, however, those who ruled at Washington.

Brilliant as these operations were, they would have missed their point and climax without the sudden transfer of Jackson's whole force, at the end of them, to join in the attack on the right wing of McClellan's army at Gaines's Mill. These operations in the Shenandoah Valley not only reduced to quiescence and inactivity the greatly superior Federal forces in that region, but made Mr. Lincoln feel anxious lest the Capital should be attacked from that quarter. To cover the heavy blows he struck within the Valley, Jackson had already so often spread false rumors of an immediate transfer of his force to Richmond that now, when really about to move there, the common rumor of his intention was not believed. The manner in which he thus mystified his enemy regarding this most important movement was a masterpiece. The one thing necessary was to disappear from all knowledge of the enemy immediately after he had delivered his last stunning blows in the Valley. For some time he left his cavalry watching the defeated enemy, whose ignorance of his whereabouts greatly increased the alarm at Washington. The effect of his ably-devised and skilfully-executed moves is fully acknowledged by Colonel Irwin, who admits that they were the cause of McDowell's forward movement to join McClellan being stopped. It will thus be seen that Jackson's 14,000 men had actually paralyzed the 80,000 Federal troops who were available in the theatre of his operations for a march upon Richmond.

Whilst Jackson's operations in the Shenandoah Valley had kept Richmond safe from alarms on that side, they had served to keep Washington in continual alarm. At last the mere terror he inspired became so far a substitute for his presence that he was able to get away to assist Lee in punishing the further error which Stanton's follies had entailed upon McClellan. The extension across the Chickahominy exposed the isolated right flank of the Federal army to the deadly blow which was about to be delivered against it. For that operation, with only the troops before Richmond, Lee had hardly sufficient strength. The transfer thither of Jackson's corps, however, effected the concentration of all the forces of the Confederacy then between Richmond and Washington. Lee was thus enabled to strike McClellan, who was left to his own resources; for the moral effect of Jackson's Valley operations was so great at Washington that McClellan could not expect any reenforcements. It was much easier to conceal from McClellan the direction of Jackson's move than it would have been that of any other force then in his front. In looking at the methods in detail by which this mystification of his enemy was secured, I am specially amused by the story which is told by General Imboden of General Whiting. After General Whiting's first interview with Jackson, and just at the moment when secrecy was absolutely necessary to the success of Jackson's transfer to the Chickahominy, we are told that General Whiting came away "in a towering passion, and declared that Jackson had treated him outrageously," and then, by way of explanation, added: "Oh, hang him! he was polite enough. But he didn't say one word about his plans. I finally asked him for orders, telling him what troops I had. He simply told me to go back to Staunton, and he would send me orders to-morrow. I haven't the slightest idea what they will be. I believe he hasn't any more sense than my horse."

How often have subordinates left their leader's headquarters under a similarly false impression! To dissemble well is an art useful to the general. Before this paper is finished it will be necessary to suggest that on one occasion General Lee himself suffered pretty severely for omitting a precaution of the kind. There are, of course, times when it is most necessary that subordinate officers should thoroughly understand and should have studied the general scope of the operations in which they are to cooperate. No pains can then be too great to insure that all thoroughly know the part to be played by every division, and how they themselves are to contribute to the result aimed at. As a rule, however, in these cases it is wise to let the plans be known as short a time beforehand as possible, and to take exceptional precautions that no knowledge even of their existence should leak out. In the case of a movement such as Jackson was then contemplating, there could be no need for a man in General Whiting's position to know it. Without knowing it at the time, he allowed his personal vanity to feel hurt because his curiosity had not been satisfied, and from this combined influence arose the unworthy want of confidence in his chief which here found vent in words. The vanity of small-minded subordinates makes them long to be consulted in the plans under consideration, and often to resent, as General Whiting did on this occasion, the reticence of their chief.

Now, these are just the kind of considerations which have to give way in war. What is known and believed in your own army is sure to reach the enemy, and before long to be known and believed in all his camps. Rumor has a thousand tongues, and it is amazing how many ears supply the tongue with information. The difficulty which arises when plans are communicated to nobody whatever must be freely admitted; for if the general be killed, his plans die with him. But this, which has been, in one or two of these papers, raised as an objection to Jackson's method, does not, I think, apply, because all his plans were known to Johnston or to

131

Lee, with whom, whilst in the Shenandoah Valley, he was always in telegraphic communication. Any one who had succeeded to his command would naturally have applied by telegraph to Richmond for further instructions. As a rule, this difficulty is easily met by imparting confidence to the one officer who is usually necessary for the execution of details. That is one reason why it is so important to have a chief of the staff of rank, as the right-hand man of a commanding general. It was evidently Jackson's practice always to communicate his plans to one confidential subordinate. Indeed, so thoroughly does this seem to have been understood by his staff that Colonel Kyd Douglas (page 622) uses the expression, "It was *my turn* this day to be intrusted with the knowledge of his purpose." A general who acts thus must reckon upon being often misunderstood, and upon exciting at least some temporary ill-feeling among those of his subordinates who do not understand his method, who have not as yet learned to trust their chief implicitly, and who have not learned from the study of war to appreciate to the full the importance of secrecy and of the mystification of an enemy. That is one of the reasons why it is so indispensable for a man intrusted with high command to have about him those who do understand and fully trust him. The arrival of a man, no matter how able a soldier he may be, who allows himself to entertain towards his commanding officer the feelings of General Whiting, is a danger to the service of a state proportionate to the importance of his rank and the influence and authority which he exercises.

The brilliancy of Jackson's moves was marred by one flaw at the last. It is clear that he underestimated by nearly twenty-four hours the time when he could get his force into position to deliver its great blow against McClellan's right flank. This mistake on his part involved Lee in a premature attack, which cost the Confederates dear. I incline to attribute this to the fact that Jackson did not know the Peninsula as well as he knew the Shenandoah Valley. Apparently the roads by which he had been previously moving were at least fairly good when compared with the execrable bush roads—and even they were few in number—over which Lee and McClellan were then moving. His marvellously rapid marches could not have been made if they had not been so. The roads in the valley of the Chickahominy were of mud, which Napoleon,

132

when suffering, during his Polish campaigns, from the same difficulty, called the "fifth element." Those marches of McClellan which created so much annoyance in Washington by their slowness —fifty-two miles in sixteen days—show how the mud was impeding movement on both sides. Relatively, therefore, Jackson's move was, in all probability, exhaustingly rapid; an effort made by his enthusiastic troops to accomplish what proved to be the impossible task for which he had pledged himself to Lee. Obviously the fault here lies in the neglect of the authorities at Richmond to have the ground in the Peninsula thoroughly surveyed and reported on. From all accounts it is clear that in this respect the Northern troops had a great advantage. Pains were taken by McClellan, whose education made him realize the importance of good maps, to have surveys and reports made of the whole country during his occupation of it. The Confederates, as so often happens with troops in their own country,—as was the case, for instance, with the French in 1870,—had omitted this precaution, and they paid dearly for the neglect. If the belief is correct that Jackson's troops had made a most exhausting effort prior to the battle of Gaines's Mill, that would account for the fact which has been so much commented on, and which produced so injurious an effect on the subsequent seven-days' battles, that Jackson did, after Gaines's Mill, "let up in the pursuit." His qualification of his own principle explains it, —"as long as your men have strength to follow." There is a point at which human energy, with the best troops, reaches its limit. Probably that limit had been passed by the end of the battle of Gaines's Mill.

It is desirable here to leave for the moment General Jackson at the end of his Shenandoah campaign and of his attack on McClellan's flank, and turn back to a period in the Peninsula antecedent to that attack. There is, obviously, some mystery which has not as yet been cleared up, which two men only can clear up, and on which they, for some reason or other, both seem indisposed to enlighten us, as to the first day's battle at Seven Pines. General Smith's account of that fight clearly throws the responsibility for the failure to crush the Federal left wing upon General Longstreet. Yet there were no written orders given to General Longstreet, and General J. E. Johnston himself seems unwilling to speak pointedly as to what his actual orders to Longstreet were. It seems to be writ large on the face of the facts that, if General J. E. Johnston's plans, as explained by General Smith, had been fully carried out during the early morning,—as it seems they easily might have been,—the whole of the Federal forces south of the Chickahominy on that morning would have been broken up, dispersed, or captured, and in all probability the slowly-arriving detachments from the north bank would, in their turn, have been driven into the river and destroyed. When two soldiers like Johnston and Longstreet decline to discuss the question, we have no business to try to set them by the ears. The deductions from the facts are in no way affected by the question as to which was to blame for allowing McClellan's forces to escape destruction. There can be no doubt, it would seem, that here, as elsewhere, bad maps and insufficient acquaintance with the ground were largely responsible for the confused crossing by the Confederate corps commanders of one another's routes, and for that dislocation of the intended order of battle which made complete success impossible.

That the position in which McClellan's army stood, part on one side and part on the other of a river liable to sudden floods, and apt in those floods to break down all means of communication across it, was a very dangerous one, is obvious at once. It is very evident that, as long as General J. E. Johnston was operating only with the army then present at Richmond, the Federal left wing was the right fraction for him to strike at. As the army defending Richmond could be wholly concentrated to the south of the Chickahominy without exposing the Capital, which lay well to the south, a sudden and secret movement against McClellan's left flank was easy, whilst an attack upon the right flank would have been tedious and difficult. The moment selected for the attack was happily chosen immediately after the river had risen in sudden flood. All that failed was the execution. In war there is in regard to almost every question a Scylla as well as a Charybdis to be avoided. When an elaborate combination of several corps over an intricate country had to be carried out by aid of very imperfect maps, it would have been better to have written orders explaining the whole situation prepared and given personally at the last moment to each of the commanders, the utmost precaution being taken against the loss of any one of the copies. It was a case in which, even if in the course of the day a copy had fallen into the enemy's hands, it would have profited him very little. Nothing could have enabled the Federal forces to the north of the Chickahominy to arrive in time to support the left, or the left to escape over the Chickahominy, if the Confederate corps had taken their proper directions. Nevertheless, here as elsewhere, one can only say that men, like mice, will often fail in their best efforts. By the second day the golden hours and opportunity had slipped away. The lost moment never returns in war.

It is interesting to compare this scheme of Johnston's with Lee's plan for attacking the right wing at Gaines's Mill. The situation had changed. This weak right wing of the Federals was now to the north of the Chickahominy River, as when Johnston attacked it it had been on the south side, and Jackson's corps was now free to move, because of the paralysis of the troops against whom he had been contending. Moreover, the course of Jackson's operations had brought him relatively near to Richmond, and Stuart's brilliant ride round McClellan had given Lee full information as to the distribution of the Federal forces. The destruction of the Federal right would cut off McClellan's whole force from his original base. It is clear that at a very early date Lee anticipated the possibility of McClellan's transferring his communications to the James River, and may have calculated on that move before he ordered the attack on the Federal right wing. Such a change of base by McClellan would not affect the fact that the defeat of that wing would deprive the Federal army of vast supplies, and would provide the Confederates with stores of which they stood sorely in need. In addition to all these reasons, the attack on the Federal right could, by the arrival of Jackson's force, be developed with better chance of its being a surprise than any attack on the Federal left could have been. It is, therefore, clear that Lee's selection for this point of attack was as sound at Gaines's Mill as Johnston's attack on the left was at Seven Pines. The fact—a fact fully reckoned upon by Lee—that McClellan was counting upon the Federal forces west of the Blue Ridge to detain Jackson in the north, and that he was continually appealing on this subject to the authorities at Washington, helped to make the movement more deadly. Lee contrived very cleverly to make it be thought in the Federal army and at

Washington that he was sending reenforcements to the Shenandoah Valley, when Jackson was in reality on his way to Mechanicsville.

The one just defence which McClellan is able to offer for the dangerous division of his army astride the Chickahominy is that, according to his statement,—and it is undisputed,—that distribution of his troops was expressly ordered from Washington, the object being that he might keep in communication with the force under McDowell, which, however, never came to his assistance. As quoted by Colonel Irwin (page 437), McClellan said: "Our men [at Gaines's Mill] did all that men could do, . . . but they were overwhelmed by vastly superior numbers, even after I brought my last reserves into action. . . . I have lost this battle because my force is too small." Clearly this assertion is not borne out by the facts. The last reserves of the whole army were never brought into action because they were then south of the Chickahominy River. The battle was lost because, owing to the separation of the right wing of the Federal army from its left by that river, it was possible to throw the mass of the Confederate army in a deadly direction upon a fraction of the army opposed to it. This answer is evident; it is complete. Without doubt the authorities at Washington were responsible for the fact that their army was too small to occupy the position which they had ordered it to assume. But, according to my views as to the powers and responsibilities of a general commanding in the field, McClellan can never be excused, under the shelter of Government orders, for placing his army in the false, and therefore the dangerous, position it was in when attacked on the Chickahominy. It was the gravest of errors, for which he had to pay in reputation, and his army in blood. Only by reenforcing his army to such an extent that the position on each bank of the river should be equal to the whole Confederate army, Jackson included, could his position astride the Chickahominy have been excusable, and even then the situation would not have been free from danger.

Most people will agree with the Comte de Paris that McClellan had a tendency greatly to exaggerate the numbers of the forces immediately opposed to him—a failing which led him frequently into a hesitating mode of action, which was of great advantage to his opponents. Just as at whist, if you know the play and temperament of your opponents, you may often score points which the mere routine play of the game would not give you, so it would seem that Lee and Jackson, who personally knew McClellan, each counted on this quality of his mind. Oddly enough, just as at whist, play of this kind may sometimes be punished, if the player against you is for once, for any reason, above his mark; so in the subsequent campaign Lee and Jackson found that they had reckoned without their host. But of this it will be convenient to speak more fully presently.

The retreat to the James was an extremely ably-conducted operation, carried out under great difficulties and, above all, in the presence of such opponents as Lee and Jackson. It ought not to have succeeded as it did: had the defeated army been pressed as it should have been, it must have been destroyed. For some reason or other, however, Jackson and his army did not show their usual quality in that pursuit; this seems to be generally admitted by those who fought in the campaign. Whether the reason suggested for this be the true one or not can never now be fully known. It is not possible now to deal fairly with the reputation of a great soldier who has left no records to explain his action or his difficulties. With the greatest respect for General Longstreet as a soldier, it must be admitted that there is at times a tone in his writing about both Lee and Jackson which grates on the ear. Any general who has commanded such numbers in the field as he has done, must know how often criticism is unjust to leaders, whose surrounding circumstances, whose motives and intentions we can never now have fully laid before us. Surely we ought to judge them by what they accomplished in those instances where we do fully know and understand all that took place. The excuse made for Jackson in one of these papers, that he was only at his best when he was acting entirely on his own responsibility, is neither satisfactory nor just to him. Not only did Lee always look upon him as his most effective agent, but the saying of Jackson about Lee, elsewhere recorded —"That man is a phenomenon; I would follow him blindfold anywhere"—shows how perfect may be the subordination of one really able general to another, when it happens to be his duty for the time to play second fiddle. It is said to be just possible that at the epoch of the War marked by the seven-days' campaign Jackson had not yet learned to appreciate Lee's genius as fully as he did later; few will, however, attach much importance to this notion.

137

Next comes one of those periods when Jackson, under circumstances most trying to an energetic man, strictly adhered to his own principles. Despatched to the north to meet the forces which were gathering under Pope, he had, in consequence of the insufficiency of his force, to remain inactive from July 12 to August 9, 1862. These are just the times when every newspaper in a democratically-governed country begins to cry out against the sloth and inactivity of a general. Nor will any previous reputation for zeal and activity save him from such charges. They were constantly and freely preferred against the Duke of Wellington in the Peninsula during some of his most wise and necessary pauses in that long contest, and after some of his most brilliant victories had shown the world of what stuff he was made, and had shown England how entirely she could trust him. Jackson, however, was strictly adhering to his own principle, "Never fight against heavy odds, if by any possible manœuvring you can hurl your own force on only a part, and that the weakest part, of your enemy, and crush it." For the latter purpose it is often necessary to bide one's time, and to have patience in biding it, which is not always easy. In this instance the time was entirely independent of anything that Jackson could do. As Lee puts it, "The uncertainty that then surrounded the designs of McClellan rendered it inexpedient to reenforce him [Jackson] from the army of Richmond." Those are facts, however, which are seldom taken into full account in the ranks of an army, and very rarely indeed by sensational newspaper writers, who, during a war, discourse so learnedly on all that goes on. Had this time of waiting been longer than, fortunately for Jackson, it actually was, his "inactivity" would doubtless have been the subject of many a savage leading article. In these days of telegraphic daily reports, even three uneventful weeks—the time during which he actually remained quiescent—may suffice to damn the fairest military reputation.

However, on July 27, 1862, A. P. Hill's division was ordered to join Jackson. As soon as Hill joined him, mark with what rapidity he acted! On August 9 he caught Banks at Cedar Mountain, and once more showed how a small army may be superior at the point of contact to the fractions of a larger. His superiority was not great, —20,000 to 17,900, according to the best estimates,—but it was sufficient. His own reputation, the confidence of his troops, and their war-tried experience under him, were elements which added indefinitely to his fighting strength. The wide-sweeping move round Pope, which followed, depended for its success, first, on Jackson's faculty for carrying out a secret manœuvre, secondly, on the trained marching rapidity of his troops, and, lastly, on the fact, which had become apparent to the Confederate generals, that the Washington authorities had so tied Pope to a post that it was safe to march round him because he could not move. It is rather remarkable that, in General Pope's description of the campaign, he appears to treat the loss of the stores at Manassas Junction as a trifling matter. In the long run, no doubt, that loss may not have been very important to the well-supplied Northern armies; but there can be no question that both by its material and moral effects it enormously increased the demoralization of the Union army after the second defeat of Bull Run. Before that battle it exercised a most disastrous influence by shaking the confidence of men and officers in their commander, however much justification he may have for throwing the responsibility for it upon other shoulders. In a campaign men do not nicely argue out questions of abstract justice; it is the broad effects which tell on the spirit of an army. There can be no doubt that, in fighting the second Bull Run, the successful raid was worth several thousand men to the Confederates, from the encouragement it afforded them and the depression it produced among their opponents. When I was with General Lee's army at Winchester, in the autumn of 1862, the soldiers in every camp laughingly spoke of Pope as "Stonewall Jackson's Commissary," so entirely had Jackson in the "Pope Campaign" depended upon capturing from that General everything he required for his men.

To put in practice Jackson's principle of bringing a small army to bear upon the fractions of a large one, it is often necessary to employ a portion of that little army, in a strong position, for the the purpose of delaying the movements of the remainder of the enemy's forces. Jackson practised this when he employed some of his troops in the passes of the mountains to hold Frémont in check, whilst with all the troops he could collect he moved to attack Banks. It is clear that this was also Lee's object at the battle of South Mountain. He sought to check the advance of the Federal Army whilst Jackson overwhelmed the garrison of Harper's Ferry.

As far as I can follow the circumstances, it seems to me that, if Jackson was to secure the desired result, Lee was right in what he did. I cannot see how, if Lee had at once fallen back in the way suggested by General Longstreet, Franklin could have been prevented from relieving Harper's Ferry. On the other hand, from the evidence before me in these papers, it would appear that several things happened which neither Lee nor Jackson had anticipated. It is interesting to note what these events were and how they came about. General Walker quotes Jackson as saying, when he knew of McClellan's advance: "I thought I knew McClellan, but this movement of his puzzles me." Though a good deal of Walker's evidence has been disputed, I do not think that anything brought forward tends to shake this statement, which is very precise, and not one about which memory would be likely to mislead. This commentary of Jackson upon McClellan, before devising the plan of campaign at Frederick, and the remark made by Lee (also quoted)—namely, "Are you acquainted with General McClellan?" —prove that both Lee and Jackson planned their course of action upon what they believed to be a just estimate of McClellan's character and of his genius for caution. The demoralization of Pope's army was well known to the Confederate generals. It seems clear to me that Lee counted upon it, and upon McClellan's slowness, to enable him to take Harper's Ferry and, perhaps, to move beyond it before McClellan had reorganized his army. In this calculation Lee was mistaken.

All the descriptions we have of the reception of McClellan by his old army as he rode out to meet it returning beaten, disorganized, and demoralized from the second battle of Bull Run, agree in this—that the fact of his presence with it restored confidence to all ranks. I would ask those who have not been in the habit of considering the conditions which determine the power or weakness of an army in war to read these accounts of McClellan's reception by his army. Let them observe the reports made by all upon the state of the army as it retreated, or rather fled, to Washington; mark the impression produced on Mr. Lincoln and Stanton as to the utter powerlessness of the Union Army to stop the Confederates and to save Washington. Let them note the conviction in the minds of Lee and Jackson that this army was so shaken that it could not be in a state to fight for at least three weeks or more; and then let them turn to that summary, made in the last article, of the blunders, the ignorant self-confidence, and the folly of Mr. Stanton at the time when he appointed Pope to the command of the Army of Virginia. All those mistakes were now coming home to roost, with consequences fatal to the power of the army. The troops had no confidence in their leader, no confidence in themselves. Here, visibly, under the eyes of the man who had caused all this disaster, though probably even then he did not realize his own absolute and complete responsibility as to the certain cause of it, the army was not going, but had gone, to pieces. He had imagined he could drive the horses of the Sun, and horses and he were being dashed to pieces. He had attempted a task for which he was absolutely incompetent. He seems to have imagined that mere self-assertion would carry him through; that the conduct of a campaign was the easiest and simplest thing imaginable, and that, if only he gave orders, the rest must go like clock-work. Suddenly the man who can drive the horses seizes the reins that have dropped from the other's incompetent hands. In a moment all is changed. Those who will be at the trouble to study the evidence for this story will see that it is no exaggeration.

Now, what must have been, what was, according to his own account, the effect of all this upon McClellan himself? The precise mistake which gentlemen like Mr. Stanton make lies in supposing that soldiers and armies are machines, instead of men living under certain special conditions—men whose ways and feelings and prejudices you must understand before you can command and lead them with advantage. But generals are as little machines as armies are. The Napoleon of 1796 and the Napoleon of Waterloo were two different men. So the cautious, rather cold-blooded, and indecisive, timid soldier whom Lee and Jackson had known at West Point, and had fought with in the Peninsula, was not the McClellan who felt himself to be the one man who had restored confidence to a beaten army. All at once he heard nothing around him but enthusiastic demands to be led forward to victory from the very men who, till he joined them, were only seeking safety in individual flight. No man could go through such an experience and not be affected by it. All the circumstances that had preceded this event tended to deepen its effect upon his mind. Failure in the Peninsula, for which he felt he was not to blame; snubbing from Hal-

141

leck, who, whenever he appears on the scene, shows himself as the very incarnation of what Shakespeare meant by "the insolence of office"; the sound of the guns of his distant army, which he was not allowed to join, while he felt it was being led to certain defeat through the incompetency of its commander; his reception at Washington, where his warnings as to the condition of the Union Army were despised; then the ample fulfilment of his worst fears, and the sight of the abject panic of those who, until that moment, were full of overweening confidence; add to all this the attempt made even at the last moment to hamper him,—and it is not to be wondered at that, when he rode out to meet his army, he seems to have regarded the proceeding almost in the light of a revolutionary act which his duty to the Nation had rendered necessary.

All these things must have sent the blood coursing through his veins, bracing him for the supreme moment of triumph over his enemies in Washington which his enthusiastic reception by his old soldiers at length afforded him. Under such conditions, a man's nature for the time may well be changed. How could McClellan help feeling a renewed confidence in himself, when he and all the army, and all those whom he believed to be his personal enemies, were thus convinced of his power by the efficiency restored to the army the moment he appeared again as its leader? Under ordinary circumstances, his methodical disposition might—perhaps it may be said certainly would—have led him to spend those weeks in re-organization upon which Lee had counted. But in the position in which he then found himself, it must have seemed to him that, as the disorganization of the army was directly attributable to his absence from it, so his presence with it—hailed as it was by all ranks—was, of itself, sufficient to restore it to order and efficiency. He may well have thought, under these circumstances, that no weeks of repose were necessary to prepare it for battle, and may well have looked only for some good opportunity to test its fighting value, now that it had been again placed under his command. It must, indeed, have been a proud event of his life, for he felt that he alone of all men was able to restore heart and life to that beaten army as it streamed back towards Washington.

All he now wanted was that Lee should afford him the opportunity to show what that army, under the spell of his name, could accomplish. This General Lee was preparing to offer him, and a lucky accident suddenly placed in his hands the full detail of Lee's intended plan of operations. The paper containing it had been picked up by chance. From it he learns that Lee, trusting to the disorganization which he believed reigned in the Federal army, had ordered Jackson to take Harper's Ferry, whilst the main Confederate army had been broken up into several disunited fragments. The evidence is supplied in McClellan's own letter to the editors of the *Century*, as to the importance which he attached to this information (page 603). Within little more than an hour after McClellan had read that paper, orders for the advance of the Federal Army on South Mountain were given.

But such moments of exaltation as that then experienced by McClellan are apt to bring their reaction after them. In this instance the character of the man reasserts itself when he arrives before the slender Confederate screen then in occupation of South Mountain. As usual, he allows himself to estimate the forces opposed to him as vastly greater than they really are, and to act as if they were so. Still, the vast numerical superiority of the Northern army could not but assert itself over the Confederates, reduced, by the straggling of the numbers of bare-footed men in their ranks, to little more than 40,000 within the fighting area.

Lee had driven back the Army of the Potomac and that of Virginia to the point from which they had started in the spring and summer. He knew how demoralized those armies had become from repeated defeats, and he was fully aware of the scare which Pope's disasters had occasioned at Washington. Mr. Lincoln was known to be very nervous for the safety of that capital. Lee felt that if he could but still further increase this fear of losing Washington, he might so retain the Federal armies in its neighborhood as to free the northern districts of Virginia from all hostile occupation during the autumn. His object was to keep McClellan's forces far away from Richmond until winter had so destroyed the roads as to render all field operations near that city practically impossible.

Although a vast amount of valuable equipment and military stores had been taken by the "Army of Northern Virginia" from Pope, it was still a very badly-supplied army, and sadly in want of transport. Notwithstanding this fact, Lee thought his best plan to accomplish the end he had in view was to invade Maryland, where the Southern cause had thousands of sympathizers, and by that operation keep the war at a distance from Richmond. Lee had, however, it seems to me, underestimated the revivifying influence which McClellan exerted over the Federal armies when again placed in actual command of them; nor did Maryland afford him the assistance he had expected. He also miscalculated the time required for the capture of Harper's Ferry—a miscalculation which placed him in a position of real danger. An enterprising commander, not impressed as McClellan always was with the notion that his enemy was vastly stronger than he actually was, would then have pushed Lee very hard indeed. McClellan, with Lee's plan of campaign in his pocket and the large force at his disposal, was in the position where a really great general would have destroyed an adversary who had crossed the Potomac and distributed his troops as Lee's were on the 13th, 14th, 15th, and 16th September, 1862.

The battles of South Mountain and Antietam proved to Lee that his army was not strong enough to carry out an aggressive campaign against the now united armies of the North. From the moment that McClellan had restored confidence to the Northern army, and, thanks to the captured despatch, had made up his mind to act, it was obviously Lee's policy to avoid fighting as much as possible and recross into Virginia. Antietam, though a battle unwittingly fought by him, was, however, unavoidable. It is necessary to estimate a general's purposes in judging what he has gained or lost by a battle. That the actual result on the battlefield was a Confederate victory seems to be little disputed. Lee had gained what he had hoped to secure by that battle, which was to make good his repassage of the Potomac. The Confederate army had won a battle, but had achieved no victory, whilst the Confederacy had failed in its intention to carry the war into the enemy's country. Colonel Kyd Douglas states the case very fairly when he says: "The prestige of the day was with Lee, but when, on the night of the 18th, he recrossed into Virginia, he left the prestige of the result with McClellan." (Page 629.)

Lee's management of the battle against vastly superior forces was wonderfully successful. His retreat afterwards was as wise and necessary as it was admirably conducted. It is only for schoolboys that retreat under such circumstances can be said to take anything from the prestige of men like Lee. He was soon to show, against generals who, as McClellan put it, "acted before they were ready," how brilliantly he could deal with the opportunities victory gave him, as well as with circumstances which, as in this instance, made it necessary to prepare the way for retreat.

I must reserve for the next article all notice of the few papers on the events in the West which appear in this second volume. They are too closely connected with those which follow in the third volume to be dealt with separately.

AN ENGLISH VIEW OF THE CIVIL WAR
PART IV

THE FOURTH ARTICLE IN THE SERIES TREATS A PART OF THE *third volume of* Battles and Leaders *and, broadly speaking, covers eastern operations in the year 1863, the middle phase of the war. A prominent topic is General James Longstreet, who himself contributed three papers to the volume—one on Fredericksburg and two on Gettysburg. With regard to Lee's "inexplicable" mistake at Fredericksburg in not pushing Burnside's army into the river or compelling its surrender, Freeman, without entering directly into the question, indicates that Lee was surprised by Burnside's crossing the river and expected him to recross and attack again.*

Wolseley scores Longstreet for his inability to appreciate Lee's military superiority, for his addiction to defensive warfare, and for a procrastination at Gettysburg that came close to disobedience. Longstreet was a paradox; incompetent to wield supreme command, he could brilliantly lead a division or wing in action, but could not "subordinate his own views" to those of his chief. The contrast of military principles held by Jackson and Longstreet is sharply made. As we have noted in the general introduction, Longstreet has recently been defended against charges that he disobeyed a "sunrise order"; the modern historian, Glenn Tucker, considers him a scapegoat instead of a culprit at Gettysburg. The point has been made in Longstreet's behalf that his men could not arrive to take up battle positions until about two o'clock on the afternoon of July 2.

149

AN ENGLISH VIEW
OF THE CIVIL WAR

IV

I WISH to remind the reader of these articles on the Civil War that they deal only with the information supplied by *The Century* magazine's history of that struggle. The story there told so graphically is treated from the military student's and the military critic's point of view, and it is earnestly trusted that no one may be offended with anything contained in these articles. Many may differ from the conclusions arrived at, and the views expressed may be often or always mistaken; but they are, at least, the honest opinions of one who has the most sincere admiration for the combatants on both sides, and for the many great soldiers and statesmen who then directed the destinies of the United States of America.

The readers of these *Century* magazine papers owe a debt of gratitude to the editors for the pains with which they have collected the various documents. The references to the parts of other papers on the same subject, and to the official publications of the losses and numbers of combatants on both sides, are very useful. But there is one respect in which I would venture to suggest improvement, if any future edition should afford an opportunity. It seems ungracious, where we have been supplied with such a large and costly number of maps, plans, and pictures, to find fault with this aspect of the series. Unfortunately, however, there is one thing needful for a military reader which has not been adequately provided. The text does not seem to have been carefully read by any editor who is in the habit of following, upon the corresponding maps, the movements described. The consequence is, it frequently happens that names of places are mentioned in the text which do not appear in the maps. It is not too much to say that for all purposes of intelligent military study, if the reader had to depend solely on these maps, there is much in the text which might almost as well be omitted. Even when, after much search, the place named is discovered in some map or other, the map in which it is found is often not that which has been prepared to elucidate that part of the narrative. One does not, consequently, get the place shown in relation to other localities described. From time to time references are given to particular maps, but these references are not sufficiently frequent. The references required to other portions of the text, in support of evidence educed, are good and ample, and it is much to be regretted that similar care has not been taken to guide the reader to the map required to elucidate the text upon all occasions.

The third volume covers a series of the most deeply interesting operations of the war. These are, in the East, Fredericksburg, Chancellorsville, and Gettysburg; in the West, Perryville, Vicksburg, Port Hudson, Chickamauga, Chattanooga, and Knoxville; to which I may add, for the purposes of this article, the papers at the end of Volume II on the Mexican campaign and the battles of Iuka and Corinth. To these battles no reference was made in my article in last month's *North American Review,* because they are closely connected with the general sequence of events in the West, which are recorded in this third volume.

For many reasons the three great battles in the East will be considered first.

General Longstreet has made certain comments upon the whole series of papers on those events, which serve as a convenient basis for a discussion of the interesting questions which rise out of them. He himself had a brilliant share in the victory at Fredericksburg. He was absent from Chancellorsville, but he tells us that on his return to the army, prior to the invasion of Pennsylvania, he propounded certain views and principles to General Lee with regard to the general conduct of future operations. I have already quoted Jackson's views as to what he considered to be the guiding principles of war. It is worth while to compare them with those that are laid before us by General Longstreet.

Neither general would probably wish to have a few sentences, such as are here given, taken to represent his whole mind on so large a subject. Nevertheless, it is always a point of some value to notice what are the aspects of the art and science of war which are most forcibly and most constantly present to the mind of an able soldier, for he is almost sure to insist on them, rather than on others, when he has to decide between the advisability of certain plans and methods.

I must, however, express a feeling, which will, I think, be shared by many of those who fought against Generals Lee and Longstreet, that it is not pleasant to read reports by the surviving general of conversations between the two in which he seems to have treated, not to say reprimanded, his great leader more like a school-boy under instruction than like one of the most brilliant commanders and remarkable men of his own, if not of all, time. Whatever other great qualities as a soldier General Longstreet may possess,— and he certainly does possess some very brilliant qualities,—that of appreciating the military genius of the commander under whom he served cannot be reckoned among them.

Most of us think that one commander has seldom been more thoroughly outgeneralled by another than General Hooker was by Lee at the Battle of Chancellorsville. No one has expressed that view more strongly than have the distinguished soldiers who served under Hooker in that battle. Even those who express the warmest appreciation of the skill which Hooker displayed in the manœuvres which brought the army to Chancellorsville think very strongly that it was the difference between the two commanders which sent the Federal Army in retreat back over the Rappahannock, as the result of that battle.

In that battle at least one Federal corps had been utterly broken up and disorganized, though the Federal Army, much better armed, and with an artillery overwhelmingly powerful, numbered 130,000, and the Confederates only 60,000, men. With such a disproportion of force, that the effect of the battle should have been, not merely to stop the invasion of the South, but to open the way for the Confederate invasion of Pennsylvania, would seem, one would say, to imply that the Federals had been "outgeneralled." Yet, on returning to the army, General Longstreet's only view, not alone of this campaign, but of that in the Shenandoah Valley under Jackson, of the first and second Bull Run, and of the Peninsular campaign, appears to have been expressed by saying that "one mistake of the Confederacy was in pitting force against force. The only hope we had was to outgeneral the Federals." "The time had come

153

(*sic*) when it was imperative that the skill of generals and the strategy and tactics of war should take the place of muscle against muscle."

"We"—that is, Longstreet and Lee—"talked on that line from day to day, and General Lee, accepting it as a good military view, adopted it as the key-note of the campaign." I do not know how it will strike others, but to me there is something unspeakably pathetic about the picture of Lee—that man alike of marvellous modesty and marvellous genius, who by his skill and daring was then exciting the admiration of all that world from which he was cut off —thus closeted with his carping lieutenant. How could Lee do otherwise than accept it as the key-note of his campaign that he must endeavor to compensate for the numerical weakness of his army by the skill of his dispositions? On what else had he to rely than the devotion of his soldiers and their confidence in him? But how cruel a blow to such a man must it have been to discover that, after all their campaigns together, the general who was now left him as the right arm on which he must rely had formed this conclusion as to all his handling of the army in the past! Apart altogether from mere personal feeling, which, seeing that Lee was human, must have been sore enough, how serious a weakness did this disclose in one of the most important elements of his possible strength! Imagine the difference between having to rely for the carrying-out of your plans upon a soldier whose judgment and estimate of you were of this kind, and upon one who had for you the feeling which Jackson showed for Lee when he declared, "That man is a phenomenon. I would follow him blindfold anywhere." Yet it was from the same campaigns that the two great lieutenants of Lee had drawn these opposite conclusions.

We are not, however, left in any doubt as to the nature of the strategy which Longstreet desired to see adopted, or the nature of the experience on which he founded it. He writes:

I then accepted his proposition to make a campaign into Pennsylvania, provided it should be offensive in strategy, but defensive in tactics, forcing the Federal Army to give us battle when we were in strong position and ready to receive them. . . . I stated to General Lee that, if he would allow me to handle my corps so as to receive the attack of the Federal Army, I would beat it off without calling on him for help except to guard my right and left, and called his attention to the battle of Fredericksburg as an instance of defensive warfare, where we had thrown not more than five thousand troops into the fight, and had beaten off two-thirds of the Federal Army, with great loss to them and slight loss to *my own* troops. I also called his attention to Napoleon's instructions to Marmont at the head of an invading army.

Now, it is certainly not wished to disparage the advantages of this method, where it can be adopted, of offensive strategy and of defensive tactics. Most generals believe distinctly in the possibility and advisability, under certain circumstances, of taking up such a position that by your doing so your enemy will be forced to elect between an attack under very great disadvantages upon your strong position and the abandonment of some most important object. But as the wise man has said of "every purpose under the sun," so it may be said of war, there is a time to attack and a time to refrain from attack, a time to defend and a time to abandon the defensive. Judged by the criticism General Longstreet offers of the action of others, his principle would appear to imply that, when an army has the opportunity of striking a series of blows against isolated fragments of its enemy, it ought to refrain from taking advantage of them in order to adopt the policy he advocates. It is needless to point out how directly that principle brings him into conflict with the admirable views on war of Stonewall Jackson, which were quoted in the article on this subject published in the July *Review.*

Of the Fredericksburg campaign, apart from the battle, we unfortunately get very little account in these papers. Most students of war will, it is thought, consider the especial brilliancy of that campaign to have depended upon the mode in which Lee succeeded in bringing up Jackson exactly at the right moment. This was done so cleverly that the Federal commander committed himself to the attack on the Confederate Army under the impression that he had little more than Longstreet's corps to deal with. Without that application of Jackson's principle, Longstreet would have intrenched at Fredericksburg in vain. It is not often you can induce your antagonist to attack straight to his front the position you have worked at for weeks to strengthen, and especially where it is a position upon which he can bring no adequate artillery fire to bear. To quote Napoleon as meaning that, when an opportunity presents itself, you ought not to strike with your own concentrated army that of your enemy before it is concentrated; that you ought not, as Jackson did at Chancellorsville, to bring an overpowering force upon the flanks and rear of an exposed wing which can be dealt with before it is supported, will seem absurd to any one who knows what Napoleon did, and why it was he so severely criticised Marmont's proceedings.

Indeed, it is difficult to believe that an able soldier like General Longstreet can really mean this. There is often an indisposition, not uncommon among able men, to play second fiddle, and to be very critical of the first fiddle. It is easiest to account for General Longstreet's proceedings by assuming that he was no stranger to this feeling. In order to enforce the wisdom of the advice he gave his chief, General Longstreet records a forecast that he made in regard to the battle of Sedan. He would appear not to have closely studied the circumstances of that battle, for otherwise he would be aware that, while he was quite right in predicting that "MacMahon's army would be prisoners of war in ten days" from the time at which he spoke, he was entirely wrong as to the method by which that result would be brought about. The Prussians at Sedan did not "force MacMahon to attack," but attacked *him* on all sides. They carried Bazeilles after fierce and bloody attacks. They carried by attack La Moncelle, Daigny, Givonne, the plateaus above Floing and Illy, and the Bois de la Garenne. They only refrained from an actual attack with their infantry upon the immediate neighborhood of Sedan because, having already secured by attack all the positions which commanded the valley, they were able to bring such an overwhelming artillery fire to bear that the French position became untenable.

In no sense whatever is the battle of Sedan an example of offensive strategy and of defensive tactics. The campaign of 1870 and the principles of war followed by the German leaders are most unfortunate authorities for General Longstreet to appeal to in support of his special views. The modern German writers on war seem to enforce a theory the exact opposite to that of General Longstreet, to an exaggeration as extreme on their side as his appears to be on the other. They for the most part seem to admit as little as he does "that there is a time for every purpose under heaven"; there is, however, this one great difference between them:

156

that, whereas he assumes the one great method of war to be that of offensive strategy and defensive tactics, they, most of them at least, continually urge that offensive strategy implies offensive tactics. They are also very strongly impressed with a view which, if we may judge from their conduct of war, appears to have been that of both Stonewall Jackson and of Grant, and perhaps that of Lee also—that defensive tactics carried on behind intrenched positions have a very dangerous tendency to unfit soldiers for all rapid offensive action. That is a serious element in the whole question which must be taken into account. It is completely ignored in General Longstreet's criticism of Lee.

In these remarks, the actions of Fredericksburg and Chancellorsville have been taken together, as the story of those battles seems admirably to illustrate Lee's principles and method, and to clear the way for the discussion of Gettysburg also.

I cannot, however, pass on to the Gettysburg campaign without calling attention to Lee's mistake in allowing the Federal Army to escape across the Rappahannock after the battle of Fredericksburg. To command in war for many campaigns and make no mistakes is impossible. General Lee, great in strategy and able in tactics, is no exception to the wisdom of this saying. Military history can only be made of use to the student of war by a close criticism of every operation, and the critic, no matter how humble, should not shrink from pointing out what he conceives to be the errors and mistakes made by even the most renowned commanders. General Lee made some mistakes in his most brilliant career, but the greatest was after the battle of Fredericksburg. The more closely his conduct then is studied, the more inexplicable it appears. The reasons he gives in his published despatches for having failed either to push the Federal Army into the river or to compel its surrender are most unsatisfactory, most insufficient. (Page 82—note.) When the last Federal attack was repulsed on that eventful 13th December, Burnside's army was at Lee's mercy. It is, however, easy to be wise after the event, and to point out what might or ought to have been done. When Wellington realized that the battle of Waterloo was won, he is proverbially reported to have suddenly shut up the telescope through which he had been looking, and to have given the order, "Up, Guards, and at 'em." He felt that the time had come for passing from the defensive to the active offensive, for he

157

saw that Napoleon's army had been delivered into his hands. Yet that army had no unfordable river, like the Rappahannock, immediately behind it. Had the French army on the evening of the 18th June, 1815, been situated as Burnside's army was on the evening of the 13th December, 1862, none of it could ever have succeeded in recrossing the Belgian frontier into France.

It has always seemed to me that, if Burnside's army had been destroyed, as it ought to have been, after its crushing repulse at Fredericksburg, the struggle between North and South would have assumed an entirely different aspect, and subsequent events would not have been as they were. That army was by far and in every way the finest under the Federal flag, and was the nucleus of that which afterwards fought at Gettysburg, and which eventually forced General Lee to surrender. The prize in front of the great Confederate general was enormous. He would doubtless have lost very heavily had he left his position of vantage to push the defeated Federals into the Rappahannock, but the losses at Chancellorsville and by many other subsequent battles might have been thereby saved. Lee does not seem to have realized how great was the Federal loss and how serious the demoralization of their army on the evening of the 13th December. He made up his mind that Burnside would renew the fight next morning, and the pages of *The Century* magazine tell us how fairly justified he was in thinking this, as they show that Burnside meant to have done so. Had the Federals attacked again on either the 14th or 15th December, judging from Lee's general mode of fighting, I think we are entitled to assume that he would, without doubt, have followed up a second repulse of the Federal attack by such an immediate and vigorous offensive as would have annihilated Burnside's army. It must be admitted that, whilst Lee's position was admirable for a passive defence, it was very bad for the sudden assumption of an active forward offensive when the enemy's attacks upon it had been even crushingly repulsed.

During the course of this long war some great opportunities were lost by the Confederacy for the delivery of a death-blow to the Northern armies. But upon no other occasion was the opportunity so apparent, or the results that would have attended success so evident, as at Fredericksburg. That battle was a brilliant success. Lee ought to have made it a crushing, if not a final, victory.

Burnside's retreat to the North bank of the Rappahannock during the stormy night of the 15th December was admirably conducted, and most creditable to the Federal generals and staff officers who carried it out.

Every one is agreed that the first day's fight of Gettysburg was brought on without Lee's having expected it. On that day two Federal corps had been severely handled by very superior Confederate forces. The Federal Army was neither concentrated nor were its corps near enough to the battle-field to be concentrated by the time that the Confederate Army ought to have been able to attack them. The evidence adduced as to the position of the Confederate corps is incontrovertible. Colonel Allen, in his reply to General Longstreet (page 355), has shown conclusively, not only that the reports of all the division commanders at the time are directly against General Longstreet's assertion that his divisions were "fifteen or twenty miles away from the battle-field on the night between the 1st and 2d July," but that General Longstreet's own official report at the time contradicts his recent statement on this point. The soldier instinctively admires the fine fighting qualities of General Longstreet, but the student of war called upon to express an opinion upon his conduct, when second in command to General Lee, sees much to find fault with. General Longstreet tells us (page 340) of his somewhat fierce discussion with his chief on the afternoon of the 1st July as to the plans that should be followed in the next day's battle. The account we have already had of his earlier conversations with Lee upon the general conduct of the war throws an interesting light upon what must have passed through Lee's mind during those discussions.

That Lee felt the necessity of keeping on the kindliest terms with his able, but argument-loving, lieutenant is evident. He bore with characteristic humility what must be termed the essentially disrespectful attitude of mind towards him of the man on whom he was obliged to rely for the most important stroke of the whole war. But that all the time Lee's own mind remained clearly fixed on the policy of adopting either offensive or defensive tactics, according to circumstances, is manifest from the firmness with which he rejected Longstreet's proposed plans. He was determined not to lose the opportunity which chance had thrown in his way, for the very doubtful possibility of being able to manœuvre round

159

the Federal army—an operation which would, at least, certainly afford that army time to concentrate against him. By all that is recorded in this volume of General Longstreet, by his whole conduct on the 2nd and 3rd July, and by the tone and temper of his present writings, it seems very evident that he quitted Lee on the night between those two days with his mind filled with the fixed idea of defensive tactics. His thoughts were apparently too much absorbed with his own plans to admit of his paying a properly strict attention to the orders and directions of his chief. Yet upon their prompt and accurate execution depended the success of Lee's far more brilliant and far wiser scheme of action.

General Longstreet has appealed to Napoleon. Those who have most carefully studied Napoleon's methods and habit will think, I believe, that Napoleon in Lee's place would have attacked in the early morning of July 2, as Lee intended to do. Those who have closely followed the history of this war will also be inclined to think that, if Jackson had been in Longstreet's place, the attack would have been delivered before 10 A.M. at the latest.

With the evidence given in this volume before us, few can doubt the truth of Colonel Allan's statement (page 356) that

General Longstreet, though knowing fully the condition of things on the night of the 1st, knowing that Lee had decided to attack that part of the Federal Army in his front, knowing that every hour strengthened Meade and diminished the chances of Confederate success, and knowing that his corps was to open the battle and deliver the main assault, consumed the time from daylight to nearly 4 P.M., on July 2, in moving his troops about four miles over no serious obstacle and in getting them into battle.

The evidence now laid before us goes far to show that General Longstreet was not only responsible for the fact that his own wing attacked so late that almost the whole Federal Army was concentrated before the stroke was delivered, but also for the fact that he was, when the attack was delivered, not properly supported by the other parts of the army detailed to cooperate in the attack.When the principal attack, on which all others depend, is delivered at least six hours later than it is ordered to be delivered, it is impossible that cooperating corps should time their movements so as to support it. General Longstreet has clinched the evidence as to the cause of the imperfect success of the battle on the second day, by urging that Lee had not ordered the attack to be delivered at the earliest possible hour on the 2d July. The direct evidence brought against him on this point is, however, very clear, although even without such evidence it would still be clear to all who closely study this great battle that the whole point and scheme of Lee's battle manifestly depended on the attack being delivered at the earliest possible moment. If General Longstreet had not been too much absorbed by his own ideas of the way in which the campaign ought to have been fought, to pay attention to the literal and prompt execution of his chief's orders, he must have seen for himself that suddenness and earliness in the attack were of the essence of that scheme.

Similarly, in the third day's battle all the evidence goes to show that, if Pickett's attack had been supported by the whole force of Longstreet's corps and the division and a half of H. P. Hill's corps, which were put at his disposal, that attack would have succeeded. The picture of General Longstreet not even able to make up his mind to order the charge of Pickett's division recalls the bitter memories of our own attack upon the Redan in September, 1855. Upon that occasion our final repulse was due to want of support. No effective arrangements had been made to reenforce the British troops engaged in the assault, who, left without support, were easily disposed of by the fresh troops of the enemy brought to bear on them. No operation in war is so bloody, nothing is so cruel to all concerned, as the weak decision which allows an insufficient force to engage in an attack from a disinclination to expose more than a small number of men to the risks it entails. How many serious disasters have been occasioned by the tender-heartedness of the commander who lacked the moral courage to launch heavy columns in support of men engaged in an attack like that attempted by General Pickett!

As to Lee's decision to attack on the third day of Gettysburg, intending that attack to be adequately supported (as, however it was not), it is very interesting to compare this battle with that of Grant at Chattanooga. Few will contend that the advantages which General Grant had gained during the first two days' fight at Chattanooga were so great as those which Lee had gained in the first two days' fight at Gettysburg. On the first day at Chattanooga, the 23d November, 1863, Thomas's force seized the picket lines of the enemy in front of him by a sudden rush. On the 24th, Hooker, on the right, drove in a small force of the enemy, and secured the evacuation of Lookout Mountain, and Sherman forced his way to a position detached from the enemy's right; but up to the moment when the successful charge was made in the centre by Thomas, General Sherman had entirely failed to force his way on the left, and General Hooker had not made good his advance on the right. No doubt the charge of Thomas, as actually ordered, was not intended to be carried forward in the way it was. But a comparison between the circumstances of Thomas's successful charge at Chattanooga with the failure of Pickett at Gettysburg will show that a large element of the uncertain prevailed in each case, and that it by no means follows that, because Pickett's charge proved in fact disastrous, Lee was therefore wrong to order it, or that, if it had been properly supported, it would not have succeeded. Even if we had not the direct and specific evidence of General Imboden, we could not doubt that the words he has quoted must have represented the secret thoughts of Lee. "I never saw troops behave more magnificently than Pickett's division of Virginians did to-day in that grand charge upon the enemy. And if they had been supported as they were to have been,—but for some reason not yet fully explained to me, were not,—we would have held the position, and the day would have been ours." After a moment's pause he added in a loud voice, in a tone almost of agony, "Too bad! Too bad! Oh, too bad!" (Page 421.)

The whole story, as told by General Imboden, of that casual meeting with Lee at 1 A.M. the morning after the last day's battle, seems to leave no doubt as to what Lee's view of the facts really was. Nothing is more characteristic of the man than that, when quietly reviewing the situation, he should realize how all-important it was to the cause of the Confederacy that no personal differences should arise between him and Longstreet, and that he should consequently have taken all the blame upon himself. Most soldiers will think that General Longstreet has not served his own cause well by appealing so much to the generous silence of his chief. He has, at least as far as all future histories of the war are concerned, deprived himself of the benefit of that silence by the way in which he has laid himself out to make charges against the chief who refrained, under the most dire provocation, from one word of reproach against him. The sneer about the appointment of Virginians to command has been well answered by Colonel Allen; the sneer about Stuart's "wild ride around the Federal army" (page 355), which General Longstreet asserts was undertaken in disobedience of his own orders, is unfortunate, as Colonel Mosby (page 251) shows from the original document that it was made by General Longstreet's own order, after the question had been expressly referred to him by General Lee: the errors he has fallen into as to the position of his own corps prior to Gettysburg are similarly confuted by the original documents. These, and not a few other matters of similar character, seem to deprive General Longstreet's statements of at least some of their value as evidence, and his criticism of all value as that of an unbiassed judge.

There is in the record of General Longstreet's battles a uniformity of incident as marked as that noticed in the case of some other generals. In the first day's fight at Seven Pines, according to all the best evidence that is before us, General Longstreet's division was so long in getting into position and preparing for attack that the whole scheme of General J. E. Johnston miscarried. General Johnston has too great a respect for his lieutenant, and is too generous a man, to reproach him for the miscarriage. At the second Bull Run, according to General Longstreet's own report (page 519, Vol. II),

As soon as the troops were arranged, General Lee expressed a wish to have me attack. The change of position on the part of the Federals, however, involved sufficient delay for a reconnoissance on our part. ... The position was not inviting, and so I reported to General Lee. ... General Lee was quite disappointed by my report against immediate attack along the turnpike. ... General Lee urged me to go in, and, of course, I was anxious to meet his wishes. At the same time I wanted more than anything else to know that my troops had a chance to accomplish what they might undertake.

And so on *ad libitum*—Lee always anxious for attack; Longstreet deliberating and postponing action. In his one brilliant and successful attack during all these battles—that at Chickamauga—Longstreet, being commander of the Confederate left wing, and having orders (page 652, Vol. III) from Bragg to "begin at day-break," did not (page 655) "advance until noon," by which time the action of the other wing had caused a gap in the Federal lines through which Longstreet, brilliantly taking advantage of the error, advanced and caused the Federal defeat. "Discovering, with the true instinct of the soldier, that he could do more by turning to the right, he disregarded the order to wheel to the left, and wheeled the other way." Destiny may have shaped these results, but one is much mistaken if there is not evident in each of these actions the hand and mind of the same man who rough-hewed each of them according to the same temperament—the hand of one man who was much better adapted to repair the errors of a second-rate commander than to carry out the purposes of such a chief as Lee. There is a greatness of soul which may be shown in subordinating even a better judgment to the perfect carrying-out of the scheme of a leader who has the right to decide. Of any recognition of that fact on General Longstreet's part in his relations with Lee, no trace is to be found in any one of these actions. That Longstreet was a brilliant leader of a division or wing in action there can be no doubt, but he seems never to have been able—perhaps from some peculiarity of temperament—to subordinate his own views heartily to the views and orders of his great chief. The impartial military critic must admit that at Seven Pines, the second Bull Run, and Gettysburg, the Confederacy paid dearly for that defect in his character.

In one respect there is a rather remarkable similarity in the incidents of the Gettysburg and of the Chancellorsville campaign. In the latter campaign nearly the whole of the Federal cavalry had been detached from the army in order to throw itself between Lee's position on the Rappahannock and his base at Richmond. The major portion of the Federal Army then crossed the Rappahannock, and the battle of Chancellorsville was fought whilst the Federal cavalry was thus absent. During the Gettysburg campaign, Stuart, with a large portion of the Confederate cavalry, had been detached round the rear of Meade's army, and the other portion of the cavalry, having been, by the course of the movements, thrown out of the line between the two armies, Lee was left with no cavalry in his front at the moment when the collision between the two armies unexpectedly occurred at Gettysburg. There is just this difference—that during the Gettysburg campaign the absence of the cavalry was contrary to Lee's intention. He had calculated upon its being possible for Stuart to return to him before the collision should take place. The difficulty which a body of men, launched like those of Stuart upon the rear of an army, find themselves in, is well likened to the position of a man turned blindfold in a room full of enemies. It was that difficulty which prevented Stuart's return till the eve of the battle. In the case of the Chancellorsville campaign, Hooker's scheme deliberately involved his being deprived of the services of the cavalry during the course of his whole campaign. In both cases alike the result seems to show that, when armies are manœuvring against one another in the field, it is a risk too great to be worth running, even for the sake of breaking in upon the communications of an enemy, to deprive the army of its eyes, as one must do if the bulk of mounted troops are sent off on some entirely isolated operation.

The case of Stuart's ride around McClellan, during the Peninsula campaign, is altogether different. There the armies were for the time stationary when opposite one another. Lee had no intention of undertaking any movement till his cavalry had returned. Stuart brought back most valuable information, which assisted greatly in the general movements of the subsequent campaign. Similarly, the partisan work of small parties like that of Colonel Mosby may serve a most useful purpose, and cannot be conducted with too much audacity. But Stoneman's raid seems to have gained advantages for the Federal Army which, though important, were dearly purchased by the loss of the battle of Chancellorsville. The more one considers that battle, the more clear it becomes that it was the absence of the Federal cavalry which made possible Jackson's turning movement. Under ordinary circumstances, the detachment of so large a force as that of Jackson's to move at first completely away from the battle-field, and then round the enemy's flank and rear, would be a very risky undertaking. It was possible and successful, first, because from the nature of the country nothing of the movement could be seen from the actual Federal position until it was too late, and, secondly, because the Confederate cavalry were able, in the absence of any corresponding force on the other side, to feel all the approaches to the Federal position and to ascertain exactly where their right wing lay. The small

165

number of possible exits from the Federal position towards that of Lee made it possible for Lee to hold them as if they were defiles, whilst Jackson, with the help of the cavalry, was working round to the vulnerable point.

The whole story of the Federal action during these battles seems to carry the same moral as that which is pressed in my first article. The decisions from Washington and the criticisms from Washington, based upon the loose and rampant public opinion of the day, were in every instance wrong, and were disastrous to the cause of the Union. Well would it be if the survivors of the Administration by which those hasty judgments were formed would now realize what the effect was of their deciding upon the course of action to be taken without having before them any of the data for such decisions. If now they would only understand the danger they entailed upon their country by their interference in the conduct of war—the most difficult of all arts—without any knowledge of its methods or of its principles, one might hope that the chastened and wise public opinion so formed would be an incalculable future benefit to all self-governing nations.

AN ENGLISH VIEW OF THE CIVIL WAR
PART V

In his fifth article Wolseley, after further remarks on *Gettysburg, surveys western operations: Corinth, Bragg's invasion of Kentucky, Vicksburg, Chattanooga, and Chickamauga. We may feel he did not grasp fully the importance of these operations—perhaps because he was not sufficiently familiar with American geography and rail connections. Vicksburg held logistical significance as the Confederacy's rail link with the southwest; so too was Chattanooga a major artery. Wolseley's assertion that the western campaigns were waged to secure recruiting districts is perhaps better applicable to Bragg's invasion of Kentucky, but here the geographical position of Kentucky, bordering on the Ohio River and a link between Missouri and western Virginia, should be recognized by the modern reader. In his essay on Sherman, written later, he described Vicksburg as a turning point in the war.*

Wolseley's estimates of three captains are notable. Henry W. Halleck, who commanded the western campaign before being elevated to the post of general in chief, receives a judgment that indicates no appreciation of the "devoted student of military art and science and of the laws of war," but rather fails to discover "the least evidence of his having ever given a decision which represented more than the embodied prejudice of the moment." Braxton Bragg, Confederate commander in the west, comes off no better: he was seen as a leader who could not inspire the confidence of his men and a soldier ignorant of the ABCs of generalship. The criticism of his failure to take Kentucky, fundamentally a result of a divided command, is sustained by modern scholars. U. S. Grant, conqueror of Vicksburg and Chattanooga, receives measured credit, though in amount far short of that allotted by his admirers. General Sherman also is handed good marks.

AN ENGLISH VIEW
OF THE CIVIL WAR

V

IN MY last article I dealt with the operations in the East, which are described in the third volume of *The Century's* papers on the Civil War. With a few further remarks on that subject, I shall pass on to consider the story of the campaigns in the West, which are also placed before the public in that volume.

The silence which was necessarily imposed upon General Burnside by loyalty to the Federal authorities has been, fortunately for us, broken through by Major Mason's highly irregular, but very interesting, personal invasion of General Burnside's headquarters. Very dramatic, certainly, is the scene described (page 101) where the Federal commander, after his terrible defeat, sitting "on an old log and being provided with crackers, cheese, sardines, and a bottle of brandy (all luxuries to a Confederate), discussed this lunch, as well as the situation," with the Confederate officer who had surreptitiously secured the interview with him.

It is very characteristic of that kind of West Point comradeship which was never wholly lost among the men who, on the two sides, were doing their best to kill one another, that Burnside should have been anxious to let the able soldiers opposed to him know, what he could not tell his own army, "that he was not responsible for the attack on Fredericksburg in the manner in which it was made, as he was himself under orders and was not much more than a figure-head."

Who, then, was responsible for this and for similar incidents? There exist in all professions certain men who make their way in the world by pandering to popular prejudices. In the army and the navy the form which this particular quality takes is one which is common in all countries, but in England and America it has a

171

special character of its own. During peace, the business of these men is to find excellent military reasons for the penny-wise economies which suit the taste of ministers who want to present a favorable budget to their countrymen. During war, their business is to clothe in military phraseology, and perhaps in army orders, the current popular prejudices of the time. Now, there is no wish to judge here of General Halleck's private character, or to say that, as a public servant, he may not have possessed many high qualities. But, taking the history of these campaigns from the time when he was appointed to the general command of the armies of the United States till the moment when, on "the coming of Grant," he was reduced to the position of a highly useful subordinate, I cannot trace the least evidence of his having ever given a decision which represented more than the embodied prejudices of the moment. There was a popular feeling that the mighty Army of the Potomac ought to brush from its path and easily destroy its numerically-inferior opponent; therefore the one thing said to be wanted was that it should go straight at its enemy and attack that enemy wherever found. Hence the orders from Washington for the disastrous attack on Fredericksburg, and hence the fatal persistence in that attack after all chance of surprising Lee, or of taking him at a disadvantage, had utterly disappeared.

When Lee began to move to his left after Chancellorsville, he offered General Hooker an obvious opportunity to overwhelm his right, which was still at Fredericksburg, and to threaten Richmond, long before any possible danger could have arisen to Washington with its powerful defences. But Lee was able to count with confidence upon the fears of a capital city and of the government within it for their own safety. The event proved that he was right. The mere suggestion by Hooker that to attack Lee's right was the proper course to pursue was sufficient to cause the removal of that general from his command. After Gettysburg, the popular impression appears to have been that the Confederate Army had been routed and that the Federal Army was virtually intact. The true state of the case was that the Confederate Army had certainly suffered very severely. It had been repulsed and defeated, but it was in no sense disorganized, and the Federal Army was in no condition for an effective general advance.

According to the evidence supplied by this volume, General

172

Meade, at Gettysburg, appears to have done all that any one but a man of quite transcendent military genius could have done to organize an effective pursuit. Few soldiers can, therefore, read without some angry feeling the letter which Halleck then sent to Meade. "I need hardly say to you that the escape of Lee's army without another battle has created great dissatisfaction in the mind of the President, and it will require an active and energetic pursuit on your part to remove the impression that it has not been sufficiently active heretofore." That feeling must necessarily be increased by his further missive in answer to Meade's natural and immediate reply, asking to be relieved from the command of the army. "My telegram stating the disappointment of the President at the escape of Lee's army was not intended as a censure, but as a stimulus to an active pursuit." Clearly General Halleck was in his wrong place. If, after Meade had won for the Federals the first great victory of the war over Lee's army, it was advisable then and there to remove him, the first letter would have been a fitting preparatory step to that end. Otherwise, to say that it was not a censure, and yet send it, was an act of feebleness, and displayed great ignorance of how a general commanding an army in the field should be dealt with. What pursuit had Halleck carried out after Shiloh? Of all men in the war, Halleck was the last who ought to have reproached another man for not adequately reaping the fruits of victory. Jackson's principle is always sound—never to "let up in pursuit" while pursuit is possible. But pursuit must have been begun in order to be followed up. An attack on the Confederates on the 4th July, if it had been possible for the Federal Army, would probably have been disastrous to the Confederates, because of their want of ammunition. No one who was not then present in the Federal Army can judge if it was possible. No one who was present at Gettysburg seems to have considered that it could be made. Under those circumstances, Halleck's business, as the chief military adviser of the government, was clearly to have pointed out to the President, "It is impossible to judge without being on the spot whether it would have been possible to do more than Meade has done; but as long as we retain him in command we must give him every sign of our confidence and all encouragement." It would have been easy so to word an earnest belief in his future success as to suggest an eager pursuit.

It is not proposed to enter closely into what is called the "Meade-Sickles controversy." There are evidently exaggerations on both sides. General Meade, having only just succeeded to the command of the army before the battle of Gettysburg, was in a very difficult position. He seems to have used considerable judgment in the mode in which he brought up his reserves to the right place and at the right time. If he was unjust, as he is charged with being, in his report of the share of the different corps in the action, he only failed in what is an almost impossible task. No general can know for long after a battle all the details of what has happened in it. On the other hand, "councils of war" are recorded under Meade and other generals in this war as though they were the most natural and legitimate things in the world. It is difficult to conceive the circumstances under which such councils as are here described, and by means of which the general in command would seem to endeavor to transfer his own responsibility to the shoulders of the majority of the council's members, can be other than a blunder and a sign of weakness. Newspaper reports of wars have, I think, often tended to create very unfortunate popular impressions as to the frequency of these councils in all campaigns, which may even affect soldiers. Whenever a number of generals are known to be assembled at headquarters, those in search of news naturally jump to the conclusion that some event is about to take place, and announce to their readers that a "council of war" is being held. Nine times out of ten the generals have only been assembled to give such information as they possess, to state their views, and to receive their orders. The character of such a proceeding is altogether changed when it is announced as a deliberative "council of war"—the abomination of all strong men, a byword for inefficiency and want of decision, and for weakness of action in all military matters. The decision of Meade's "council of war" on the second day at Gettysburg, like that arrived at by most councils of war, was not to attack, and, therefore, as it fortunately proved, to remain where they were and accept battle. This decision cannot be taken as a model for future imitation, though it happened in this instance to be the right course, as it turned out.

On one point more there is a word to be said before we pass from the East to the West. The evidence appears to be clear that on the afternoon of the first day of Gettysburg, at 4 o'clock, General Ewell had his corps, 20,000 strong, ready in column of attack to assault Culp's Hill. (Page 411.) The evidence is equally clear that, in all human probability, if that attack had then been delivered, it would have been successful, and that, if successful, the whole of Cemetery Ridge would have become untenable. Further, it is clear that Lee stopped that attack against Ewell's judgment. As the case arose, and as the facts were, there can be no question that this was an unfortunate decision. Lee was aware of the advance of Slocum's corps to the support of the Federals, and knew that his own army was not yet concentrated, but that, in all probability, it would be concentrated more effectively than the Federals could be by the following morning. This was the evidence before him at the time, and the reasoning to be inferred from it, under all the circumstances of the case, leads one to think that he was justified in postponing the attack as he did. If Lee had then known what we now know, it may be assumed that he would have attacked; but had we been in his position then, it is tolerably certain that most generals would have done as he did. It is not by the knowledge we now have of all the circumstances that such a decision as that of Lee must be judged, but by the knowledge of the facts which he himself then possessed. That this knowledge was not more accurate was, no doubt, due to the previous absence of Stuart and his cavalry. It was the only campaign of the war in which Lee fought blindfold, and he bitterly paid the penalty for so fighting. It would be rather interesting to know whether disappointment at losing the precious opportunity did or did not, during the following days, somewhat affect the vigor of Ewell's cooperation. Something of the usual energy of the Confederates seems to have been missing on that side, and though it may be attributed chiefly to the delay and the uncertainty of the hour of Longstreet's attack, other causes probably contributed, and this disappointment on Ewell's part was most likely among them.

There seems to be this general peculiarity about these campaigns in the West—that they were fought very much to secure recruiting districts. Where the condition of feeling was such that it made all the difference whether the district was in the occupation of the Federal or the Confederate troops, and whether the State authorities were in sympathy with Washington or Richmond, it is obvious that the conditions are very unlike those which usually obtain in European warfare. The only very analogous wars to which one can go back for similar conditions in this respect are those of Wallenstein and Gustavus Adolphus. Gustavus, when he died, left to his successor several armies, though he had entered Germany with but one. It made all the difference that he had been able to clear the Protestant districts of the Imperial troops, and to establish recruiting depots there. It is obvious that the wisdom of military movements, and the relative importance of certain campaigns, cannot, under these circumstances, be judged on precisely the same principles on which one would judge contests between the different nations in Europe.

If the statements as to the condition of popular sentiment in California and in the West during the earlier years of the war, which are furnished us in some of these papers, are to be relied upon, it is evident that the so-called New Mexican campaign was a much more important matter, small as were the forces engaged in it, than it has been supposed to be. As General Grant has said, the Confederacy, without large territories to extend into, was doomed, even if it succeeded in establishing its independence. It looks as if, but for the judicious arrangements made by the Federal commander, the Confederate forces, after their successes at San Augustine Springs and Valverde, might have formed an imposing army in New Mexico and Texas. Such an army, if properly supported from Richmond, might have enabled the various Confederate sympathizers to make head in California, and to secure the all-important Pacific Coast, with its important gold supply. It is scarcely possible to overrate the difference which that would have made in the conditions of the war. Probably the Confederacy, cut off as it was from all the outside world by the original mistakes of Mr. Davis's administration, could not have afforded to furnish supplies for this New Mexico campaign. But considering the initial success which attended it, and that it failed almost entirely from lack of material resources, one is led to think it would have been worth a more serious effort.

The junction of Van Dorn and Price with General Beauregard's forces, after the battle of Shiloh and the retreat from Corinth, seems to show clearly how easy would have been that junction in the mode suggested in my first article, prior to the Pea Ridge campaign and the battle of Shiloh. Then it would, in all probability, have been decisive as far as the battle of Shiloh itself was concerned, and at least for the year it would have left the whole West in the hands of the Confederacy. Considering the state of feeling prevailing at that time, it is impossible to gauge what might not have been the effect in the creation of new Southern forces. The retreat from Corinth seems to have been an extremely skilfully-contrived movement on the part of General Beauregard. General Halleck appears to have done about as little as it was possible for a man to do with the imposing forces and the able soldiers, Grant, Sherman, and Sheridan, who were with him. The regathering of the Confederate forces at Tupelo, and the scattering of the great Union Army, are among the most curious incidents of the war. General Beauregard had done great things for the army under his command during the halt at Corinth and Tupelo. Under his fostering care it had vastly improved both in discipline and in military training. It was a Confederate misfortune when ill-health obliged him to leave and hand over command to General Bragg. The whole of Bragg's ill-advised invasion of Kentucky and the simultaneous movements which led to the battles of Iuka and Corinth, in September and October, 1862, can, it seems, be only justly judged by taking into account the question of the recruiting districts. Bragg's advance into Kentucky was a mere flash in the pan, not because of any strategical or tactical considerations, in the ordinary sense of the term, but because Kentucky did not rise in support of the Confederate cause. Whatever may have been the reason,—whether the actual amount of anti-Union feeling in the State had been exaggerated, or because, as Bragg thought, the bluegrass region was too rich to allow men readily to sacrifice their wealth and ease for any cause,—the fact remains that Bragg's invasion was undertaken to gain recruiting districts; that is, in other words, to afford the people of Kentucky the chance of rising in support of Southern independence. The attempt was a failure; the people did not enlist even in sufficient numbers to make up the waste which the campaign itself entailed. It is, therefore, difficult to see how any change in the handling of troops could have made much difference in the final result. "The people have too many fat cattle and are too well off to fight," was General Bragg's commentary upon the conduct of the Kentuckians.

177

Van Dorn's movement on Corinth to make a direct attack upon it, instead of manœuvring Rosecrans out of it, was a mistake that seems obvious on the face of the facts. When Bragg had been intrusted with the chief command in the district, it was an enormous blunder on the part of the Confederate Government to place Price's forces under the command of Van Dorn. This arrangement, made without notice, suddenly deprived Bragg of the support upon which he had counted; that is clear enough. It distinctly violated the principle so well expressed afterwards by President Lincoln, that it is not wise "to swap horses whilst you are crossing a stream." As far as one can now judge of the relations of time and place, there was not time, it would seem, for Price to have moved with considerable effect upon Nashville, as Bragg had ordered him to do. At all events, his long circuitous movement to join Van Dorn was a waste of force, even apart from the disastrous termination of that movement in the battle of Corinth (October 4, 1862). Buell's army was exposed to very serious risk in the movement from Nashville upon Louisville, and that risk would have been greatly increased if Price had moved as rapidly as possible upon Nashville. General Bragg was a commander who seems to have been very uncertain in his action. At times he was both skilful in his arrangements and enterprising in his movements. Suddenly his skill deserted him at the most critical moments. During his bold but useless invasion of Kentucky, he was, no doubt, right in considering that everything depended on a proper cooperation between him and General Kirby Smith. No doubt the authorities at Richmond were largely to blame for not definitely appointing one man to command the joint expedition from the moment the invasion of Kentucky had been determined upon. Nevertheless, from the evidence before us, it seems clear that Bragg was supplied with sufficient information as to Buell's move to have enabled him to fall upon Buell's flank during his march from Nashville to Louisville.

The decisive effect of such a move was so obvious that Bragg would clearly have been able to call upon General Smith to support him, and the junction of the two forces ought to have been made by Smith's junction with Bragg rather than by Bragg joining Smith. It is difficult to see how, if Bragg, supported as rapidly as possible by Smith, had fallen upon Buell during the march,— still more, if simultaneously, as Bragg wished, Price had moved upon Nashville, instead of moving round to join Van Dorn at Corinth,—Nashville or Louisville could have escaped falling into the hands of the Confederate generals. Probably in that case they would have been able to strike back in time to intercept the retreat of the Union force from Cumberland Gap. If, as the Confederate writers seem to believe, the effect of so great a success would have been to induce Kentucky to throw itself heartily into the cause of the South, the result would have been most important. Without that, it is obvious that just as Lee's invasion of Pennsylvania caused numbers of the local militia to come to the aid of the Union forces, so the approach of Bragg's army to the borders of Ohio and Indiana tended to raise fresh armies against him. No doubt much of the relative ill-success, in proportion to numbers, which subsequently attended Buell's movement may be attributed to the rawness of that general's troops, who were little better than mere recruits, whilst Bragg's men had been trained to war in several campaigns. In the action of Perryville (October 8, 1862), which followed upon Buell's gradual concentration of force at Louisville, and the consequent retreat of Bragg, Buell evidently succeeded in imposing upon Bragg as to the direction in which he intended to move. Bragg's success in the fight and his successful retreat afterwards appear to have been very much the result of his possessing an army much better in hand and more experienced in fighting than it was possible for Buell to have collected under the circumstances at the time.

Though not prepared to modify the opinion expressed elsewhere, that General Lee was the most remarkable man the Civil War produced, and though I cannot admit that General Grant possessed at all the same genius for command, yet it must be at once confessed that it is an immense relief to turn from the mirage of these indecisive battles and movements in the West to the story of the Vicksburg campaign. It is very natural that General Sherman should rate very highly the military genius of General Grant, for the great services which, in the summer of 1863, Grant rendered to the Union made him tower head and shoulders over all others who could possibly be placed in supreme command of the Federal armies. McClellan had become by this time a political character, and as long as Mr. Lincoln remained President it was impossible that he should be again appointed Commander-in-Chief.

179

The elections had already begun to show the effect which the depression caused by Fredericksburg and Chancellorsville was producing throughout the North. Halleck, applying to a campaign which he could not stop till its success was assured the mischievous interference which had been in the East so fruitful in disaster, at last palpably stultified himself, even in the eyes of the President and the Cabinet. The scheme of the Vicksburg campaign was both original and brilliant in conception, and vigorous and fortunate in execution. Sherman, loyally anxious to acknowledge his own opposition to it, contributed, no doubt, largely to cause the military skill which Grant had shown to be appreciated throughout the country.

In its general character of sudden movement, by which he enlisted on the side of his army the advantages of surprise by a concentrated force, unentangled by any line of supplies, the Vicksburg campaign closely resembles many of Jackson's operations. It had something of the character of his campaign in the Shenandoah Valley, and something that recalled his movements which preceded the second Bull Run. The news of such strokes as Grant delivered in rapid succession at Port Gibson, South Fork, Fourteen-Mile Creek, Raymond, Jackson, Champion's Hill, and Big Black River, coming at a moment when gold had gone up to a figure hitherto unknown, and in the very weeks which immediately succeeded Chancellorsville and preceded Lee's invasion of Pennsylvania, must, indeed, have seemed like a sudden break of light through the darkest of clouds. No wonder, therefore, that public attention became concentrated on the siege of Vicksburg. The very fact that six weeks elapsed before the surrender was probably in favor of Grant's reputation. It gave time for representative people from the North to gather in the besieger's lines, and hear from the victorious army all the particulars about the successful campaign, and to learn how entirely it depended for its conception and execution upon the skill of one man, and upon the confidence which he had inspired in his subordinates.

When, almost at the same moment, the fall of Vicksburg and the battle of Gettysburg made the 4th of July, 1863, almost a new birthday for the Union, the general self-congratulation of the North made all hearts crave for a hero—for some one in whom to feel confidence. All this tended greatly, and very naturally, to increase the importance of Grant's position. In the West, the work accomplished and the victories achieved were palpably Grant's own, but from the first the general public, at least, seem to have refused to Meade the honors of the battle which had been won under his orders. When, in consequence of the defeat at Chickamauga, the virtual investment of Rosecrans's army in Chattanooga, and the unhappy condition of Burnside's army at Knoxville, the aspect of affairs in the West again became gloomy and threatening, it followed as a matter of course that General Grant should be intrusted with the task of restoring the Union affairs in the West.

General Bragg seems to have shown, in the campaigns which had intervened since his retreat from Kentucky, a strange mixture of qualities. At the battle of Stone's River he successfully planned and carried out an attack upon the right flank of Rosecrans's army. But when everything was going in his favor, he abandoned his advantage, and, instead of crushing in the defeated wing upon the other wing, made a gratuitous attack upon the strongest intact position left to the enemy, and at a point where his previous success gave him no advantage. Rosecrans skilfully manœuvred Bragg out of his defensive positions, and forced him back beyond Chattanooga in June and July, 1863. The art of finding out the position, movements, and intentions of the enemy is the ABC of generalship. Of this art General Bragg was not only ignorant, but he lacked even the power to put together into one intelligible whole the information daily supplied by his outposts and obtained from other sources. At Chickamauga the victory was clearly in no way due to Bragg, and his incapacity to realize the nature of the situation presented to him was very much alike at the two battles of Stone's River and Chickamauga. He seems in the first instance to have contrived with considerable skill the virtual investment of Rosecrans in Chattanooga, but it is difficult to understand why, if his force was sufficient to allow him to detach Longstreet at all, he should not have attacked Bridgeport before the arrival of Hooker's troops. To have done so would have deprived the Union troops of their only means of constructing boats within reach of the beleaguered army. Bragg seems to have relapsed into a condition of careless confidence after the important positions round Chattanooga had been, in the first instance, secured. So much so that things were left in a condition which only required that a vigorous leader should restore confidence to the army of the Union to make it certain that the besiegers would lose all the results of their previous successes.

So far as one may judge from the papers contributed to this series, those who fought under Grant at Chattanooga are by no means disposed to credit him with any great share in the work of opening the "cracker line," or even in planning the battle itself. I am disposed to think that they hardly do General Grant justice. It may be very true that the apparently splendid effect which, as the broad results only were heard of at a distance, appeared to attend the placing of Grant in command of the army and the dismissal of Rosecrans, was something of a *coup de théâtre*. It may be very true that the arrangements for opening communications had been at least partly planned under Rosecrans before Grant's arrival at Chattanooga, on the 23d October, 1863, and that they were mainly the work of subordinates. It may be true that, in the actual moment of victory at that place, the successful charge of Thomas was due to the spontaneous enthusiasm of the men, and that it was actually carried out in excess of Grant's intention or order. If it be assumed that Grant trusted entirely for his success to Sherman's attack upon the Confederate right, or trusted for success even to the combined effect of Sherman's and of Hooker's movement, it is no doubt true that Grant's original plan was not carried out. Grant certainly made many changes in his plans of attack, but surely this sort of criticism is not by any means fair to a general commanding an army in battle! The changes of plans seem to have been only such as the changing circumstances rendered necessary. General Grant acknowledges that Rosecrans offered him many most valuable suggestions, and rather pithily says: "My only surprise was that he had not carried them out." This may or may not be quite fair to Rosecrans, and it may be the case that the arrangements were being worked out as rapidly as circumstances admitted before Grant's arrival. But, taking the whole of the facts as they stand, it seems clear that while Grant, as any sensible man in his case would have done, took advantage of whatever had been effected before his arrival that promised to be useful, and listened to all suggestions that were likely to assist in the solution of a very difficult problem, nevertheless it was his energy and skill which carried the whole of the scheme through the great victory of Chattanooga. No doubt, as continually occurs in war, things did not happen exactly in the way he had designed they should happen, but he was ready to do the best thing that was to be done under all the fresh circumstances as they arose. The actual working-out, the general superintendence of the whole scheme, were his and his alone.

The panic which appears at the last in that battle to have seized upon a portion of the Confederate Army was not, I think, the improbable event General Bragg seems to have considered it. Nothing tells so much on the confidence and courage of an army as the conviction that their general has been outmanœuvred by the enemy. Now, his army, it seems, never had any very special confidence in Bragg, and every misfortune is possible to the army that has no confidence in its leader. The battle of Chickamauga, and the knowledge that he had actually absented himself from the field under the belief that the battle was lost, must have greatly diminished their faith in him, even in the moment of victory. Then, after their successful investment of the Union army in Chattanooga, with everything to raise their spirits and depress those of their opponents, there came upon them one blow after another; first, the opening of the "cracker line," which meant, as they well knew, that there was no longer any hope of seeing the Federal Army surrender from want of food and ammunition; then the successive reenforcements of the Federals, the arrival of Hooker and of Sherman, the most unwise withdrawal of Longstreet's force, and of the detachments sent afterwards to reenforce him, just before Grant was ready to attack. Then came the successful ruse and surprise by which Thomas carried the outposts and picket-lines of the besiegers, and took up a threatening position all along the front of their works; then General Hooker, by the successful employment of superior forces against a weak part of the Confederate line, necessitated the withdrawal of their troops from Lookout Mountain; and then came Sherman's successful surprise of their pickets on the right, by means of which he contrived to get his troops across the river without loss, and to establish them, unknown to his enemy, on their right flank.

I think one may well guess what must have been the effect of all these Federal operations upon the minds of the Confederate soldiers. It is quite true that little material advantage was actually gained by Grant by his attack on the Chattanooga position. But each succeeding event tended to depress the spirits of the Confederate Army, to shake their confidence in their leaders, whilst, on the other hand, every fresh move of Grant's tended to restore confidence to the Federal troops, and to make them believe they were being skilfully led. There is a sense in which, with armies as with individuals, deep depression, when once relieved, tends to pass rapidly into a condition of high exaltation, all the more effective because of the reaction from the previous opposite feeling. The army under the command of General Thomas, after all the misery and starvation they had courageously endured, seem to have passed through these phases. Nothing could have been better calculated to excite in them an extreme and passionate desire to go through any sacrifice for victory than that they should be kept for some time idly waiting in front of the enemy, whose forward position they had already seized, and compelled to witness the fighting being done for them by the armies that had come to relieve them—by Sherman on their left, and by Hooker on their right.

Those are circumstances under which you may securely trust Anglo-Saxon troops, at least when once released from the leash, to go forward, as those of General Thomas did, with a bound that carries everything before it, and that probably exceeds both your wishes and your orders. The apparently-sudden change in temperament of their opponents seems to have been all that was needed to convert the discouragement of the Southerners into actual flight. Grant certainly deserves all possible credit for having, within the time between his arrival and the battle of Chattanooga, done so much thus to change the condition of the *morale* of his own army, and that which was opposed to it. He further deserves the credit of having realized how important that change was to him, and how advantage could best be taken of it. The story told in these papers is a fitting introduction to the time when Grant was to be transferred to a yet higher command, and to be pitted against very different opponents from Generals Bragg and Pemberton.

It is rather curious that this third volume on the Civil War should close with an account of Longstreet's first independent command, in which, far from remaining perpetually on the defensive, he committed himself to the particularly bloody attack upon Knoxville, which, ill-prepared and ill-advised, ended in failure.

AN ENGLISH VIEW OF THE CIVIL WAR
PART VI

It is in his sixth article that Wolseley makes his unusual appraisal of the strategic significance of the Charleston operations, wherein he sees involved the question of naval attack versus land defense. Charleston, to him, was a modern instance for Britain, a nation still drawing lessons from the days of Nelson and earlier. The battle proves, Wolseley thinks (doubtless with a side-glance at the British admiralty) that naval fire alone is unreliable and that army and navy must cooperate and support one another in bombardment of harbor forts. He cites Charleston instead of New Orleans because Admiral Farragut did not have to reduce the forts below New Orleans to take the city; and Mobile Bay he considered "almost purely an affair of ships against ships."

We find here, too, renewed admiration for P. G. T. Beauregard, the great Creole general and skillful defender of Charleston.

But above all, the critic analyzes the beginning of the "last act" of the war: the sledgehammer blows Grant struck in Virginia in the spring and summer of 1864. A leading theme is the contrast of Union and Confederate command systems that placed Lee at so marked a disadvantage; and although Grant brandished a hammer, Lee's army was a worthy anvil until Cold Harbor. Up to the date of Cold Harbor (June 3, 1864) advantage lay with the South.

189

AN ENGLISH VIEW
OF THE CIVIL WAR

VI

THE LAST volume of this most interesting series of papers begins with an account of the attack upon and defence of Charleston. Were I bound to select out of all four volumes the set of papers which appears of most importance at the present moment, not only from an American, but also from a European, point of view, I should certainly name those which describe the operations at Charleston.

All European powers, England especially, are deeply interested in this question of naval attack *versus* land defence. Since the time of the Civil War many changes have, no doubt, taken place; many inventions have been made which greatly affect the relations between ships and forts. The size of guns has enormously increased. Torpedo work in all its forms has been immensely developed, and the use of the electric light has materially helped all night operations. Ramming has been taken more and more into account in the construction of all men-of-war. Various forms of armored ships have come into existence and have been subjected to all such experiments as peace admits. It is never very safe, however, to assume that anything will take place in war precisely as the result of peace trials would lead one to believe. It would be no good reason, however, for refusing to adopt new plans or novel inventions in our next war because they have not been tried and found to answer well in some former one. To act upon such a principle would be to handicap very heavily the nation that adopts it. It would be to hand over many great advantages to a more courageous, a more intelligent, and a more enterprising enemy. But it is only possible safely and usefully to apply the results of peace experiments to war preparations by studying as closely as we can the experience with which past wars supply us. Now, since the great Civil War in America came to an end, there has been no contest in which, on anything like the same scale, many of the points which the efforts to take Charleston illustrated have been tested by actual fighting. It is interesting to summarize the facts as they appear in these papers. We have ample evidence both from the side of the defence and of the attack. Practically there is no important difference in the conclusions to which the serial papers lead us.

If there was in the whole of the South one fortified harbor which the government of the Union was anxious to seize, that harbor was Charleston. The whole resources of the Federal dockyards—it may be fairly added, of the outside world also—the inventive genius of the most inventive people upon earth, and especially of the most able constructors, were unstintingly employed in preparing an armada for the attack which it was intended should be irresistible. The ablest naval officers who could be found were placed in command. In only one respect can it be considered that the attack was deficient. It was not possible to spare for the cooperating army more than a relatively small military force. Practically, therefore, the success of the attack depended on the fleet, increased to the fullest strength, being able to reduce the land defences. During four years of war, despite all these efforts, Charleston held out, and it only fell at last because the advance of General Sherman's army and the common progress of the war necessitated the withdrawal of the garrison.

Nor is it possible to consider that these records represent at the present time only "ancient history." We in England have lately had much discussion on the relations between land defences and the employment of fleets. Almost all our arguments are taken from the time of Nelson, or from even earlier days. No one who looks into the matter can fail to see that at least these records of the Civil War represent facts much more closely analogous to the present relations between fleets and land batteries than any other operations of the kind in previous wars. Many of the details of the story add greatly to its interest and value. General Beauregard, the successful defender of the place, is able to show that in many respects the defence was under serious disadvantages. He speaks of the "inadequate force under him" (page 4), whilst it was the boast of the

Secretary of the Federal Navy that the preparations of the North by sea were of a kind "such as the hand of man had never yet put afloat." (Page 5.) The result of the first attack was wholly unexpected. "The repulse had not been looked upon as a thing possible by the North," and the news of the failure "engendered a heavy gloom of disappointment and discouragement." The Admiral was, of course, sacrificed by the Navy Department. He, however, like many other unjustly-used commanders, might securely trust that time would brings its revenge. The evidence of all those whose judgment can weigh with posterity tends to blast the reputation of the men who, by suppressing reports and perverting facts, continued to make it appear that the fault lay with the navy and its commanders.

As Admiral Rodgers says, not only had Admiral Du Pont been selected because of his well-founded reputation, but the commander of every turret ship and of the "Ironsides" was a man of known and approved skill and courage. None of these doubted the necessity for Admiral Du Pont's retirement from the unsuccessful attack. All of them consider that he was unjustly dealt with; and that the simple cause of the failure lay in the fact "that, whatever degree of impenetrability" the ships might have, they possessed "no corresponding quality of destructiveness as against forts." It is the serious duty of all our officers of the sister service to consider these experiences. If history has any value as a guide to the fighting of the future, it goes to prove how dangerous it will be to all naval officers if by any action of theirs they create a false public opinion as to the relative powers of ships and guns. If, as it would seem some of them wish to do, they succeed in making the public think that one gun afloat is worth several ashore, it is they who will have to make good that claim by success, when they are asked to attack heavily-armed and well-planned coast batteries.

The estimate in America at the time of the attack upon Charleston was altogether different; and most certainly the engines of war which have been invented since those days do not tend to redress the balance which during the Civil War told against the Federal Navy. The practice from guns fired from a floating target can never be reliable, and most certainly not as reliable as the practice from guns ashore. None but a fanatic on the subject will deny this, and the experience we gained by the bombardment of Alexandria in 1882 proves this conclusively. Our firing on that occasion may, I think, be fairly described as erratic, although the conditions as to sea and weather were most favorable, and the enemy's return fire was extremely feeble—indeed, beneath contempt.

The one success which attended the naval attack upon Charleston is at least as significant as the general failure. The attack upon the Confederate batteries on Morris Island, which paved the way for the bombardment of Fort Sumter, was successful precisely when the fleet and army were able to combine in the attack, and because they did so combine. If this story be compared with that of Admiral Farragut's great success at New Orleans, when he passed the forts below that city, it will be seen that there was nothing in those events which tends to affect the force of the lesson taught by the attack on Charleston. As mentioned when discussing the capture of New Orleans in a former article, Admiral Farragut's success was mainly due to the moral effect produced by his gallant passage of the forts. Ship against fort, and gun for gun, he never reduced those forts, and seems to have inflicted very little damage upon them. Again, taking the whole story of the operations on the Mississippi together, it is clear that, while it was vitally important to the success of the Federal military operations throughout the vast theatre of war that the Federal, and not the Confederate, navy should dominate the waters of that great river, the result could not be secured by the navy alone. It was General Grant's reduction of Vicksburg and his capture of the other forts on the Mississippi which converted that river into the exclusively Federal highway that cleft the Confederacy in two. This cooperating action of the naval and military services, mutually supporting each other, and the fact that neither can be neglected without direct detriment to the other, seem to be among the most important lessons taught in the whole history of the American Civil War. Those lessons are of world-wide interest. I do not think they are affected by the story of Admiral Farragut's brilliant success at Mobile Bay, into the details of which I must not allow myself to enter, as it was, practically, almost purely an affair of ships against ships.

Before leaving the subject I may venture, however, to express the admiration which all unprejudiced readers of these papers

must feel for the skill and judgment with which General Beauregard conducted the defence of Charleston. It may be gathered
from his article that he agrees in thinking that when forts are
fairly pitted against fleets the general officer in command on shore
ought to consider that he has a task before him which, with brave
men under him, he ought successfully to accomplish. And, further, that, as a rule, the naval commander intrusted with the attack of a well-fortified harbor will evince a prudent wisdom if he
arranges for the cooperation of such a land force as will clear
away some of the opposition with which his ships, if alone, would
have almost insuperable difficulties in dealing. Our own expedition to Kertch, during the Crimean War, supplies the very experience which is wanting to complete the lesson taught by the
attack on Charleston. At Kertch it was possible for a land expedition, supported by the full power of the navy, to gain just
those advantages which are illustrated by the successful second attack upon Morris Island. As the result of our combined attack on
Kertch, the navy secured a passage through the Straits of Yenikale,
which they could not have obtained for themselves, or without
the cooperation of the land force that had advanced upon Kertch.
On the other hand, the army could not have acted without the assistance of the navy, both in securing a point for landing and in
the direct support obtained from the guns of the fleet during the
disembarkation. The success of this combined operation opened
out the Sea of Azof to our gunboats, which, to use Mr. Kinglake's
graphic phrase, "carried the invasion into the very heart of the
Czar's dominions, and produced a material and moral effect almost
equal to all that was achieved by the terrible sufferings and fierce
struggles before Sebastopol."

The one thing, as General Beauregard has well pointed out,
which he could not have resisted would have been a well-appointed
and powerful Federal army, that would have cooperated with the
Federal navy in an attack upon his works on James Island. The
lessons as to the power which lies in the combined action of army
and navy, and as to the importance, at least for the purposes of
local defence, of a certain number of coast batteries, cannot be
ignored. It would be, however, a great injustice to one of the best
soldiers, most skilled engineers, and ablest strategists who fought

in the Civil War, were it not to be freely admitted that the defence owed much of its memorable success to the genius of General Beauregard, the Todleben of Charleston.

Through the scenes still to be enacted before the war was brought to an end, we enter now directly upon an examination of what must always be regarded as the "last act" of this great human drama. In this study, it is interesting and instructive to compare General Grant's own account of the preparation for "The Campaigns of 1864" with General Sherman's paper on "The Grand Strategy of the Last Year of the War." Again and again in the course of the great struggle between Grant and Lee one is struck by the relative disadvantage of the position occupied by the Confederate leader in one important respect. The "grand strategy" of which General Sherman speaks covered the whole field of war, and General Grant took upon himself the immediate supervision of the most important of all the operations upon which the several Federal armies were employed. General Sherman's Atlanta campaign and Butler's movements on the south of the James River were as much under his general direction as General Meade's Army of the Potomac. On the other hand, Lee does not seem to have had any actual control over the movements of the Confederate forces that did not belong strictly to his own army. One naturally somewhat hesitates to accept evidence which is given by other generals who cooperated with Lee, since we have had no corresponding evidence from himself. It has always struck me, however, that in some respects even Lee's very greatness made his position tend to at least one unfortunate result. Lee was so great, not only in character, in genius, and in reputation, but in the affections of the whole Confederacy, civil and military, that, if he was not to be the commander-in-chief of all the armies of the Confederacy and to direct and control their movements, no one else could effectually take that place. The importance of this fact comes out perhaps most clearly in the period after Cold Harbor, and in General Beauregard's evidence as to the proposals he made at Richmond, of which I shall have more to say presently.

The military student must not forget that Lee was not at the focus of information in regard to the general course of the war outside his own immediate field of operations; that he had no responsibility with regard to it, and could not take upon himself to act from moment to moment throughout the whole theatre of war, as General Grant did on his side. Whilst this was the case, no one in Richmond, on the other hand, liked to act in any decisive matter without consulting Lee. This seems to have given rise to a certain headlessness which, I think, is to be observed in the conduct of the Confederate authorities, civil and military, during this year of the war. It does not appear that this headlessness can be reckoned as the fault of any one particular man in Richmond. This fact could be illustrated by incident after incident throughout this volume, and those who read these pages with care will see for themselves what is meant. The majority will probably agree to some extent with what is said here, both as to the fact and as to the cause of it. The enormous superiority in the mechanical means of intercommunication throughout the States under the Federal Government made that possible for Grant which was not possible for Lee. All must agree with General Sherman that Grant's great merit as a commander was the ability and clearness of vision with which he grasped the whole of the situation. He saw not only the position of vantage in which he stood, but the fact that it was well worth while, and that it would be an economy of life in the long run, for the Union to pour out life and treasure unstintingly; that by so doing he must in the end wear out the Confederacy. Surely the Union owes its life to having found the man who was ready and able so to direct its overwhelming resources.

Whilst fully recognizing General Grant's clearness of perception and his boundless pluck and determination, it seems to me that, when the actual campaign from the Wilderness to Cold Harbor is closely and critically examined, few impartial educated soldiers will deny that throughout it Lee simply and completely outgeneralled his great opponent. To judge, as I must do, from these papers, it would seem that many very able Northern soldiers concur in this opinion. Which shall we take as the fairest summary of the feelings of the Northern army on this point? Major-General McMahon states:

The men could not help reading and discussing certain facts. Two years before, this same army had been placed much nearer Richmond with comparatively little loss. During Grant's advance from the Rapidan he had the advantage, of which he freely availed himself, of order-

197

ing troops to his assistance, not begging for them as McClellan did in vain. He depleted the defences of Washington at his pleasure, and of new troops more than the number of men with which he commenced the campaign joined him before its termination at Appomattox. The line of the peninsula and the advance to Cold Harbor and the Chickahominy had been McClellan's second plan. His first had been a movement from Urbana, with the possibility in view of crossing to the south side of the James and compelling the evacuation of Richmond and its defences. This plan had been overruled in Washington, and that of the peninsula, also suggested by McClellan, had been approved as a compromise. But the plan of an overland march to Richmond, while protected navigable waters within our control led to the very door, was fully tried between the 3d of May and the 15th of June and had failed. (Page 220.)

Then, again, let us turn to the briefer summary by Major-General Smith. It is more technical in its language, but it is, fully as much as the other, supported by a detailed examination of the conduct of the campaign. He writes, at page 230: "In speaking of a concentration much better than the one which was made by the Army of the Potomac, Jomini says: 'The logistics were contemptible.' "

Turn now to the other side, and see what was the feeling of the Southern army regarding each battle of the campaign. See how the evidence given us proves that at the Wilderness Lee had exactly anticipated the very point where Grant would cross the Rapidan. (General Law, page 118.) See how, taking advantage of the very movement he had anticipated, Lee flung his army upon the flank of the crossing enemy in such a direction that a part of Meade's army, had the whole operation been worked out as he intended, must have been cut off from the remainder, and driven into the river or the Wilderness in a condition of complete disorganization, if not to utter destruction. But the operation was not worked out as he intended. No; the course of the battle repeated incidents with which we are now familiar. General Longstreet's wing, arriving in magnificent order, was just a sufficient number of hours too late to produce the decisive result which Lee had justly reckoned upon. If analogy has any value, it is tolerably safe to say that, had Jackson been in Longstreet's place then, Jackson's troops would have reached the field, not perhaps in the magnificent order which

198

Longstreet had the art of imparting to his men, but exactly at the very hour when Lee expected them. Had Longstreet arrived in time, the Wilderness would have been, as an offensive stroke, as brilliantly successful as that of Cold Harbor was as a defensive one.

Probably the most severe risk which Grant ran throughout the campaign, and the most brilliant stroke which Lee had prepared, was at the passage of the North Anna River on May 24. Lee allowed both wings of Grant's army to cross the river unopposed. They were completely separated one from the other, for the centre had been successfully checked. Both wings were at Lee's mercy. But Lee was ill, too ill for action, and I think it may be said that this illness, which confined him to his tent and rendered him incapable of action for the time being, in all probability saved Grant's army from a blow that would have postponed, at least for that campaign, the advance on Richmond. If that operation had been postponed, it is difficult to see how Butler's army could have escaped destruction. That great results have arisen, and that the very course of history has been on several occasions seriously influenced, through the illness of generals commanding in the field, is well known. It would, however, be difficult to find a more striking illustration of the fact than is here presented to us.

I think it would not be unfair to sum up as follows the story of this campaign: On May 3–4, 1864, soon after midnight, the Army of the Potomac moved out from its position north of the Rapidan, and prepared for the passage of that river at the very point where Lee, watching it, had fully anticipated it would cross, and where he wished that it should cross. General Lee had deliberately chosen as his battle-ground the very place where Grant's army was now about to arrive. He knew this tangled wilderness well, and appreciated fully the advantages which such a field afforded for concealing his great inferiority of force, and for neutralizing the superior strength of his antagonist. General Grant's bold movements across the lower fords into the Wilderness, in the execution of his plan to swing past the Confederate Army and to place himself between it and Richmond, offered Lee the expected opportunity to strike a blow upon his flank, while his troops were stretched out on a very long line of march. Undoubtedly Lee expected that Longstreet's corps would be up at daylight on the following morning, May 6, but in point of fact it was still at least two hours' march away. That delay gave the Federals time to commence the attack, and partly to intrench themselves on the ground where they had been attacked upon crossing. As a result, the losses were not materially different on the two sides, or, at least, the action was relatively indecisive.

Nevertheless, Grant was foiled in his first attempt and began his movement towards Spotsylvania, to march round Lee's right. He was again anticipated in this movement, and nothing very decisive happened until June 11, after the failure of the two Federal attacks on June 10. Lee then somewhat anticipated the moment at which Grant's fresh turning attempt actually began, and the "Bloody Angle" on the 12th was the result. That was the only means, and it was but a partial success gained by the Federal general throughout the campaign. Despite the capture of 4,000 Confederates at this point, no impression could be made upon the interior lines. Grant again moved eastward, and for five days the two armies manœuvred, one against the other, with little fighting. On the 18th June a final attempt on Spotsylvania was terribly repulsed. On the 24th and 25th June occurred the incident of the North Anna, to which I have already alluded. For two days at least Grant's army was in as critical a position as such a force could well find itself in. Once more Grant slipped away, and once more he found his opponent facing him. This time the position on the Totopotomoy River was too strong to be assailed; so he moved off towards Cold Harbor.

It is alleged on page 228, by General W. F. Smith, on the authority of General Meade's own statement, that Meade, annoyed by the credit which Grant was acquiring for a campaign which had been entirely worked out in its details by him, deliberately made no arrangements for the attack which Grant had ordered. Whether this be actually true or not, there can be no doubt from all the evidence that, from some cause or other, in the concentration of the Federal Army before Cold Harbor, and in the attack on Lee's position, the Federal Army was simply mismanaged and sent to useless butchery. Grant himself appears to admit the mistake made there. Nevertheless, it would be most unfair to assume that he was responsible for the disastrous details of that action. He throws the blame upon no one, and his silence on the subject is highly honorable to him. His method consisted, and wisely consisted, in a general superintendence of the whole campaign against the South, whilst he left the details to the several commanders of armies. He especially abstained from removing General Meade from the command of the Army of the Potomac. As it stands, General Smith's statement is a most appalling indictment of General Meade. It amounts to this: that, because the newspapers did not do him the justice to which he considered himself entitled as regards the movements of the army he personally commanded, he allowed that army to have a dire disaster inflicted upon it. The one merit of the campaign was the firmness and sternness with which it was carried on—elements which were imported into it entirely by Grant, and not by Meade. If General Meade, from sheer, jealous sulkiness, did really allow the army under his command to be exposed to the awful slaughter it experienced at Cold Harbor, through lack of proper care and proper orders as to details, the crime was one for which no punishment, no condemnation, could be too severe.

It is quite true that by the end of the campaign Grant's doggedness had produced a certain effect upon the Confederate soldiery. All acknowledge it. But what was that effect? Undoubtedly they had begun to realize that, if the North would allow its soldiers to be exposed to such frightful butchery, the North might at that price triumph. But not for one moment did it modify the confidence of the Southern soldiery in their own great leader; and not even at the fatal moment of the surrender at Appomattox did a Southern soldier doubt that everything that any general could do for his army had been done by Lee. I fancy that if at Cold Harbor the proposal of the Irishman after the battle of the Boyne, "to swop leaders and fight it over again," could have been put to the two armies, there would not have been one hand on the Southern side held up to accept the offer. Would there have been none on the Northern? I fancy few of the Northern generals who knew all the circumstances would like much to put the question of the greatness of the two leaders to any such test. Of course, the opinion of armies is not always a fair one as to the capacity of generals. It is, however, a very important element in the actual power and effectiveness of a general in command. In this instance the opinion of the hour has been confirmed by the careful and critical examination of many able soldiers.

Meantime, while the Wilderness campaign had been proceeding, a very heavy blow had been struck against the South in the appointment of General Sheridan to the command of the Federal cavalry. Its organization as what is known in Europe as mounted infantry enabled the incomparably superior resources of the North in men, horses, and equipment to be developed with decisive effect. When, on the 9th May, 1864, at 6 A.M., Sheridan, with 10,000 horsemen, started on his Richmond raid, there was no force with Lee's army fitted to cope with him. Three days afterward the death of Stuart marked the end, at least as far as the Eastern campaigns were concerned, of the ascendency of the Southern horsemen. For an army like Lee's, already shortened in its supplies, this fact was of dire consequence.

It is interesting to compare the circumstances under which this raid was carried out with those which attended the cavalry raid under Stoneman. Both to some extent partook of that characteristic of all such movements, that "to take the enemy by surprise, and to penetrate his country, was easy enough; to withdraw from it was a more difficult matter." (Page 153, Vol. III.) In that respect General Sheridan had the important advantage which the position of Butler's army south of the James River gave him. He was thus provided with a secure point to make for, where he could obtain supplies and a safe starting point for his return march. Stoneman, on the other hand, was launched simply against the enemy's communications without a force sufficient to draw the whole of Stuart's cavalry after him. He therefore left them behind him, to serve Jackson admirably at Chancellorsville at the very time that the Federals were deprived of Stoneman's services. On the other hand, from the first the purpose of Sheridan's move was even more to ease Meade's fears as to the safety of his wagon-trains during the passage of the Rapidan in presence of Stuart's cavalry than to harass the enemy by attacking his communications. The movement was so made as to encourage and employ Stuart's cavalry during the general advance of the army. "Circumstances," as usual, "alter cases," and the practical difference of these two cases is well worth the thoughtful study of soldiers. Stoneman's raid, whatever its destructive effects, was a dangerous withdrawal from the Northern army of its eyes and ears at the very moment when it most needed them. Sheridan's raid contributed essentially to the general objects of the march of the Northern army, by keeping the

Southern cavalry fully engaged at a moment when they might have seriously hampered Grant's movements by attacking the enormous train which his lavishly-equipped army left stretching out behind it beyond the Rapidan.

Taking all other parts of the theatre of war into consideration, the balance of advantage this year, up to the date of Cold Harbor, was heavily in favor of the South. Sherman had certainly pressed Johnston toward Atlanta, but had gained no decisive advantage over him. Beauregard had heavily defeated Butler at Drewry's Bluff, and had, as General Grant happily expressed it, sealed him up between the James and the Appomattox rivers as completely as if he were in a "bottle tightly corked." The unfortunate expedition to the Red River had come to an end before the Cold Harbor campaign was over, and had not improved the general situation. In the Shenandoah Valley for the moment the Northern forces were certainly advancing successfully, but the number of troops there was altogether small, and General Early had been already ordered to begin the movement which was to take him up to the walls of Washington.

AN ENGLISH VIEW OF THE CIVIL WAR
PART VII

The SUMMER OF 1864 WITNESSED THE LAST GREAT CRISIS OF THE *war. Grant's losses of men, accompanied by his inability to inflict a mortal wound on Lee's army, and Sherman's slow advance upon Atlanta, evoked deep and bitter criticism of Union policy. Lincoln's grim determination to continue his policy and to support his generals "decided the fate of the war."*

President Davis, having grown impatient with General Joseph E. Johnston's Fabian retreat from Dalton, Georgia, replaced him with General Hood. Wolseley here censures Davis for relieving Johnston from command of a masterly retreat, and he discovers fresh substantiation for his aspersions on the Confederate "headlessness" of command— a fact that contributed so heavily to Lee's final failure to withstand Grant's numerical superiority and unified command.

In addition to the Atlanta campaign, Wolseley treats in his concluding article Early's and Sheridan's operations in the Shenandoah Valley, the Petersburg campaign, and the closing of the Federal net in early 1865.

AN ENGLISH VIEW
OF THE CIVIL WAR

VII

THE situation, however discouraging to the North it was for the moment, was soon now about to change. The siege was about to begin that was eventually to entail the fall of the Confederate capital and the capture of Lee's devoted army. By the end of June, 1864, it is not surprising that much pressure was brought to bear upon President Lincoln to remove Grant and, somewhat later, to stop General Sherman's southward movement. It was then that Mr. Lincoln's historic phrase, that he would not "swop horses whilst crossing a stream," settled the policy of the Federal Government. It decided the fate of the war.

If for the moment we turn our attention from the Army of the Potomac to the campaign of General Sherman against General Joseph E. Johnston, we there find plenty of very interesting and instructive matter. It is difficult to believe that the army of which General Johnston assumed command when the campaign began could have been altogether in the splendid condition of that period which is attributed to it by General Hood. It was the same army which had been disastrously defeated by Grant at Chattanooga, and since that event no circumstances had occurred which could have tended to restore its *morale,* heavily shaken as it was by that disaster. There may or may not have been some errors of detail in the disposition of the army for the defence of Rocky-face Mountain, but with forces so superior to him as those of Sherman's were at this period, it is difficult to see how Johnston could have adopted any other role than the defensive one he actually assumed. According to the careful calculation of Major Dawes (page 281), his own army stood to Sherman's as 64 to 100 in point of numbers, but certainly in every respect inferior in point of equipment, and more especially in the supply of ammunition. His own estimate, which puts the figures as low as 4 to 10, though it is probably too low, marks, no doubt, his opinion, at the time, of the fighting powers of the two armies. It is not quite fair (as Major Dawes seems to do) to reckon up the casual replacements and reenforcements which reach a general during a campaign as, necessarily, additions to his original strength. The total number of men "to be accounted for" as "available for battle," given by Major Dawes as 84,328, leaves an entirely false impression on the ordinary reader, as though it meant that General Johnston had at some one moment an army of that size under his orders. As regarded his day-to-day fighting strength, he was very much in the position of the man who, with a very inadequate income, should receive small sums of capital at different times which he had to treat as income. In the aggregate those small sums might possibly reach a considerable amount, and if he had received them altogether and early in life, he might have lived handsomely upon the interest. But, as it was, his necessities obliged him to use up from time to time those sums for which critical friends said afterwards he should "account." Without, therefore, attempting to decide too positively between the estimates of General Johnston and of Major Dawes as to the available strength of the Confederate Army, I think it may safely be assumed that the fighting force of General Johnston's army was such that, for the time at least, a defensive and watching position was enforced on him.

It is difficult for a stranger to discuss the character of a country regarding which one of the two opposing generals who fought over it says:

Mr. Davis and General Sherman exhibit a strange ignorance of the country between Dalton and Atlanta. Mr. Davis describes mountain ridges offering positions neither to be taken nor turned, and a natural fortress eighteen miles in extent, forgetting, apparently, that a fortress is strong only when it has a garrison strong enough for its extent; and both forget that, except Rocky-face, *no mountain is visible from the road between Dalton and Atlanta.*

Yet in the middle of this very paper we have a picture of the Confederates dragging guns up "Kenesaw Mountain," which certainly conveys the impression that the "mountain" was at least a very steep and considerable hill. According to the map which faces page 250, "Kenesaw Mountain" looks as if it ought to be pretty clearly visible from the road in question. The whole map indicates a series of ridges which appear to be mountainous. The word "mountain" is also scattered over it almost as thickly as peas in a pod. The words "Chattoogata Mountains," "Horn Mountains," "Pine Mountain," "Carnes Mountain," "Lost Mountain," etc., leave one in utter bewilderment between the meaning of General Johnston's expression and the meaning of the term "mountain" as locally used in those parts. One is obliged, therefore, to follow the campaign at some disadvantage in these respects. However, allowing for all differences as to the views of the writers and map-makers as to what is and is not a mountain, it seems tolerably clear that General Sherman successfully manœuvred Johnston out of his first positions at Dalton. They were not, however, positions which Johnston had any intention to hold seriously, for he very naturally considered them as too extensive for the force under his command.

The one opportunity for striking an offensive blow which presented itself to Johnston occurred at Cassville, and he took every step that was possible to him in order to take advantage of it. Either owing to some misunderstanding on General Hood's part or from some other cause not explained, Johnston's orders were not carried out, but the opportunity was lost through no fault on the part of General Johnston. No other presented itself up to the moment when he was deprived of his command, at which time he was busily engaged in preparing to take advantage of a temporary separation of General Sherman's army into two parts. The defects in execution which attended General Hood's attempt to strike this very blow, which had been suggested to him by Johnston, would have been much less likely to occur had Johnston remained in command. It was for the Confederates a fatal illustration of the danger of "swopping horses," either when you are "crossing a stream" in the figurative sense, or when your enemy is actually crossing a stream and you lose the chance to attack him. It does not seem from these pages that General Johnston can be fairly charged with any undue preference for a purely defensive course of action. In command of an inferior army, he wisely waited on the defensive, watching for time and opportunity to strike back at his skilful adversary. It was the faults of others and the impatience of the Confederate Government which snatched from his grasp the chances that were presented to him.

In this history he appears simply as the Fabius of the war, whereas he was, in fact, only pursuing a Fabian policy at a time when it was the sole course open to him to avoid certain defeat. Always on the lookout for an opportunity to assume the offensive, he seems to have been always anxious to act in a very different manner from what he did, had circumstances favored his doing so. There are, however, some very interesting points which arise out of the events of this campaign, especially as to the effect which operations like those carried out by Johnston are likely to have upon the fighting value of an army. Many of the ideas and reasons which influenced his action could not have been known to his troops,—a condition of things which from the earliest ages has often turned soldiers against their commander. There has been, unfortunately, so much angry discussion over the events of this campaign, and so many contradictory statements as to fact and so many private reputations are involved, that it is peculiarly difficult to arrive at the truth. In attempting, therefore, to state the case as it is given in *The Century* papers, the military student is obliged to trust very much to his own judgment in the rejection or acceptance of the conflicting statements. One is naturally prejudiced in favor of those which appear to fit in best with the story as a whole and those which are most in accordance with the general experiences of war.

The first question that naturally arises is, What was the state of the Confederate Army when Johnston handed over the command to General Hood? The conclusion to be drawn as to the practical success or failure of Johnston's strategy up to that period will be very much influenced by the answer given to that question. As far as one can judge of the facts from the evidence we derive from General Sherman's own account, together with that supplied by General Johnston and in the main by others, it is that a most difficult task had been set before the Federal Army. It seems abundantly clear that, as long as General Johnston commanded against it, very little success that was of much value had been achieved. But, on the other hand, it is difficult not to attach some importance to the plea put forward by General Hood that the desertions from the Confederate Army had reached a most alarming figure, in consequence of General Johnston's continued retreat. His war of intrenchments, one line made after another, and always further and further to the rear, though it was terribly annoying to the Federal general, had, it was said, told seriously on the *morale* of the Southern troops.

It seems clear that, if the campaign were to be looked upon merely as a great game of chessmen, Sherman, by his long advance from Chattanooga to Atlanta, had rather weakened than strengthened his position. He seems to admit as much himself when he says: "Johnston had meantime picked up his detachments, and had received reenforcements from his rear which raised his aggregate strength to 62,000 men, and warranted him in claiming that he was purposely drawing us far from our base, and that when the right moment should come he would turn on us and destroy us." (Page 252.) And again: "No officer or soldier who ever served under me will question the generalship of Joseph E. Johnston. His retreats were timely, in good order, and he left nothing behind." (Page 253.) Of course he says also, as any good soldier would, "We were equally confident, and not the least alarmed." (Page 252.) But there is no mistaking the meaning of the sentence, "At this critical moment the Confederate Government rendered us most valuable service. Being dissatisfied with the Fabian policy of General Johnston, it relieved him, and General Hood was substituted to command the Confederate Army." That clearly represents the view of a most able and generous opponent as to the management of the Army of Tennessee by General Johnston, from the beginning of May, 1864, to July 18, 1864, when Hood succeeded to the command. But I do not see that any answer has been made from within the Confederate lines to General Hood's statement (page 336) that when on the night of the 9th of July the Confederate Army crossed the Chattahoochee River, "with one-third of their number lost," the men were "downcast, dispirited, and demoralized. Stragglers and deserters, the captured and killed, could not now, however, be replaced by recruits, because all the recruiting depots had been drained to reenforce either Lee or Johnston."

It is difficult to see what better Johnston could have done than adopt a Fabian policy during this time. If only it were possible to

213

make the rank and file of an army understand the wisdom of such a policy at such a time, and to understand the advantages it would confer if discipline were strictly maintained, and if its adoption did not tend seriously to discourage them, such a policy would be followed more frequently than it is, and it would often be a sure means to victory in the long run. But there are too many "ifs" in this proposition. The soldier is a human being and not a soulless machine; and a lengthened retreat, no matter how skilfully carried out, has always injured his fighting spirit, and I believe will always do so. The quotations I have already made from General Hood are strengthened by his reference, which can hardly be inaccurate, to the opinion of all his corps commanders. On the 15th of October they expressed the opinion that, although the army "had much improved in spirit, it was not in condition to risk battle against the numbers reported by General Wheeler." (Page 426.) It is true that in the meantime Hood had engaged in a series of offensive operations around Atlanta, but they were, at best, of doubtful value.

Taking the story as a whole, it seems to point out very clearly the practical danger, in its effect upon troops, of the most brilliant series of defensive actions, and that this is especially the case when those actions are fought behind earth-works constructed at each succeeding stage of a campaign, and further and further to the rear. I incline to think that something of the same kind of effect is to be noticed even in the army of General Lee from the time when the long series of earth-work operations began around Petersburg. General Hood's view of the condition of the Army of Tennessee at the time when he took over the command has been so far accepted, because it appears on the whole to be confirmed by other evidence and to be in accordance with the general experience of war in such cases. Moreover, General Sherman, with all his respect for Johnston, speaks of the superior *morale* of his own army at this time. General Hood accounts for his own ill-success on every occasion by pouring out blame upon his subordinate leaders. This sort of explanation cannot be accepted as strictly impartial history. In a recently-published volume of the Duke of Wellington's conversations there is a remark about Napoleon's campaign of 1814, which our great captain, like most educated soldiers, regarded as one of the most brilliant, if not the most brilliant, of all the performances of that great master of the art of war. The Duke, answering some characteristically flippant remark of Croker's on the subject, refers to the series of victories which Napoleon gained over army after army in that campaign, and then, speaking from his own vast experience, says: "I know *the nice calculation* of time and distance which is necessary to the working-out of such combinations."

Some commanders are said to be "unlucky," which may sometimes mean that fate has really been continuously adverse to them. Far more often, however, it means that, whilst in conception their paper schemes may have been brilliant, they have failed in those nice calculations of time, distance, and other points to which Wellington attributed Napoleon's victories. Hood was certainly an "unlucky" commander. It is unfortunate for his reputation that his old classmates of West Point, represented so largely in the Federal Army opposed to him, should have fully anticipated from the first that he would be "unlucky." In speaking of a general who had been continuously unsuccessful, Lord Beaconsfield said to me: "They say he is unlucky, but my experience leads me to believe that want of luck is too often only a want of skill." It is impossible to say at each point where fate and where miscalculation caused General Hood's ill-luck. His original scheme for moving into the heart of Tennessee, with a view to draw Sherman after him, was dashing in the extreme. It is, however, very difficult to believe that he could have successfully carried his army "through the gaps in the Cumberland Mountains" to "attack Grant in rear" (page 427), and so on to Petersburg, as he appears to have contemplated. This is just one of those elaborate combinations of which Napoleon has said that their only defect is that they never succeed. Fate certainly struck him hard when, having urged that the railway to Decatur should be repaired, and that large supplies of stores should be gathered at Tuscumbia, he found on his arrival that nothing had been done.

This is one of those cases in which the want of one effective military head to the Confederacy, of which I have spoken heretofore, appears to have been disastrous. The Confederacy should have been governed from Lee's headquarters. In any case, it is clear that General Sherman's calculations of time, distance, and the resisting power which the stalwart Thomas would be able to gather in Tennessee against Hood, were right, and that General Hood's were fallacious. On the whole, it would seem that, for once at least, fate decided between the commanders with the blind eyes of Justice. From the moment that General Sherman had decided upon the bold step of allowing Hood to do his worst in the rear of the Federal Army, the march of that army to the sea is a most interesting feat of arms, and had a most decisive effect on the result of the war. He justly urges that its importance did not depend so much on the success of his march from Atlanta to the sea as on the fact that at Savannah, after destroying the resources of the South, he was in a position to join hands with Grant by a march northward from Savannah to Goldsboro'. As he says, after the complete destruction of Hood's army by Thomas on December the 16th, 1864, this march from Savannah was "like the thrust of the sword toward the heart of the human body; each mile of advance swept aside all opposition, consumed the very food on which Lee's army depended for life, and demonstrated a power in the National Government which was irresistible." (Page 259.)

Let us now return to the doings of Lee's army, which we left at Cold Harbor after the successful issue of its Wilderness campaign. Unfortunately for the readers of these papers, it requires a good deal of careful collation to get from them a clear picture of that most interesting period between June 3 and June 18, 1864—that is, between the end of the Wilderness battles at Cold Harbor and the time when, on June 18, at 11:30 A.M., Lee in person joined Beauregard before Petersburg. It was then that the siege of Lee's army by Grant may be said to have fairly begun. (Page 543.) It is necessary to compare Beauregard's "Four Days of Battle at Petersburg" with "General Grant on the Siege of Petersburg." In order to realize the circumstances under which at this time General Early was detached into the Shenandoah Valley, General Imboden's account of "The Battle of New Market" must be studied. The movements in the Shenandoah Valley, which, since Lee's retreat from Gettysburg, had led up to the battle of New Market and to the events which followed it, are also of importance. Briefly stated, it may be said that the Shenandoah Valley—one of the possible openings for supply which it was essential for Lee to keep open—had been for the moment secured to him by a success gained by Breckenridge over Sigel on May 15, 1864. It was not an unimportant event, because, during the Wilderness campaign, Lee could not have spared men to stop Sigel had he proved successful. But on

216

May 21 Hunter superseded Sigel in the command of the Federal forces in the Shenandoah Valley, and began a series of movements which resulted, on June 5, in the defeat of the Confederates at Piedmont. Hunter pushed on with increased forces across the Blue Ridge, and moved upon Lynchburg.

It was under these circumstances that General Early, with Jackson's old corps, was despatched to reenforce the Confederates in the Shenandoah Valley, at the moment when Grant was arranging for the transfer of his army to join Butler before Petersburg. The battle of Cold Harbor had been fought on June 3, 1864, and on June 12 Early was despatched to the Shenandoah Valley. Then followed on that side what was the last offensive effort of the dying Confederacy, Early's march on Washington. By July 12 Early's retreat had begun from before Washington; by September 19 Sheridan had defeated him at Winchester, and on September 22 at Fisher's Hill. Despite an at first successful surprise of Sheridan's forces on October 19, Early's army on that day had been almost annihilated. Its destruction meant that one more of the avenues for food and supply was cut off from Lee's doomed army.

Meantime Grant's army had been transferred to the south of the James River, and for the time the Federal commander seems undoubtedly to have given Lee the slip. The movements began on the very day, June 12, that Early had started for the Shenandoah Valley. Up to this time General Beauregard had completely worsted Butler in all his attempts to employ his army against Petersburg or Richmond. The scheme which Beauregard describes on page 198, under the title of "The Defence of Drewry's Bluff," was proposed by him on May 12, 1864, for the destruction of Butler's army. It seems to have been wise and clever, and, as far as one can judge, it was then *the* scheme most likely to give a brilliant result. General Beauregard's idea was that an immediate, though temporary, transfer of 10,000 men from Lee's army, together with the addition of the troops in Richmond, to his own army south of the James River, would make him strong enough to destroy Butler. After Butler had been disposed of, his plan was that with this combined force he should fall upon the left of Grant's army. Until Butler had been disposed of, Lee was to fall back and take up a defensive position covering Richmond. This plan of operation certainly looks as if it were not only feasible, but one that would have

217

afforded the best opportunity which the situation offered to the two Confederate armies. If carried out, it would have taken place during the five days' lull which succeeded the battle of Spotsylvania. If we are to judge by the success with which at Drewry's Bluff, on May 16, Beauregard rolled back Butler's army, and the narrowness with which that army avoided destruction,—owing its escape, in fact, to the error of General Whiting,—there does not seem any reason to doubt that General Beauregard's proposal, if vigorously carried out, might have been big with great results for the Confederacy. The only doubt seems to be whether food and transport could have been provided for Lee's already starving soldiers during the movement.

In any case, it seems clear that here again the want of a commander-in-chief over all the Confederate armies interfered with the possible execution of such a plan, and, indeed, it would seem, with any adequate and effective cooperation between the two armies of Lee and Beauregard, till they actually effected their junction. The situation when Grant's army began to re-enforce Butler, and the four days' fighting before Petersburg commenced, is very noteworthy. A comparison of General Grant's account of those days' proceedings with that given by General Beauregard will show that, whilst, on the one hand, Lee was not aware that Grant's army had left his front, on the other, the Federals were completely imposed upon by the slender force which was interposed between them and Petersburg. The incident is thoroughly characteristic of the history of war, and suggests, not any hostile criticism of the commanders, but rather a reflection as to the strange conditions under which the command of great bodies of men had to be exercised in a country such as was then the field of operations.

The importance of the advantage which Grant had over Lee in this all-decisive matter of unity of command comes out strikingly here. First, when apparently, on May 12, it might have been possible for a large detachment from Lee's army to reenforce Beauregard, and, after defeating Butler, to join in an attack on Grant—an attack which, if successful, would have had decisive results. In the almost pathetic correspondence (pages 244–245) between Lee and Beauregard, there is in Lee's telegrams something almost like irritation at the fact that General Beauregard wanted some one at

Richmond to give him definite orders as to the force he should then send to Lee. Lee evidently felt that the event was one of such paramount importance that it ought to have been entirely and exclusively in his own hands. Yet he was compelled by a faulty and disastrous system of military administration and command to leave the question in Beauregard's hands. "The result of your delay will be disaster. Butler's troops will be with Grant to-morrow," is the expression of a man intensely anxious, who feels that at a critical moment he can only request assistance from a coequal ally, whilst his opponent has the absolute disposal of all the forces in his theatre of war. It is not to find fault with Beauregard that this is written. His great ability as a general, his loyalty, and his honesty of purpose are beyond criticism. The object is to emphasize the necessity of unity of command in war, for without it success must always be doubtful.

When General Grant, on June 12, began his transfer of force towards Petersburg, it is clear that his success in effecting that movement was due to his being able to act as commander-in-chief of the two armies of Meade and Butler. General Lee, on the other hand, could only act as commander of the Army of Northern Virginia, and was at a disadvantage when he received from Beauregard—to whom he could not send orders—only warnings of what was taking place in his own immediate front. Information so received could not affect Lee's mind with the same force or certainty as the daily collected information received at his own headquarters would have done, had he been the commander-in-chief of all the armies in that theatre of war. To those who are not familiar with the systematic working of the headquarters of a large army in these respects, it may be difficult to convey an idea of the enormous practical difference between the two sets of facts. The political exigencies of the moment often render the temptation very strong to adopt some such arrangement as that of the Confederates at this time, in which a sort of general headquarters for the two armies is established at the political capital. It is well, therefore, to insist here upon the important effect which it produced upon this part of the campaign.

The situation in the South at this time, when Bragg was acting as Mr. Davis's "chief of the staff," was almost exactly analogous to the situation at the North until General Grant took supreme com-

219

mand. During all the time that elapsed between the appointment of General Halleck to a position nominally more dignified, but practically that of chief of the staff to Mr. Lincoln, and the moment when Grant assumed command of all the armies and took the field, General Halleck, in Washington, virtually directed all military operations under the President's authority. Grant reduced Halleck to his proper position, that of staff officer to himself, the commander-in-chief in the field. That in each instance the result was disastrous few who seriously study these papers will deny. There is so much in the arrangement that is plausible to a cabinet of civilians, and as it is one that may entail the most fatal consequences upon a nation, attention cannot be too forcibly drawn to it. To consider it rightly, the circumstances under which Halleck was appointed, apparently very much at the suggestion of General Pope, should be carefully studied. We have no explanation afforded as to the circumstances which led to the appointment of General Bragg, but probably they were very similar to those of which we have in General Pope's paper a full account in the case of General Halleck.

The final struggle now fairly began. The fate of Lee's army, despite the heroic resistance which it offered and the alternate successes and failures of the Crater battle and the sally against Fort Stedman, was being surely decided by events beyond its own immediate field. The fall of Fort Fisher on January 15, 1865, cut off an avenue of supply without which Lee had declared it would be impossible to feed his army. The advance of Sherman's army and the destruction of General Early in the Shenandoah Valley were events that closed in the net tighter and tighter around Lee's army, until, as Sherman says (page 259), by March, 1865, there was only one move left to Lee, viz., to abandon Richmond, join Johnston in North Carolina, and, if possible, destroy Sherman, and then turn upon Grant. General Sherman assumes that political considerations alone deterred Lee from carrying out this programme, although Sherman himself suggests that its success was problematical at best. All the evidence goes to show that Lee's troops were already starving, and almost without any means of transport. He, therefore, most probably did not attempt this move because he knew it had become impossible. After General Sheridan's gallant attack upon and capture of Five Forks from the famished and broken men of the old Army of Northern Virginia, the impossible had then to be attempted by Lee, and it soon became apparent how hopeless was the attempt. The military interest of the great struggle was over; the forces had become too unequal. The closing scenes were strikingly dramatic in their character; but all operations that could be of interest to the military critic ended long before Appomattox Court-House was reached.

The perusal of these papers has revived my remembrance of this great struggle and of the impressions it left upon me at the time. The routine of military duty had stationed me in the neighboring Dominion of Canada while this mighty fight was going on. It is not easy to describe the breathless interest and excitement with which from month to month, almost from day to day, we English soldiers read and studied every report that could be obtained of the war as it proceeded. No doubt many of our impressions of the facts, as we received them at the moment, required to be corrected by subsequent investigation. It takes a long time before the facts can be thoroughly threshed out from the mass of evidence bearing upon the complicated events of a great war that spread over a mighty continent. Nevertheless, in one respect, at all events, the broad impressions then formed are confirmed by the conclusions since arrived at, both from the more elaborate histories and from this most valuable series of papers. I refer to the opinion that, amid the crowds of able men, of gallant soldiers, and of clever statesmen whom the epoch of the American Civil War produced, the two men Abraham Lincoln and Robert Lee stand out a head and shoulders above all others. Neither of them was free from human error. Experience and the teaching of history warn us that perfection is a myth. But how great were both of these two great men in their several spheres! How modest, how wise, how self-restrained, how generous, how large in their views, and how grandly patriotic, as each understood patriotism!

An eminent Greek master taught that mortals are to be judged happy or otherwise according to the ending of their lives. Judging by this test, is it Abraham Lincoln or Robert Lee that we should regard as the favorite of the gods? It was Mr. Lincoln's fate to be struck down by the assassin at the moment when the cause for which he had lived and struggled had absolutely triumphed—a circumstance which has forever identified his death with the life of his country. Was this a nobler death than Lee's? He, the foremost man in the Confederacy, the General, the idol of the South, retired from his high command to a private, a humble position. He refused repeated offers of wealth and comfort, in order to devote his remaining years to serve his ruined State in the way in which he believed he could be most useful to it—namely, the education of her sons and the training of her citizens, by his great example, to have faith in Virginia's future. One hardly knows which ending the Greek master of old would have admired the more.

One other remark before closing this series of articles, which have at least afforded me most interesting work, whether my humble criticism shall or shall not be profitable to others. I make it with considerable diffidence, both because I am a soldier and because I am not a citizen of the United States. As a soldier, it may be thought that I am prejudiced in what I say, and as an Englishman, that I can only speak of the effect of the great American Civil War from the outside rather than from within. What I have to say is that if one were compelled to choose between condoling with American friends on the terrible misfortunes they underwent in that war, or of congratulating them upon the ennobling effect which that war has had upon their people, one would unhesitatingly congratulate them upon the fact that such stirring and ennobling incidents as those which fill the volumes I have reviewed did occur in American history, a quarter of a century ago.

It has been said—foolishly, I think—that the nation is happy whose annals are uninteresting. If anything so preposterous could be true, we should thank God to have been born in a country every page of whose history was replete with heart-stirring events. To eat the fruits of the ground in a warm, balmy climate, with all sorts of comforts round one, may furnish the materials for a happy, passive, uneventful, almost vegetable existence in equatorial Africa. But would there be any pride in belonging to the Anglo-Saxon race if we had no Crécy, Agincourt, Armada, or other glorious achievement of our ancestors to look back upon? What would England be if there had been no Marlborough, no Wellington, no Nelson, no Chatham, Pitt, or Clive, or Warren Hastings— no "men of action"? And since the greatest writers have always breathed the patriotic spirit of their own times, no Shakespeare, no Milton either? How could any Miltons or Shakespeares have been born in a country of purely bovine delights, whose history was a blank? Without war, there would, in fact, be no history at all. And yet, without any doubt, the statesman or the soldier who would not devote all his energies to save his country from what all must regard as the appalling calamity of civil war, or indeed from any war, would be an unprincipled villain. But when all has been done that can be done by statesmen or soldiers to stave off the calamity, surely the effects of war upon the country are not all bad. It is a fearful evil, but an evil for which greater good often compensates. Would the United States now prefer to have had no Washington, no Lincoln, none of the many heroes of the War of Independence and of the Civil War, in order to blot out the record of all war from the pages of its history? Would it be better for the future generations of American citizens that, as mere characters, all such heroes as Robert Lee and Stonewall Jackson should never have lived and fought?

In the nation that has never gone through the fiery ordeal of war,—if there be such a nation,—that has never had to encounter circumstances of difficulty and of danger which have threatened its very existence, that has never endured calamities which have tested its men's fibre, there can be no great characters, no lofty figures. It is not a noble, a glorious, or an admirable epoch in the history of any people when the great hero of the hour is the best platform orator or the best money-grubber.

I close the pages of this volume with a sincere feeling of thankfulness and pride that I belong to the race from which sprang the soldiers and sailors who fought upon both sides in this memorable struggle. Who can say which to admire the more—the Southern pluck and daring, or the stern, sober determination which eventually led the North to victory?

INDEX

Albemarle Co., Va., 24
Allan, William, 160, 162; reply to Longstreet, 159
Amphibious warfare, 107-11, 191-94
Antietam, battle of, 31, 32, 65, 144
Army organization, Confederate, 21-22, 218-19

Baltimore and Ohio Railroad, 37
Banks, N. P., 37, 46, 128-29, 138
Beauregard, P. G. T., 203; battle of Shiloh, 81-95; quoted, 91, 96; at First Bull Run, 95-97; battle of Charleston, 192-96; defense of Petersburg and Richmond, 217-19
Blackwood's, xii
Blucher, Gebhard L. von, 83
Bragg, Braxton, 164; battle of Shiloh, 89-91; invasion of Kentucky, 177-79; Tennessee campaign, 180-83; as chief of staff, 219-20
Breckinridge, John C., 216
Buell, Don Carlos, 81, 83, 84, 85, 86, 90, 178-79; quoted, 82
Bull Run: first battle, 62-63, 95-100; second battle, 119, 163, 164
Burnside, Ambrose: battle of Fredericksburg, 157-58, 171
Butler, Benjamin, 196, 199, 202-3, 217-18

California, 176
Cedar Mountain, battle of, 138
Chancellorsville, battle of, 152-53, 164-65
Charleston, battle of, 191-96
Charlottesville, Va., 24
Chattanooga, battle of, 161-62, 181-84

Chickahominy River, 21, 130, 132, 134-36
Chickamauga, battle of, 181-82
Civil-military relations, 77-80, 99-100, 120-21, 166
Civil War, end of described, 220-21
Cold Harbor, battle of, 200-201
Command systems, 215-16, 218-19; Union and Confederate compared, 196-97
Comte de Paris, cited, 136
Confederate army, xxxvii, 21-22, 37-41; cavalry, 44-45
Corinth, battle of, 81, 85, 86, 177-78
Cox, Jacob D., 100
Cross Keys, battle of, 129

Davis, Jefferson, 48, 67-68, 113, 176; Wolseley's estimate of, xxxii; replies to Wolseley, xxxii; "a third-rate man," 76-77
Dawes, E. C., 209-10
Douglas, Kyd, quoted, 132, 144
Drewry's Bluff, Va., 22, 203
Duncan, J. K., 109
Du Pont, Samuel, 193

Early, Jubal A., 97, 98, 203, 216-17
Elzey, Arnold, 97
End of the war described, 220-21
Ewell, Richard S., 127, 174-75

Falkenstein, Vogel von, 80
Farragut, David, 107-11, 194
Fisher's Hill, battle of, 217
Forrest, Nathan B., Wolseley's estimate of, xxxiii
Fort Donelson, 80-81
Fort Fisher, 220

Franklin, William B., 140
Fredericksburg, Va., 14
Fredericksburg, battle of, 64, 155-57, 171
Freeman, Douglas S., appreciation of Wolseley's writings, ix, xxiv
Frémont, John C., 129
Fry, James B., xxxvi-xxxvii; quoted, 98-99

Gaines's Mill, battle of, 18-19, 115, 129, 133, 135
Gettysburg, battle of, 159-64; Longstreet's views of, 152-57
Gordon, Charles, compared with Lee, 69
Goss, Warren Lee, "Recollections of a Private," 113
Grant, U. S., 81-86, 89, 92-93, 216-20; Wolseley's estimate of, xxi; Sherman's estimate of, xxix; at Vicksburg, 179-81; Chattanooga, 182-84; advantaged by unified command system, 196-97; campaigns of 1864, 197-203; at battle of the Wilderness, 198-99; Cold Harbor, 199-200
Great Britain and the Civil War, 40-43, 48
Gustavus Adolphus, of Sweden, 176

Halleck, Henry, 46, 119-20, 141, 171-73, 219-20
Harper's Ferry, W. Va., 31, 33, 139-40, 143-44
Harrison's Landing, Va., 21-22, 32, 64
Henderson, G. F. R., xxxi
Hill, A. P., 138, 161
Hill, H. P., mistake for Hill, A. P.
Hood, J. B., Atlanta campaign, 209-18
Hooker, Joseph, 153, 162, 165, 172, 183
"Hornet's Nest," 93
Hunter, David, 217

Imboden, John D., 116, 216

Irwin, R. B., 115, 130, 136; defends Lincoln's handling of McClellan, 111-13

Jackson, T. J. ("Stonewall"), 7, 30, 31, 37, 75, 86, 114-15; principles of war, xxii, 116; interview with Wolseley, 35-36; Valley Campaign, 127-30; role in Peninsula Campaign, 130-33, 137; battle of Cedar Mountain, 138-39
Johnston, Albert S., 80-92, 96
Johnston, Joseph E., 81, 96, 127, 131, 163; First Bull Run, 97-99; Peninsula Campaign, 133-37; Sherman's campaign, 209-16
Jordan, Thomas, 88; quoted, 87

Kentucky, Bragg's invasion of, 177-79
Kernstown, battle of, 128
Kinglake, Alexander, 107, 195; quoted, 94
Knoxville, Tenn., 185

Law, E. M., 198
Lee, "Light Horse Harry," 55
Lee, Robert E., 36, 40; Wolseley's estimate of, xxvii-xxix; interview with Wolseley, 30-35; "General Lee," 53-69; Peninsula Campaign, 131-37; at Antietam, 143; battle of Fredericksburg, 155-58; at Gettysburg, 159-64; disadvantaged by Confederate headlessness of command, 196-97; campaigns of 1864, 197-203, 216-20; Wolseley's final estimate of, 221-23
Lincoln, Abraham, 8, 32, 40, 47, 48, 55, 60, 66; Wolseley's changing views on, xxx; Wolseley's final estimate of, 219-20
Long, A. L., 53, 60
Longstreet, James, 33, 119, 133, 137, 198-99; views on Fredericksburg and Gettysburg, 152-57; battle of Gettysburg, 159-64

Lookout Mountain, battle of, 183
Lyon, Nathaniel, 76

McClellan, George B., 21, 31-33, 34, 45-46, 65, 100-101, 111-17, 127-37, 140-44, 179; Wolseley's estimate of, xxxi-xxxii
McCulloch, Robert, 78-79
McDowell, Irwin, 98-99, 114-15, 129, 136
McMahon, Martin T., quoted, 197-98
McMahon, Maurice, of France, 156
Maine, Sir Henry, 100
Manassas Railway, 98
Marlborough, Duke of, 61-62
Mason, W. Roy, 171
Mason, James, 37
Meade, George G., 164, 181, 198, 200-201; at Gettysburg, 172-75
Mechanicsville, Va., 136
Mitchell, John K., 108-10
Mosby, John S., 163, 165

Napoleon, 68, 84, 87, 141, 158, 160, 214-15
Nashville, Tenn., 81
Nelson, Horatio, 192
New Market, battle of, 216
New Orleans, 194; capture of, 107-11
Norfolk, Va., 11
North American Review, ix

Palmerston, Lord, 43
Parks, Joseph H., on Polk at Shiloh, xxi-xxii
Patterson, Robert, 98-99
Pea Ridge, battle of, 78-79
Pemberton, John C., 184
Peninsula Campaign, 111-20, 130-37
Perryville, battle of, 179
Petersburg, siege of, 216, 219-20
Pickett, George E., 161-62
Pittsburg Landing, Tenn., 83, 85
Polk, Leonidas, 87-89
Pope, John, 31, 32, 46, 63, 141, 143; succeeds McClellan and fights Second Bull Run, 117-20, 138-39

Port Republic, Va., battle of, 128
Porter, David D., 108
Price, Sterling, 78-79, 176, 177-78

Randolph, George W., 19, 23
Red River, expedition to, 203
Rhett, Robert B., article in Century cited, 77
Richmond, Va., 15, 20, 39, 100, 113, 129, 144
Robertson, William B., 108
Rodgers, C. R. P., 193
Rosecrans, William S., 100-101, 181-82

Savannah, Ga., 216
Schenck, Robert C., quoted, 129
Scott, Winfield, 34, 57, 58, 60, 98
Seven Pines, battle of, 115, 133, 163, 164
Shenandoah Valley, Va., description of, 26-30
Sheridan, Philip: Richmond raid, 202-3, 217; at Five Forks, 220
Sherman, William T., 66, 162, 192, 203, 220; Wolseley's estimate of, xxxiii-xxxiv; campaign against Johnston and Hood, 209-18
Shields, James, 129
Shiloh, battle of, 81-93, 176-77
Sickles, Daniel, 174
Sigel, Franz, 78, 216-17
Slocum, H. W., 175
Smith, Gustavus W., 97, 133
Smith, Kirby, 178
Smith, W. F., 198, 200-201
South Mountain, battle of, 139, 143-44
Stanton, Edwin, 46, 114-15, 141; relieves McClellan and appoints Pope, 120
Staunton, Va., 25-26
Stoneman, George, 165, 202
Stone's River, battle of, 181
Stuart, J. E. B., 44, 45, 97, 135, 163, 164, 175
Sumner, Charles, 47

Thomas, George H.: Sherman's estimate of, xxix; battle of Chattanooga, 162, 183-84, 215

Tucker, Glenn, on Longstreet at Gettysburg, xxv

Van Dorn, Earl, 79, 81, 176

Vicksburg, battle of, 95, 180, 194

Virginia Central Railroad, 14, 24

Walker, John G., quoted, 140

Wallace, Lewis, 83, 84, 85, 86

Washington, D.C., 128-29; defense of, 114-15

Wellington, Duke of, 36, 68, 83, 138, 214-15

West Point, military academy, 56, 57, 65, 141, 171

Whiting, W. H. C., 130-32, 218

Wilderness, battle of, 198-99

Williams, T. Harry, on Lincoln as strategist, xxx

Wilson's Creek, battle of, 78

Winchester, Va., 14, 36-37, 128, 139, 217

Wolseley, Garnet J.: his life, x-xvi; place in Civil War literature, xvi-xix; his views on significance of Civil War, xix-xxxvii; on strategy and tactics, xix-xxvii; his war heroes, xxvii-xxxiv; on preparedness, xxxiv-xxxv; civil-military relations, xxv-xxxvii; shortcomings as military critic, xxxvii; on battle of Charleston, xx; First Bull Run, xx-xxi; Shiloh, xxi-xxii; on Jackson's Valley Campaign, xxii-xxiii; McClellan's Peninsula Campaign, xxiii-xxiv; on Fredericksburg, xxiv; Gettysburg, xxiv-xxv; command systems, xxv-xxvi; end of the war, xxvi-xxvii; on Lee, xxvii-xxix; Lincoln, xxx; Jackson, xxx-xxxi; McClellan, xxxi-xxxii; Jefferson Davis, xxxii; Forrest, xxxiii; Sherman, xxxiii-xxxiv